AF470692

The Holy Boys

Dedicated to every one of the Holy Boys and Vikings;
past, present and future

The Holy Boys

A history of the Royal Norfolk Regiment
and the Royal East Anglian Regiment
1685–2010

Jonathan Sutherland and Diane Canwell

Pen & Sword
MILITARY

First published in Great Britain in 2010 by
PEN & SWORD MILITARY
an imprint of
Pen & Sword Books Ltd
47 Church Street
Barnsley
South Yorkshire
S70 2AS

ISBN 978 1 84884 212 0

A CIP catalogue record for this book is available from the British Library

Printed and bound in the UK by
the MPG Books Group

Pen & Sword Books Ltd incorporates the Imprints of
Pen & Sword Aviation, Pen & Sword Maritime, Pen & Sword Military,
Wharncliffe Local History, Pen and Sword Select, Pen and Sword Military Classics,
Leo Cooper, Remember When, Seaforth Publishing and Frontline Publishing.

For a complete list of Pen & Sword titles please contact
PEN & SWORD BOOKS LIMITED
47 Church Street, Barnsley, South Yorkshire, S70 2AS, England
E-mail: enquiries@pen-and-sword.co.uk
Website: www.pen-and-sword.co.uk

Contents

Acknowledgements

The authors wish to thank Kate Thaxton and her volunteers at the Royal Norfolk Regimental Museum in Norwich, Lieutenant-Colonel Tony Slater, OBE and Major Dick Gould at The Keep in Gibraltar Barracks, Bury St Edmunds, as well as Andy Merkin from the Royal Anglian Regimental Museum at Duxford. Many thanks to all of these individuals for their support and enthusiasm during our research, and for providing such stunning photographs.

Introduction

On 25 April every year the Royal Anglian Regiment celebrates Almanza Day. In this modern regiment it is most closely associated with the 1st Battalion, the battalion that has the closest links with the 300-year history of the 9th Foot. It is from Almanza that the 9th Foot, later the Norfolk Regiment then the Royal Norfolk Regiment and ultimately the Royal Anglian Regiment, became known as the Holy Boys.

The Battle of Almanza took place in 1707, during the War of the Spanish Succession. Britain, Portugal and their allies lost the battle against the French and the Spanish. The 9th Regiment refused to surrender and covered the retreat of the defeated army, and these actions were honoured by Queen Anne. She awarded it the badge of Britannia and henceforth Britannia was displayed on its colours.

But why then is the regiment known as the Holy Boys? There are two legends regarding the origin of the nickname. Both of these are plausible, but both probably incorrect. The first relates back to the Peninsular War, at the beginning of the nineteenth century. Soldiers of the regiment, in order to buy liquor from the Spaniards, traded in their Bibles. The other, more accepted explanation, relates to the same period. Spaniards and Portuguese were said to have mistaken Britannia on the regiment's colours for the Virgin Mary.

There is, however, a far more compelling reason why the nickname the Holy Boys came about. We can trace this back to Lieutenant E Watson. He was born on 9 January 1792 in Quebec and was the fourth son of Lieutenant-Colonel J Watson. His father was on the staff of the Duke of Kent, who was then in Canada. The Watsons moved to Ireland in 1794 and settled in Wexford. The lieutenant-colonel was killed fighting rebels in 1798 and at the age of 13 Watson joined the Royal Military College. In 1808 he was commissioned in the 9th Foot and joined the 1st Battalion, which was then in Portugal. Watson left England via Deal in Kent and made for Corunna. From there he was assigned to one of the detachments of troops that were guarding the funds sent over to pay the British army. Several detachments from different regiments made up the guard party which was commanded by Colonel Peacock of the 71st Regiment.

The journey promised to be a treacherous one. Peacock learned that the route had been blocked by a French force. Consequently it was decided not to risk the treasure but to make for Vigo, where British transports were known to be moored.

The march over the mountains was arduous, but the hundred or so men, under Captain Drew of the 45th Foot, set off. As Watson later wrote in his *Personal Adventures of a Young Officer during the Peninsular War*: 'The soles of my boots were completely worn out, and I might be said to have walked barefoot, though for appearance sake I wore the uppers in a poor state in which to contend with the season and snow.'

They managed to reach Vigo and embarked for England, nearly coming to grief three times on the rocks. When Watson arrived home he again rejoined the 1st Battalion. At this point it consisted of only a hundred men, but soon 400 new men were recruited from the East Norfolk Militia. The battalion was then sent to Walcheren in the Netherlands and was involved in the capture of Flushing. Later, in March 1810, the battalion was bound for Portugal. Watson met up with them at Lisbon and was shocked to discover that his fellow officers were more interested in the local girls than preparing for battle. He later wrote: 'At Thomar my regiment was quartered in a large monastery on a hill over the town and I occupied a cell which had been the wretched dormitory of a monk; its furniture consisted of an old table, a chair, a few boards, intended for a bed.'

Watson was clearly a religious man, but was concerned that in the theatre of war there was no spiritual guidance for the men:

> There were no chaplains to the regiment, no religious observances whatever, and, circumstanced as we were, life being peculiarly uncertain, none needed religious instruction more than the soldiers. I was, therefore, led to make enquiries if there were any amongst the men of the brigade that cared for their souls. The result was that I was enabled to induce a few to attend at my cell to receive such few hints as I could communicate. The Lord was pleased to bless the attempt, and in a very short time my apartment could not contain the numbers that attended, and they frequently thronged around the door. The soldiers attended each evening and I read and expanded the scriptures to them. The matter now began to obtain publicity, and to rouse hostile feeling. Some of the officers, excited partly by curiosity, came to witness what was going forward, and to make a mock of what they considered so extraordinary and uncalled for. However, they were restrained on witnessing the orderly manner of our meetings.

At this time the regiment was in the lines of Torres Vedras (a chain of forts that had been built in 1809–10 to defend Lisbon) and with more men attending these scripture meetings Watson looked for a more suitable building. Men from other regiments also attended the meetings and a Lieutenant Witley offered to help. But all was not well:

> The 1st Battalion of the 9th, with which I was, had been for some months under the command of Brevet Lieutenant-Colonel Crawford, the senior

major of the regiment, Colonel Cameron being in England on sick leave. The former was a brave man, and one who seemed to have his whole mind occupied with military concerns, taking little interest in anything else. The young officers being now determined to arrest, if possible our public religious proceedings, went in a body to the colonel, and represented to him that such extraordinary doings in the regiment would subject him to be called into question for permitting them, and would bring a reproach on the corps throughout the whole army. So he sent for me, and asked me 'what is this I hear of you? I understand that you are in the habit of assembling soldiers in a Roman Catholic Church, and there preaching to them.' I said, 'the charge is true, but if there were chaplains with the army to instruct the soldiers, I should feel happy to enjoy the place of a hearer, and not a teacher'.

The situation was referred to more senior officers who thought that it was not an officer's place or duty to discuss religion with the men. Eventually the issue went up as far as the commander in chief, Arthur Wellesley, who decided that the religious meetings could continue as long as the officers and soldiers performed their duties. From that point on the religious activities, now well known to many of the regiments, earned the 9th Regiment its nickname of the Holy Boys.

In today's Royal Anglian Regiment a sense of history and tradition could have easily been lost during the course of successive amalgamations with other regiments. Today's Royal Anglian Regiment includes regiments that are linked not only to Norfolk but to Suffolk, Essex, Cambridgeshire, Lincolnshire, Leicestershire, Northamptonshire, Bedfordshire and Hertfordshire. Two companies among the

A close up of a brass belt buckle, showing Britannia. It is simply inscribed IX Regiment

A silvered brass belt buckle of the 9th Regiment, as worn during the 19th century

three battalions have the closest association with the tradition of the Holy Boys: A Company of the 1st Battalion and A Company of the 3rd Battalion.

The term Holy Boys is no longer applied to the current regiment; instead each of the battalions has its own nickname. The 1st Battalion is known as the Vikings, the 2nd the Poachers and the 3rd the Steelbacks. But the men of all the battalions can now commemorate the many campaigns and traditions of the regiments that have become part of the Royal Anglian Regiment.

This book takes the story back to 1685, years before any association with Norfolk had been made. Over the course of nearly 300 years, the regiment went through at least nine incarnations, from Colonel Henry Cornwall's Regiment of Foot through various associations and names related to Norfolk, to its modern association with the East Anglian region. It is a complex and fascinating story of one of the senior regiments in the British army which served successive monarchs and fought in some of the most important wars, campaigns and battles in British history.

A close up of the Edith Cavell memorial drum, belonging to the Royal Norfolk Regiment and now held by the regimental museum in Norwich

1

Origins 1685–1750

The Royal Norfolk Regiment, formerly the 9th Foot, can trace its ancestry back to the time of the Monmouth Rebellion in 1685. As Colonel Cornwall's Regiment of Foot, it was the second of eight regiments specifically raised to deal with the internal disorder. However, by the time the regiment had been fully raised, organized and trained, Monmouth had been executed at the Tower of London after his defeat at Sedgemoor.

The regiment, like so many others, excepting those with permanent titles, had a shifting identity. Ultimately, the regiment would become known as the 9th Foot, a title that it would retain for many generations. Before this, there were family connections that tied the fabric of the regiment together. During the period that Cornwall commanded the regiment, five family members served. Later, when Colonel Steuart commanded, no less than eleven family members were commissioned officers.

Colonel Henry Cornwall was, in 1685, a captain in the Royal Horse Guards. He was first commissioned on 19 June 1685 and over the next few days company captains were commissioned. Each of the officers was authorized to raise their own company, consisting of 100 private soldiers, three sergeants, three corporals and a pair of drummers. Once the company was up to strength it was then to march to Gloucester and muster.

Eleven companies were initially raised under Colonel Henry Cornwall (he would command the regiment and a company of his own). Lieutenant-Colonel Sir John Morgan, Major James Purcell, Captains Richard Kidley, John Powell, Cox, John Booth, Jerom Bubb, Thomas Williams, Daniel Wicherly and Sir Francis Edwards commanded the other companies. Once the Monmouth Rebellion had been crushed there was a general order to reduce the size of the bulk of the regiments. Each command was reduced in strength, bringing the company strength down to sixty privates on 16 July and then to fifty privates, two sergeants, three corporals and a drummer on 25 July 1685. Cornwall had been order to disband three companies on 18 July in order to effect these reductions.

The regiment marched from Gloucester to Hounslow Heath on 22 August. It arrived there six days later. They were then ordered to proceed to Kingston-on-Thames. James II received the regiment before it was given orders to march on to

Berwick-on-Tweed. It was also to provide a detached company to garrison Holy Island.

On 17 March 1686, after being relieved by the Princess Anne of Denmark's Regiment, it headed off for St Albans. Again the regiment took part in a review by the king. On 11 June it was sent south to overwinter at Portsmouth. In July one man per company was discharged to fill the ranks of two companies that were being raised for operations in New England.

By May 1687 the regiment was in Bramley, Surrey, and then marched to Hounslow once more. By this stage an additional company had been attached to the regiment, in the form of Grenadiers under the command of Captain Henry Villiers. In August the regiment marched north to York and then moved on in the September to Kingston-upon-Hull, to work on fortification construction under Lord Dartmouth. Its duties there over, it was back in York by December.

There had been some personnel changes in the ranks of its officers. Sir John Morgan had left to join a Welsh regiment that had just been raised. His position was taken by Major James Purcell, whose company command in turn was taken by Captain Lacy.

Between March and September 1688 the regiment provided detached companies for Carlisle, Berwick, Chester, York, Tynemouth, Scarborough and Chepstow. Nominally, the regiment's headquarters and undetached companies were stationed at either Carlisle or Berwick. September also saw the strengthening of the regiment: ten privates, one sergeant and a drummer were added to each company. This meant that the average company was now up to sixty privates, three sergeants, three corporals and two drummers. It was still significantly under-strength compared to its establishment size in 1685. At around the same time, two new companies were added to the regiment. This meant that including the Grenadier Company the regiment was now up to thirteen companies.

The Glorious Revolution

A new crisis swept England with rumours of the impending invasion by the Prince of Orange. The regiment was ordered to pull in the detachments and make for London as soon as practicable. These orders were rescinded in a letter from the Secretary of War (4 December 1688) to Lieutenant-Colonel Purcell. It also confirmed a change in the leadership of the regiment:

> The regiment is given to Colonel Nicholas [promoted from Lieutenant-Colonel in the Prince George of Denmark's regiment], Colonel Cornwall having laid down his commission [Cornwall had resigned on 20 November just after William of Orange had entered London; other family members stayed with the regiment] as have two captains and five other officers.

As it was, Nicholas's command of the regiment was extremely brief; he could not decide which horse to back, James II or William of Orange. Consequently, John Cunningham (Lieutenant-Colonel in Werden's Horse) replaced him on 31 December 1688. By this stage the bulk of the regiment was in Worcester with one detached company at York. The regiment received orders to march towards Liverpool on 3 January 1689.

The regiment would now see combat for the first time. Admittedly, under Lieutenant-Colonel Purcell, part of the regiment had put down a riot in York in March 1687; Purcell had been rather heavy-handed and had subjected prisoners to military punishments, such as being forced to sit on a wooden horse, designed to inflict pain rather than equestrian training. During the quelling of the riot Ensign Ord smashed a rioter over the head and had been admonished by the Secretary of War and ordered to be confined to barracks for a month.

It would not be England that was the regiment's first taste of battle, but Ireland. By the beginning of 1689 the regiment was close to Liverpool and it was ideally placed for the short voyage across the Irish Sea. The civil war in Ireland was already raging; William III had the support of the Protestant north, whilst James II was favoured by the Roman Catholics of the south and west. Orders came on 3 February 1689 to get the regiment up to full strength and to prepare for embarkation. The detached company rejoined the regiment and by 1 March the regiment was up to thirteen companies of sixty men.

It is important to understand that this period saw the beginnings of the transition from predominantly pike-armed regiments to musket-armed units. In terms of the mix between pike and musket, this was left to the discretion of the regimental colonel.

The situation in Ireland was fluid, as James II had landed at Kinsale on 12 March and had been welcomed when he entered Dublin. He now proposed to move on Londonderry. The city was commanded by Colonel Robert Lundy, who was in favour of William, but he faced difficulties due to the poor state of the defences.

Cunningham's regiment, along with a regiment commanded by Solomon Richards, was earmarked for the defence of Londonderry. On 12 March Cunningham received orders to take command of the expedition and to embark for Londonderry: 'To be there employed for our service as the governor of the said place and you shall think fit.' Cunningham was told only to land if Londonderry still remained in Protestant hands:

> You are to land the said regiments and stores, and to take care that they be well quartered and disposed of in the said city, following such directions as you shall receive during your stay there from our said governor, Lieutenant Colonel Robert Lundy, in all things relating to our service. You are to make the best defence you can against all persons that shall attempt to besiege the said city.

If Cunningham found that Londonderry had fallen or that the landing would be disastrous then he was to attempt to land either at Carrickfergus or Strangford. If this were not possible he was to return to Liverpool.

Cunningham, the regiment and Richards's 17th Regiment sailed on 3 April 1689. Prevailing winds forced them to put into Hoy Lake. The force made a second attempt on 10 April and they were off Londonderry by 15 April. The situation had radically changed at Londonderry and Cunningham's indecision and reluctance to risk the regiments would cost him dear. Lundy had fled after a rising in Londonderry. Cunningham refused to take on the governorship and, worse, he refused to disembark his force. Instead he sailed back to Liverpool, where he was promptly arrested on 24 May 'on suspicion of dangerous practices against the government'.

This ended Cunningham's career with the regiment, ushering in William Steuart, formerly the Lieutenant-Colonel of the 16th Foot. Meanwhile, Major-General Kirk (2nd Foot) was despatched to Liverpool to take control of the situation and relaunch the planned landings. Kirk had been sent on 29 April and he planned to land at Londonderry at the head of the 2nd Foot, the 9th and Sir John Hammer's 11th Regiment. He would take enough ammunition and supplies to withstand a long siege. Major-General Percy Kirk had been earmarked for the original operation. He already had a reputation for his exploits at Tangiers, but neither his regiment nor a fourth regiment were immediately available, hence the operation had fallen to Cunningham to mismanage.

As far as London was concerned, Kirk was taking too much time preparing for the landings. On 13 May he received a terse letter from Lord Shrewsbury telling him to sail immediately and not to wait for the stores to come up. The letter seems to have had little impact on Kirk, as he only set out on 31 May. He appeared off Londonderry on 15 June, after encountering poor weather out to sea.

Kirk was still prevaricating on 19 June; he was unwilling to force the boom that was blocking the River Foyle. Kirk received a letter begging for help on 26 June from Londonderry. He replied that he intended to land behind the enemy at Lough Swilly. The 9th was sent there on 7 July. Captain Echlin, Lieutenant Biggett and Ensign Hart, along with sixty musketeers, were sent six miles inland to seize a number of cattle at Rathmulton.

Meanwhile the rest of the force began landing on the island of Inch. Here they built fortifications. Kirk set about mustering local Protestants and formed them up into companies, eventually raising fifteen of them. By 20 July 1689 all of the 9th was ashore and they were manning the defence works on the island. Londonderry was just six miles away and the position of Kirk's force was causing considerable concern for James's besieging force.

James was already planning moves against Kirk's command. Under the Duke of Berwick a sizeable force of 1,500 Dragoons had set out on 17 July. Steuart began evacuating Protestant refugees from the mainland and he reinforced the detachment under Echlin at Rathmulton. Preparations were made to defend the village and an attack by the Dragoons was repulsed on the morning of 20 July. Steuart now concentrated on bringing in cattle to deny the enemy food. At the end of the month the boom across the River Foyle was forced and the siege was raised. As James's troops fell back they set villages on fire.

The 9th now marched into Londonderry and then on to Dundalk on 7 September 1689. The regiment would now join a force under Count Mainhard Schomberg. He had landed at the head of 10,000 men at Bangor on 12 August. They marched towards Belfast, reaching the city on 17 August. He then marched on to Carrickfergus and then to Dundalk. Schomberg's force now reinforced by the 9th, sat in poor fortifications until a large enemy force appeared on 21 September. For a fortnight the two armies stared at one another, each of them steadily losing troops to fever, dysentery and desertion. In a relatively short period of time Schomberg's force had dwindled from a high of 14,000 to around 8,000. James's army had dropped in strength from 40,000 to just 25,000.

On 5 October James retreated to Drogheda. On 7 November the 9th marched toward Newry and moved into billets at Greencastle and Rostrevor. Here the regiment overwintered until the end of January 1690 when Steuart began organizing a major raiding party. He pulled together 500 infantry and cavalry for a cattle raiding expedition. Steuart's troops managed to round up large numbers of cattle despite the enemy lighting bonfires to give people time to hide their livestock.

The campaign itself did not get under way again until June 1690. King William landed at Carrickfergus on 14 June 1690 and began advancing on Dublin. The 9th was in action on 22 June when some 200 troops, made up of Dragoons and Captain Farlow's company of the 9th were advancing from Newry to Dundalk. They were ambushed and in the running battle Farlow and another officer were taken prisoner and twenty-two men were killed.

Meanwhile, James's troops had fallen back towards Dublin. He decided to stand his ground on the southern bank of the Boyne, near Drogheda, on the afternoon of 30 June 1690. James's force is estimated to have been around 26,000, comprising of Irish and French troops. William's army, around 36,000 strong, was comprised of English, Dutch, Danes, Irish Protestants and French Hugenots. As it was, the 9th played only a small role in the battle; it was held in reserve and did not suffer any casualties.

The battle was a disaster for James and by 9 August William's army was threatening Limerick. On 12 August the 9th was part of a force sent to capture Castle Connell. It was four miles from Limerick and the fortification surrendered without a fight. By 18 August the 9th was entrenched around Limerick, along with seven other regiments. The 9th was nearly routed by a sortie launched by the enemy on the night of 18 August. The regiment, caught unawares, fell back in confusion only to be fired on by Danish troops from their own army. The 9th fired back at the Danes. Eventually the chaos subsided and the enemy sortie was beaten off.

A breach in the defence works of Limerick had been made at St John's Gate. It was decided to launch an assault on 27 September 1690. Again the 9th was involved; the attack was to be led by 500 Grenadiers, amongst which was Captain Farlow's company. The attack was hopelessly mismanaged, Farlow was killed along with Captain Lindon of the 9th and several other officers or men were either killed or wounded.

The 9th spent the winter in Tipperary. It emerged on 9 April 1691 to mount operations in County Leitrim. Fifty musketeers, supported by twenty Dragoons, ran into a couple of troops of Irish Dragoons and some infantry near Mohill. It was a resounding success; the 9th killed thirty of the enemy, took five prisoners and a number of horses. The regiment's next operation was at Athlone as part of the besieging force. A breach had been made in the defences on 20 June and the regiment was to be part of the storming column that would attack the bridge. In the action Steuart, now a brigadier, was severely wounded and had to be evacuated to Dublin for treatment.

James's army was by now under the command of the French General St Ruth. By July 1691 he could muster some 20,000 infantry and 5,000 cavalry. St Ruth took up defensive positions at Aughrim on 12 July and in the ensuing battle the 9th occupied a position at the centre of the English line. The enemy position was across the lower slopes of Aughrim Hill, behind boggy ground and enclosures. The 9th was part of the general assault at around 1800 that day. Incredible bad luck struck the Irish army when St Ruth was killed by a stray cannon shot. Confusion spread as the English army advanced and in a short space of time the Irish army was running. Huge numbers were killed; for the 9th Major Cornwall was killed along with an ensign, a captain and an ensign were wounded, thirty-six other ranks were killed and a further forty-three wounded.

It was now determined that Limerick should be dealt with. On 15 September 1691 the English army attempted to force a crossing of the Shannon, around two miles from the city. The attack was led by 400 Grenadiers, including a detachment from the 9th. Behind the Grenadiers were 600 engineers with pontoons and these in turn were supported by the 9th and then other regiments.

Work got under way on the bridge by midnight and at daybreak the English army began crossing. The enemy withdrew without much of a fight. A second English force was despatched across the bridge on 22 September, but by then the 9th had been withdrawn to the reserves. Limerick fell and the war in Ireland was over. Operations in Ireland were not, however, over for the 9th as they would become garrison troops before they spent the winter of 1691 to 1692 at Fenagh, Kavan, Killeshandra, Strangford, Lough Foyle and County Donegal.

By this stage the regiment still had a nominal thirteen companies; the establishment strength being recorded in 1692 as 928 officers and men. In truth the regiment could muster less than half this strength. They had 411 effective soldiers, 138 were sick and 231 had died.

War in Europe

A year later, in 1693, the regiment was in Dublin, but yet another twelve months would pass before a new posting was confirmed. In a letter written by Steuart in Dublin on 13 March 1694 he expressed his hopes that the regiment would be bound for Flanders. In a second letter, on 19 March, Steuart reported that they had landed at Neston to the south of Birkenhead. He also wrote that on 18 March they had reached Chester and on the following day he had mustered some 800 officers and men.

The regiment received a fresh draft of 130 recruits and then marched south to Portsmouth. Here it would have to wait for its new posting. In June 1694, with Brigadier Steuart in Flanders with another brigade, the regiment was under the command of Lieutenant-Colonel Hussey. The 9th would be part of an invasion force that would attack Brest on the French coast. The operation was an unmitigated disaster and the English losses were heavy. The 9th, amongst other regiments, was evacuated to the Isle of Wight.

By October 1694 the regiment landed at Chatham in Kent. After a short rest two companies marched to Bristol and other companies were detached to various places around Somerset, including Taunton and Bridgewater.

On 6 December eight companies were at Bristol and on 19 December the regiment was sent to Hampshire and Wiltshire. Two companies were based at Winchester, two in Southampton and three in Salisbury. This was a short-lived posting, as at the end of 1694 Steuart received orders to prepare to move to Portsmouth. Confirmation of the order was received on 12 March 1695. The 9th was part of a force that sailed out of Portsmouth on 18 March; a month later they were at Cadiz in Spain. The fleet reached Barcelona on 18 May, with the plan to attack the French at Toulon. A change of plan and poor weather meant that instead the 9th would be involved in an attack on Palamos (on what we now know as the Costa Brava). It had been taken by the French.

On 9 August the regiment was part of a 4,000 strong force that landed at Blanes. Even after Palamos had been bombarded by the English fleet it was still clear that the French were in too great a strength to be forced out and the attack was called off. After a frustrating overseas campaign the 9th had home postings across the West Country and in Ireland (in fact the 9th would have several Irish postings between 1691 and 1805).

War of the Spanish Succession

A new war was looming in 1701 and the catalyst was the squabble over the succession to the Spanish throne. The French King Louis XIV favoured his grandson Philip of Anjou. Emperor Leopold of Austria supported his own grandson, Archduke Charles. The bone of contention was that if Philip succeeded it would bring France and Spain together and upset Europe's balance of power. In

August 1701 England, Holland and Austria proclaimed their support of Archduke Charles, pledging to throw the French out of Flanders and Italy.

The 9th embarked from Cork on 15 June 1701 and headed for Spithead. Initially the 9th had been earmarked for operations in Holland, but instead four companies were sent to Windsor. The Prince and Princess of Denmark were to be there on a state visit. The remaining six companies were to go to the Tower of London.

On 15 July two newly recruited companies joined the six companies at the Tower. The whole regiment was reunited on 6 February 1702. Its strength was around 700 officers and men and this time it was bound for Holland. They had hardly disembarked when news arrived that King William III had died on 8 March 1702.

England did not declare war on France until 4 May 1702. The 9th was now part of a 25,000 man force commanded by the Duke of Marlborough and facing them were estimated 60,000 French. The 9th was involved in the storming of Liège on 23 October 1702. Again the Grenadiers of the 9th had led the way. The French governor surrendered his sword to a lieutenant of the regiment.

The 9th was back in England by January 1703 and went to Windsor to receive honours from Queen Anne. Their part in the war of the Spanish succession, however, was not over as operations would now switch to Spain itself.

In January 1704 preparations were well under way to send six foot regiments, the Royal Dragoons and Archduke Charles to the peninsula. The force arrived at Lisbon on 29 February 1704 but it was not until the May that they were ready for operations, due to a combination of sickness, poor supply, arguments between the allies (Dutch and Portuguese) and the dreadful state of the Portuguese troops. The 9th found itself garrisoning the small fortress of Castello de Vide by late June 1704; it was under siege by the French. The garrison, comprising of the 9th and two Portuguese units, was under no real danger, as the French lacked the fire power to effect a breach. The Portuguese governor had other ideas, however; he sent out a Portuguese colonel and Lieutenant-Colonel Hussey (by now commander of the 9th) to negotiate terms. The French insisted that the whole garrison would have to give up their weapons and become prisoners of war. Hussey refused, but his hand was forced when he found out that the governor had ordered that the reserves of gunpowder be thrown down a well. The 9th surrendered and was marched off into captivity. On 29 September 1704 Marlborough had agreed to exchange English prisoners taken in Portugal for French prisoners taken at the battle of Blenheim (13 August 1704). The 9th was certainly at Bordeaux in November 1704, but was then shipped back to Portugal under the agreement.

There had been a number of developments in Spain and Portugal whilst the 9th were prisoners of war. Gibraltar had been captured by the English and the campaign was going well. The 9th was involved in the sieges at Valencia de Alcantara, which was taken in early May 1705, Albuquerque (20 May) and Salvaterra (21 May).

On 12 July 1705 the 9th was reinforced when it received 227 men from the 11th Regiment. It is clear that the 9th was still in Spain, although it is difficult to know precisely what they were doing, as they are not specifically mentioned in any of the engagements. The 9th was still involved in the campaign in the spring of 1706; it was to be events in 1707, however, that were to have a marked impact on the progress of the war.

Battle of Almanza

The 9th was involved in a major battle at Almanza on 25 April 1707. It was to become the most decisive engagement of the war of the Spanish succession. The allied force consisted of 4,800 English troops, 1,480 Dutch, 1,100 French Huguenots, 250 Germans and a number of Portuguese; the total force amounted to some 22,000 men. Opposing them was the Duke of Berwick, at the head of a Franco-Spanish force of 25,000. The 9th was positioned to the right of the centre of the allied army. The engagement went disastrously wrong for the Earl of Galway in overall command of the allied force. Each of their attacks was beaten back with heavy casualties until all that was left intact was some 3,500 men, including most of the 9th, who were able to retreat over twenty miles to relative safety. The 9th had taken heavy casualties; a number of officers and men had been killed and several had been taken prisoner. The remnants of the force marched to Alcira on 26 April. Lieutenant-Colonel Steuart (a nephew of the colonel) had succeeded Hussey as lieutenant-colonel of the 9th and he was left at Alcira with 800 infantry, made up of what remained of the 9th and other English and Dutch infantry. Steuart held out as long as he could. There was no hope of reinforcement and he was desperately short of food and ammunition. He finally accepted terms and was to be repatriated to Catalonia to rejoin Galway. The commander had managed to pull together around 2,000 survivors of the ill-fated battle. When Steuart's men marched into Galway's camp on 16 September 1707 there were just 386 officers and men left.

The 9th was one of the regiments that were sent home during the winter of 1707 to 1708. Back in England, on 15 September 1707, recruitment had got under way to bring up the regiment to full strength and they were to muster at Hereford. From 24 December 1707 the regiment's establishment strength was set at thirteen companies. It is not clear exactly when the remnants of the 9th returned home, although it was probably early in 1708.

The next clear information we have of the regiment is in March 1708. The recruits were sent to Winchester, possibly in anticipation of linking up with the survivors returning home. An order was issued on 15 September 1708, authorizing the regiment to be recruited up to full strength. More recruits left London in November and December to join the regiment, which now seems to have been based at Worcester. Three more companies recruited at Hereford were sent off to join the regiment at Worcester on 22 January 1709. Another order, on 12 February 1709, instructed the regiment to march to Portsmouth. This order was cancelled ten days later; four of the companies were to go to Stockport and the remaining nine to Manchester. The regiment was reduced in strength on 24 April 1709 to twelve companies; the thirteenth company was to be given over to another regiment. By June 1709 the bulk of the regiment was at Chester; it was ready for transfer to garrison duties in Ireland.

The regiment was probably stationed in Ireland throughout the period 1709 to 1718. During that time there were a number of changes. The precedence of the 9th was confirmed as being ninth in the list of line regiments. In 1715 Steuart sold his commission as Colonel of the 9th to Colonel James Campbell, who was lieutenant-colonel of the Scot's Greys. However Campbell was only with the 9th until February 1717 when he rejoined the Scot's Greys. The new colonel was the Honourable Charles Cathcart, later Lord. He retired in January 1718 and was replaced by Colonel James Otway.

Minorca

Overseas postings once again beckoned in July 1718; the 9th was transferred from Ireland and posted to Minorca. The regiment embarked on 8 May 1718, reaching Gibraltar on 12 July. This was a peacetime posting and the regiment had twelve companies. The companies were much reduced in size, with no more than forty private soldiers, except the Grenadier Company that had closer to forty-five. An order was issued on 20 May 1718, with the purpose of bringing the regiment up to strength. It was to receive a new draft of nearly 100 men.

Colonel Otway died in 1725 and was replaced on 25 December by Brigadier Richard Kane, who was already the commander in chief of Minorca and the lieutenant governor of the island. Minorca had become an English possession in 1713. Kane was a brilliant administrator; he had directed the improvement of the island's infrastructure and the regiment was in good hands.

On 25 September 1729, the strength of the 9th was fixed at ten companies, each of them, including the grenadiers, were fifty privates, three sergeants, three corporals and two drummers. Brigadier Kane died in 1737 and was replaced by Colonel Hargrave (formerly of the 7th Fusiliers). Hargrave only remained with the regiment until 28 August 1739 when he was replaced by Brigadier-General George Reade. Another war was looming, this time with Spain. War was declared in early August 1739, by which time the 9th had been reinforced to the extent that it now had sixty privates in each of the companies. In all, the regiment now mustered some 815 officers and men. The Minorca garrison was increased from four battalions to five in anticipation of an attack. It never came, but in 1746 the regiment was transferred to Gibraltar.

Troops manning Gibraltar had been posted to America and the 9th replaced the two that had been sent even further from home. On 1 November 1749, Reade was transferred to command the 9th Dragoons and his place was taken by Sir C A Powlett. On Christmas Day, the regiment was informed that they were to be sent to Ireland. This would be their posting for the next six years.

By 26 January 1751 it was Powlett's turn to move on and the regiment was now commanded by Hon. J Waldegrave. At the beginning of July 1751 a number of major changes for all regiments came into effect. Up until this point, the name, uniforms, weapons and flags had not been fixed. The new regulations changed this forever. From this point, regiments would not be directly associated with their own colonel. The King's colour would be carried, as would a second colour featuring the facing colour of the regiment and the union flag. The number of the regiment was embroidered on the second colour inside a wreath of roses and thistles. Further regulations covered the uniforms worn by the drummers, the grenadiers' caps and the drums.

Henceforth, the regiment would be known as the 9th Regiment of Foot. The regiment's facing colour would be yellow. This would be just the first step on a road to establishing the identity of the regiment. Over thirty more years would pass before its association with Norfolk would begin and a hundred until the title of the 9th Regiment transformed into the Norfolk Regiment.

2

The 9th Foot 1751–1827

If the regiment had any connection with a county at all it would have been Gloucestershire, rather than Norfolk, as it had been raised there in the first place. This association with Gloucestershire is even more muddled than would first appear. In August 1807, a Sergeant Hale stated that he and another 170 men had volunteered to join His Majesty's 9th or Britannia Regiment of Foote. Hale and the other were all members of the North Gloucestershire Militia.

The 9th, along with seven other regiments, were recalled from Ireland in 1755. In December 1754, the strength of the regiment had been established at seventy private soldiers per company. Less than a year later, in October 1755, two more companies were added to the regiment, each with a complement of non-commissioned officers, but with a hundred private soldiers each. The regiment had also had another change of commanding officer. Sir Joseph Yorke took over as colonel on 18 March 1755 after Waldegrave had been transferred.

Shortly afterwards, the regiment landed at Bristol, the companies were distributed around Bristol itself, Exeter and Tiverton. The 9th had been inspected on 18 October 1755 at Bristol by Lieutenant-General Sir J Mordaunt. He had not liked what he saw: he thought the bulk of the men were unsoldierly and he doubted whether the regiment was fit for active service. Ten days later, and confirmed on 1 November 1755, the regiment was ordered to march to Carlisle; the eventual destination would be Scotland. A large number of the regiment still remained in Ireland, too sick to be moved. Consequently, they did not rejoin the regiment until 1756. By 1756, the regiment was in Glasgow, but once again it was bound for Ireland, returning there in the spring of 1757.

The 9th made another return to the West Country at the end of their tour of duty in Ireland in 1759. In February, the regiment marched out of Bideford with companies being spread out at Oakhampton, Dartmouth, Falmouth, Tavistock, Launceston and Penrhyn. The four companies assigned to Falmouth were sent to replace three companies from another regiment (Lord George Bentinck's) that were guarding French prisoners at Falmouth and Penrhyn. On 6 March, a company of the 9th from Oakhampton and another from Launceston marched to take up duties as prisoner of war guards at Bideford (replacing companies of Lieutenant-General Wolfe's regiment).

The ornate head of a ceremonial axe that would be carried by a senior non-commissioned officer of the regiment in the late 18th and early 19th century

A close up of a late 18th-century wooden powder flask, which would have been worn by regular soldiers in the regiment, from the Royal Norfolk Regimental Museum

By June 1759, the whole regiment was at Plymouth. In the same month, the new establishment strength was set at nine companies of 100 soldiers, plus four sergeants, four corporals and two drummers. The grenadier company had an additional two fifers. At this stage, the 9th's paper strength was 1,034 officers and men.

Bay of Biscay

The regiment received new orders on 7 June 1760; it was to march to Chatham in Kent. It remained encamped until 13 October and then took up residence in Chatham barracks. On 24 January 1761 Major-General Hodgson was issued an order, giving him the power to move the 9th Regiment and four other regiments to embarkation ports, ready for an overseas expedition. The 9th itself did not leave Chatham until 5 March and it arrived at Hilsea barracks, close to Portsmouth, in two groups between 16 and 17 March. The 9th would be part of a secret mission, which aimed to capture a French island called Belleisle, off Quiberon Bay in the Bay of Biscay.

The expedition would consist of 10,000 men, made up of the 9th, 19th, 21st, 30th, 67th, 76th, 85th, 90th, 97th and 98th Regiments of Foot, along with members of the 16th Light Dragoons. The 9th would make up a sizeable proportion of the force, with some 800 men under the command of Lieutenant-Colonel R Phillips. The force left Spithead on 29 March, arriving off their objective on 7 April 1761.

A reconnaissance was carried out that day and the island resembled a fortress. The French had been feverishly working on the defences. In overall command were Hodgson and the naval commodore Keppel. Together they decided that the weakest point was close to the village of Lomaria, on the south-eastern end of the island. The fleet was led by HMS *Valiant* and consisted of eight frontline battleships and a number of frigates.

The fleet opened fire on the fort at Lomaria and the shore batteries on the morning of 8 April. Grenadiers led the amphibious landings but immediately they ran into difficulties; the cliffs were simply too steep. The initial attacks all failed and bad weather began to set in that evening. Stormy conditions scattered the fleet and not much could be done until 22 April, by which stage four more units had arrived as reinforcements for the invasion force.

The French had around 2,500 regular troops and 4,000 militiamen. They also had a number of artillerymen, engineers and coastguards and were commanded by Chevalier de St Croix. It was now decided that the English troops would attack the coastline at several points, hoping that one of the targets would be unguarded.

The attacks began at 1700 on 22 April and this time, despite some setbacks, the landings were largely successful. The French fell back towards the citadel at Palais. Hodgson now concentrated his force and began to advance. Delays in landing the siege artillery gave the French time to build redoubts to protect the approaches to the town. The English now began the painstaking duty of digging trenches and siege works and bombarding the town until a breach was made. A practicable breach was made on 7 June and by this time St Croix, having held out for two months, knew that the game was up and that he could not hope for any salvation; he surrendered and was given honours of war. His troops were repatriated to France.

It is not clear as to the precise movements or activities of the 9th during this siege. What we do know is that by the time the campaign was over two officers had become prisoners of war and twenty-two of the 9th had been killed. The only clear account of the 9th's involvement, *The Historical Records of the Ninth Foot*, states: 'The Ninth leapt on the beach in the face of the enemy's entrenchments, and rushed up the steep acclivity to storm the works, but were unable to gain the summit without ladders.' Undoubtedly this quote refers to the initial attacks which failed on 8 April and it was probably during this time that the two officers were taken prisoner.

The 9th stayed on Belleisle as part of the garrison until the beginning of 1762. On 25 December 1761 their strength was set at around 1,034 officers and men in nine companies. The 9th had an appalling return journey to England; an order to the governor of Portsmouth, dated 9 January 1762, states that he should station one company of the regiment at Arundel, four at Chichester and four between Petersfield and Havant. However not all of the 9th had made it home by this time; four transport vessels, with members of the 9th onboard, were still missing after being hit by a gale. It seems probable that these men did not make it back to England until 16 January 1762 or later.

Caribbean

Overseas service was to be the 9th's lot for many years to come. The governor of Portsmouth was issued with orders to send out officers of the regiment to collect drafts of new recruits and concentrate them at Chichester. The 9th would become part of another overseas expedition, this time commanded by the Earl of Albemarle. They would soon be marching towards an embarkation port. Albemarle had been given the responsibility of launching an expedition against Spanish-held Cuba. The English had long since believed that Spain would ally itself with France and that it would declare war. As a result preparations were well under way when war was finally declared on 18 January 1762. Albemarle received secret orders dated 18 February 1762.

Albemarle's force sailed from Spithead on 5 March. It reached Barbados on 20 April and here it was supposed to join up with another English force based on Martinique. These troops had been ravaged by disease and shortage of supplies, so Albemarle took his own force to Martinique to join up with them. Another 4,000 men, under General Amherst, had also been supposed to rendezvous with Albemarle from North America, but they had not appeared. Albemarle found himself in the difficult position of having to mount the expedition against Cuba on his own. The force left Martinique on 6 May and arrived off the coast of Cuba, close to Havana, on 6 June 1762. Part of the fleet blockaded Havana harbour, whilst the rest of the force landed the army, without opposition, along the coast. Albemarle had left a number of men on the Leeward Islands and had with him four infantry brigades, including the 9th. At this time the 9th could muster around 977 officers and men and together with the 34th Foot was the strongest regiment in the force.

Without waiting for the troops from America or Jamaica to join them, Albemarle set off towards Havana on 8 June. They ran into 6,000 local militiamen, formed up along the River Coximar. The militia were driven back and the English pressed on.

The first target would be Fort Moro, the main defence point protecting the entrance to Havana harbour. A number of the men of the 9th Regiment were assigned the task of becoming mounted infantry; in effect they would operate like Dragoons. They were commanded by one of the regiment's officers, Captain Suttie, and they would carry out patrol work and engage in cattle raids.

The Spanish garrison in Havana was strong; there were 4,600 regular troops, 9,000 Spanish sailors and 14,000 militias. The British concentrated on building batteries to bring fire down on Fort Moro and prepared to storm the redoubts. A breach in the fort's defences was the main priority. By mid-June the English batteries were just 250m from the fort's walls. The major danger to the English force was not the Spanish, but the hot and humid climate, the persistent rain and the lack of proper shelter. In fact by the middle of July nearly half of the English force was sick.

The British also occupied the Cavanos Ridge, overlooking Havana city itself from across the harbour entrance. This posed an even greater threat to the Spanish. On 22 July 1762 the Spanish launched 1,500 men at daybreak against the British defences along the ridge. They also launched a diversionary attack against the British troops besieging Fort Moro. By the time the attacks petered out the Spanish had lost at least 400 killed and at least that number wounded. The 9th's Grenadier and Light Companies were directly involved in beating off the attacks. The Spanish tried again on 30 July; this time their losses were even higher, with at least 700 killed or wounded. A number of key Spanish officers were also lost.

That day there was a sad episode, as members of the 9th Regiment took part in the assault on Fort Moro. The storming party was led by Lieutenant C Forbes. Two of his close friends, Lieutenant Holland of the 90th Regiment and Lieutenant Nugent of the 9th, were tragically killed just as victory had been sealed. They were shot by Spanish troops firing from the lighthouse. Forbes led a storming party into the lighthouse and killed everyone inside. Nugent was part of the Grenadier Company which had been among the leading units to storm the fort.

With the capture of Fort Moro, Havana was doomed. The English opened up on the town and Punta Fort, a smaller defence works on the opposite side of the harbour entrance to Fort Moro. Preparations were now under way for an assault.

Albemarle summoned the Spanish to surrender on 10 August 1762, but they refused. On 11 August the English opened fire, with forty-three guns and eight mortars. They quickly silenced Fort Punta. Realizing that this would be the fate of the city itself, the Spanish ran up white flags at 1400 hours and asked for surrender negotiations to commence.

Although a number of the English troops had been killed in the fighting, at least 3,000 had died from disease by October 1762. The 9th had lost a number of officers and men; nineteen private soldiers had been killed in the fighting, twenty-four had been lost to disease.

Bizarrely, however, Cuba would be returned to Spanish possession. A peace treaty was signed in Paris on 10 February 1763; Spain would regain Cuba but would lose Florida. The 9th was to accompany the 35th Regiment to occupy Florida and take over from the Spanish administration. The 9th was sent to Fort St Augustine on the coast of east Florida. It was a far healthier posting than they could have hoped for and the regiment would remain here for six years.

Records of this period are very sketchy, but we do know that by March 1764 the regiment had six companies based at St Augustine. There was another at Fort Apalache, another on New Providence Island and a third on Bermuda. By 1765 each of the companies was no stronger than three sergeants and forty-four privates. This was as a result of disease and lack of reinforcement. There was a marked difference from the thousand or more that had landed in Havana in 1762. Bt the time the regiment reached Florida in August 1763 they had been reduced to sixteen officers, sixteen sergeants, nine drummers and 234 private soldiers.

This was to be a miserable period for the regiment; it was constantly ravaged by disease and what few reinforcements arrived did not last long in the difficult climate. A draft of new recruits certainly did arrive in June 1766, under a Captain Peyton, but the commander in chief in North America, Major-General Gage, complained bitterly about how poor these recruits were.

Ireland

By late 1768 it appears that the regiment was bound for Ireland once again. Officially the regiment joined the Irish contingent on 25 December 1768, but the regiment had not even left Florida. Gage was ordered to reduce the size of the regiment before sending it across the Atlantic. He was instructed that the regiment should consist of no more than nine companies. Each of these companies should have two sergeants, two corporals, a drummer and twenty-eight other ranks. Any men belonging to the 9th in excess of this would be given a bonus if they volunteered to transfer to another regiment in America. It was not until January 1770 that the 9th finally landed in Ireland, where it was brought up to strength, now with nearly 150 men in each of the companies.

On 8 August 1771 Viscount Ligonier became colonel of the regiment. The regiment was based at Limerick by January 1772 and by the March it was stationed in Dublin. Lieutenant-General Dilkes inspected the 9th on 15 July but he was not impressed: 'The regiment is really a very bad one. Notwithstanding, they fired and marched well. By the plan laid down by the Colonel it must certainly improve.' Less than a year later, on 18 March 1773, he inspected them again and said that the regiment was: 'Very much mended since the last review, and I doubt not it will be better against the next, as most of the old men are discharged.'

In July 1773 the 9th moved to Waterford and on 26 May 1774 they were again inspected, this time by Lieutenant-General Lord Blayney. He commented that the men were: 'Of good appearance, saluted well, uniforms correct.'

Canada

In 1775 the regiment was at Dungannon and later in Dublin, but they were bound once again for overseas active service. They were shipped down to an embarkation port between January and April 1776. The regiment set sail from Cork on 8 April 1776, bound for Quebec in Canada. By this stage the regiment consisted of twelve companies. Two companies were to remain behind in order to recruit more men for the regiment. The new recruits were to be offered a three-year time of service, or for the period of the war, whichever was the shorter. The colonies in North America were in rebellion against the Crown and even Canada was threatened.

At the time of embarkation the regiment mustered its lieutenant-colonel, a major, seven captains, ten lieutenants, six ensigns, an adjutant, a quartermaster, a surgeon's mate, thirty sergeants, twenty-two drummers and fifers and 462 other ranks. Some sixty-six men had deserted the regiment as soon as word had been received that they were to make for Canada. The regiment arrived off the coast of Newfoundland on 18 April 1776. The transports took them up the St Lawrence River and they reached Quebec on 29 April.

The rebels had taken Fort Ticonderoga, which lay between Lake George and Lake Champlain, in the previous year. They had also tried to take Montreal, but had failed. 6,000 rebels were laying siege to Fort St Johns, on the north of Lake Champlain. The fort had surrendered and the rebels were advancing toward the St Lawrence River, in an attempt to cut Montreal off from Quebec.

The new British reinforcements enabled Sir Guy Carleton, the British governor, to launch his own offensive at the beginning of June 1776. He advanced towards Three Rivers and we know that the 9th disembarked on 5 June close to Three Rivers and marched into the settlement on 6 June. At 0300 on 8 June the rebels launched a surprise attack with 2,000 men against Three Rivers. They were beaten off with high casualties. The 9th now embarked on ships and sailed for Sorel at the southwest end of St Peter's Lake. They hoped to catch the rebels there and bring them to battle. The regiment landed on 14 April, just two hours after the rebels had evacuated the settlement.

Carleton's troops, supported by those under Burgoyne, pursued in three columns. The rebels were forced to abandon Fort St Johns. The British, lacking sufficient boats to follow, watched the rebels fall back to Crown Point, to the south of Lake Champlain and to Fort Ticonderoga, guarding the north entrance of Lake George.

The British had managed to collect together a large enough fleet by the end of September 1776. After a naval battle between 11 and 13 October, the rebels evacuated Crown Point and fell back towards Ticonderoga. By this stage the British army amounted to some 12,000 men. Winter was now drawing in and the 9th spent the winter months on Isle Jésus, close to Montreal.

Over the winter months Sir William Howe and his troops captured New York and plans for a new campaign in 1777 were now being formulated. It was proposed that Howe move up the Hudson River from New York whilst Burgoyne would close in on Ticonderoga, head for Saratoga and then on to Albany. Meanwhile a third force was to capture Fort Stanwix. This would mean that the rebel army would be trapped between three British forces.

The 9th was to be part of General Burgoyne's force operating out of St Lawrence in June 1777. The 9th was the senior regiment of the command and would operate on the right of Brigadier-General Hamilton's brigade and work with the 53rd and the 47th Foot. The army assembled close to Lake Champlain and was ferried across to Crown Point, landing on 27 June 1777. There were still around 3,000 rebels under General St Clare, at Ticonderoga and at Mount Independence, which was on the opposite side of the entrance to Lake George. Some distance away, near Albany, was another rebel force of up to 12,000 men.

Burgoyne's troops got under way on 30 June, closing in on the forward rebel positions. By the evening of 5 July the British had established artillery batteries on Sugarloaf Hill, which overlooked both of the rebel positions. Too late, St Clare realized his mistake; he knew that the British would bombard him and there would be nothing that he could do about it. He ordered a retreat during the night of 5 to 6 July. The British moved into the unoccupied forts the following morning and sent troops ahead to probe and find the rebel columns.

We know that the 9th, along with two other regiments, landed at South Bay as part of the pursuit force. Elements of the 9th were thrown forward under Brigadier-General Simon Fraser and they ran into a rebel rearguard, where a number of members of the regiment were killed. Captain Stapylton was mortally wounded and Lieutenant Rowe was also wounded. Both men were officers in the 9th Regiment. Lieutenant-Colonel Hill, commanding the 9th, moved towards Fort St Anne to engage the enemy. Burgoyne promised that two other regiments would be sent up in support, but they arrived too late, as Burgoyne explained in a letter dated 17 July 1777:

A violent storm of rain, which lasted the whole day, prevented the troops from getting to Fort St Anne so soon as was intended; but the delay gave the 9th Regiment an opportunity of distinguishing themselves by standing and repulsing an attack of six times their number. The enemy finding the position not to be forced in front, endeavoured to turn it; and from the superiority of their numbers that inconvenience was to be apprehended; and Lieutenant Colonel Hill found it necessary to change his position in the height of the action; so critical an order was executed by the regiment with the upmost steadiness and bravery. The enemy, after an attack of three hours, were totally repulsed and fled towards Fort Edward, setting fire to Fort Anne, but leaving a sawmill and a blockhouse in good repair, which were afterwards possessed by the King's troops. The 9th Regiment acquired, during their expedition, about thirty prisoners, some stores and baggage, and colours of the 2nd Hampshire Regiment.

According to Sergeant Lamb of the 9th, the regiment had captured a number of rebel boats in Wood Creek. They advanced to within a quarter of a mile of Fort Anne. A rebel deserter told Hill that the fort was garrisoned by 1,000 men. Hill sent off a despatch to Burgoyne. In all probability Hill's command amounted to no more than 190 men. Hill, to avoid being outflanked, retired to a hill as the rebels closed in on him. His position was close to being overrun when the rebels were spooked by the sound of Indian war cries. Burgoyne had sent an officer of the 9th Regiment, Captain Money, who was one of his staff officers, ahead with a number of Indians. As the force approached the rebel lines the Indians refused to advance any further. Money proceeded on his own, screaming and crashing around. In the engagement the 9th had lost eleven killed and nineteen wounded. One officer had been killed and four others had been wounded.

The British now had to advance towards Albany; it was extremely difficult terrain, thickly forested and laced with rivers. By 13 September 1777 Burgoyne's force had reached Saratoga. The rebels, under Gates, were twelve miles to the south at Stillwater. The 9th was now part of a force that amounted to some 5,000 effective troops. They were supported by thirty-five guns and howitzers and six mortars. On 19 September Burgoyne began to move towards the rebel positions on Bemmis Heights. The British force closed in on Freeman's Farm. The 9th was part of the centre of this force, but as Burgoyne approached the farm the 9th was pulled back into reserve. At the farm the British encountered a large rebel force. The woodland around the farm was so thick that it was difficult to see if either side was being outflanked. Consequently much of the fighting took place in the dense woodland. The British were hopelessly outnumbered and Major Forbes, Captain Swetenham and Lieutenant Price, all of the 9th, were among the officers killed. Eventually the rebels fell back, but the British were too exhausted to pursue.

A close up of the flintlock mechanism of an early musket used by the Royal Norfolk Regiment, from the regimental museum

The fight resumed on 20 September 1777, this time with the British throwing themselves against new defence works. Burgoyne had hoped that Sir Henry Clinton would bring his force up to support him, but Clinton was in no position to move and if he had been it would have been too late. All Burgoyne could hope for was that Gates would attack him and suffer the same kind of casualties that the British had endured when they had taken the offensive. Burgoyne still wanted to move on Albany but he lacked sufficient strength.

On 7 October, in an attempt to turn the rebel left wing, a sharp fight developed. Again casualties were high and by the evening the British could barely muster 4,000 effective troops. Burgoyne was forced to pull back. Gates was continually being reinforced and had with him around 16,000 men. If Burgoyne was not careful he would find himself entirely surrounded. Burgoyne dug in around Saratoga. The 9th Regiment operated as a central reserve that would be rushed to any point under threat.

By the night of 13 October the situation had got even worse. Allied Indians and Canadian troops had deserted and only around 2,000 British troops were fit for duty. Burgoyne was all for falling back towards Fort Edward and Fort George but to his horror he now discovered that the road was held by the rebels. Ticonderoga had already fallen and reluctantly Burgoyne began to negotiate the surrender. Gates insisted that he would allow them to march to Boston for embarkation provided none of the men ever served in North America again. In all, some 4,420 men, including the sick and wounded, surrendered. They were moved towards Boston and imprisoned in Rutland County in the summer of 1778. It was the officers that would get home first; Major Forbes, Captain Sheldon, Lieutenant Fife, Lieutenant Prince, Lieutenant McNeill, Lieutenant Murray and Lieutenant Hoy, along with Ensigns Fielding, Waddle and Spencer, were exchanged sometime after 25 October 1780. Another batch of officers was sent of home on 3 September 1781. The rest of the men were to be held in captivity for a number of years.

Incredibly the 9th had not lost its colours after the surrender at Saratoga. Lieutenant-Colonel Hill had hidden them in his own personal belongings. He kept them safe until he returned to England in 1781 when he presented them to the King and in return was promoted to the rank of Colonel on 16 May 1781.

The two companies that had been left behind in Ireland had been sent to England. Lord Ligonier, the colonel of the regiment, was given instructions on 31 October 1780 to establish headquarters at Stoke Newington in London.

East Indies

In January 1781 a company of the 9th was despatched from Portsmouth under the command of Major-General Medows, bound for the East Indies. The unit arrived in India on 24 June 1781 and became the responsibility of the East India Company.

Moves were afoot to link many of the regular regiments with specific counties.

The following letter was sent out on 31 August 1782:

His Majesty having been pleased to order that the Regiment of Foot, which you command, shall take the county name of 'Ninth or East Norfolk Regiment' and be looked upon as attached to that division of the county, I am to acquaint you it is His Majesty's further pleasure that you shall in all things conform to that idea, and endeavour by all means in your power to cultivate and improve that connection, so as to create a mutual attachment between the county and the regiment which may at all times be useful towards recruiting the regiment; but as the completing of the several regiments, now generally so deficient, is in the present crisis of the most important national concern, you will on this occasion use the utmost possible exertion for that purpose, by prescribing the greatest diligence to your officers and recruiting parties, and by every suitable attention to the gentlemen and considerable inhabitants, and as nothing can so much tend to conciliate their affections as an orderly and polite behaviour towards them, and an observance of the strictest discipline in all your quarters, you will give the most positive orders on that head; and you will immediately make such a disposition of your recruiting parties as may best answer that end.

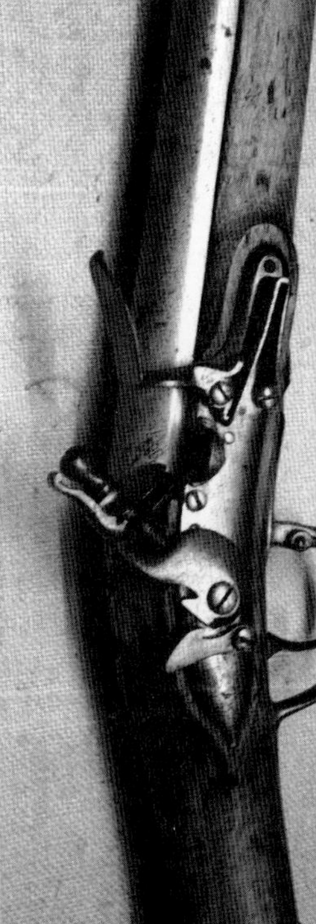

A close up of a typical musket that would have been used by soldiers in the regiment throughout the early part of the 19th century

A brass waist belt buckle, as worn by a soldier of the 9th East Norfolk Regiment during the Napoleonic period, between c.1808 and 1813

An 18th-century painting of a drummer of the West Norfolk Militia

It is worth remembering that the 54th Foot was given the title 'The West Norfolk Regiment'. It was actually to become the Dorsetshire Regiment. Regardless of the instructions to try and recruit from east Norfolk, recruiting parties were sent to Ireland and to Lancashire. In fact in 1803 a whole battalion was raised for the North Lancashire Regiment from men living in Norfolk. The actual marrying up of the regiments with counties seemed to be rather haphazard. Admittedly when the regiment had returned to England it was sent to Norwich, which may well have been the principal reason for its territorial title in 1782. Before then it had no connection with the county at all and had never even served there. If anything it should have become the Gloucestershire Regiment.

The regiment, however, would have a brief association with East Anglia. Although a company was ordered to leave Norwich and head to Watford on 15 April 1782 (it would then go on to Windsor on 20 June), many of the other companies would remain in East Anglia. Four companies were ordered to go to Great Yarmouth, Lowestoft, Pakefield and Gorleston on 4 April 1783. We know that in June that year a sergeant and seven men from the company based in Great Yarmouth were sent to Southwold to help out revenue officers against smugglers. This was also one of the major tasks of the company based in Lowestoft.

In September 1783 the detached companies mustered at Norwich and on 22 September the regiment was given its marching orders to head for Berwick and for Tweedmouth. The regiment arrived there on 1 November 1783. By 1785 the regiment was once again bound for Ireland. Major-General C O'Hara reviewed them in Dublin on 28 July 1786, commenting: 'The general appearance of this regiment is smart and soldierlike, with great attention, both in officers and men; but from the inferior size of many men in the rear rank it is at present, upon the whole, not very fit for active service.'

Nearly a year later, on 10 May 1787, Major-General J Paterson reviewed the regiment, once again in Dublin. He commented that the regiment looked very smart and added: 'The regiment is particularly well disciplined in the field.'

West Indies

The regiment was once again earmarked for duties abroad and in 1788 they would go to the West Indies. In June 1788 the bulk of the regiment was on the island of St Kitts, with a detached company on the island of Nevis. It would remain here until the spring of 1793 when it became involved in the war against France, which had spread as far afield as the West Indies.

Under the overall command of Major-General Cuyler and ferried by vessels under Admiral Laforey, two companies of the 9th, under Major Baillie, left St Kitts for Barbados. They were to be part of an expedition that aimed to seize Tobago. The force sailed on 12 April 1793, arriving off the island at 1300 hours on 14 April. The troops were disembarked by 1500 and advanced towards a fort protecting the town of Scarborough. It was a relatively small British force, comprising of some Marines, nine companies of the 4th Battalion of the 60th Foot and the two companies from the 9th. They lacked siege equipment and Cuyler decided that he would try to storm the defences. The troops formed up at 0100 on 15 April and the men had been told not to open fire, but to attack with the bayonet. In the ensuing attack the soldiers of the 9th rushed the French fort and the French garrison surrendered. Only one officer, a drummer and three men were wounded from the regiment out of a total force of 394 and four officers.

The companies of the 9th returned to Barbados, but were back in action in the June; this time the target was Martinique. Again the two flank companies of the 9th were involved and the overall expedition was under the command of Major-General Bruce. The force landed to the northwest of Fort Royal, amounting to some 1,100 men. The British had hoped that royalist sympathizers on the island would assist them against the French republican troops. It was quickly decided that with little royalist help and a larger than expected French garrison it was prudent to withdraw. Consequently the flank companies of the 9th returned to the regiment at St Kitts, via Barbados.

At the beginning of the following year, 1794, a larger expedition was planned. Lieutenant-General Sir Charles Grey, who had been appointed the commander in chief in the West Indies in the previous September, would lead an attack against Martinique, Guadeloupe and St Lucia. The fleet would be commanded by Sir John Jervis. In preparation for the expedition the 9th was reinforced by new recruits. The British had mustered around 7,000 men by the end of January 1794 and their first target would be Martinique. The force sailed out of Barbados on 3 February, arriving off Martinique two days later.

The French on the island were commanded by Rochambeau, who was known to be a competent commander and who had a regular force and irregulars at his disposal. The flank companies of the 9th landed near La Trinité under Colonel Campbell. They were involved in the storming of Morne le Brun before advancing on Gros Morne, further inland. The British continued their advance toward Fort

A watercolour of an 18th-century Royal Norfolk Regiment soldier

Royal (Port de France), the principal harbour of the island. The French evacuated Morne Bruneau and the 9th beat off some frenzied French counterattacks. There was still much more fighting to do; the 9th was engaged in vicious fighting around St Pierre, but this town eventually fell, although Campbell was killed. Rochambeau finally surrendered Fort Bourbon on 23 March and now the British could look towards their next target, St Lucia.

The troops began embarkation on 30 March 1794 and elements of the 9th were attached to brigades under Major-General Dundas, Colonel Sir Charles Gordon and Colonel Coote. The first of the 9th to get ashore was the Light Company with Coote at 1900 on 1 April. They were involved in storming a redoubt and two batteries, at Anse de la Tocque. The French commander, Ricard, quickly realized that he was faced with insuperable odds and surrendered. Some of the 9th remained on St Lucia as part of the garrison, but the bulk returned to Martinique.

Again elements of the 9th were involved in the landings on Guadeloupe on 11 April. Guadeloupe resembles two islands, connected by a narrow causeway around 300m across. It is difficult to be clear as to the precise movements of the 9th on Guadeloupe, or indeed their casualties, but they were certainly engaged in the attack that seized Grande Terre, and then attacks against Basse Terre, the remaining half of the island. The French governor, Collot, capitulated on 21 April and the expedition was now over, but as dangerous as combat might be for the soldiers of the 9th, it was disease and fever that were the main threat.

As the expedition made plans to break up, news was received on 31 May that a French force had landed on Grande Terre and taken it back. Again soldiers of the 9th sailed out of St Lucia, aiming to retake the island. The troops landed without incident and stormed the French outposts. Six companies, commanded by Colonel Fisher of the 9th, worked around the French rear and despite several French counterattacks all their attempts to dislodge the British failed. The fighting continued. By now it was the rainy season and conditions were dreadful on the island. With losses mounting, the 9th withdrew to St Lucia.

It was clear that there were going to be considerable problems with these islands. The French were intent on taking them back and slaves were offered freedom and French citizenship if they rose up against the British. There was a rising on St Lucia on 9 September 1794. Major Baillie commanded a force of the 9th and the 6th against some of the rebels and managed to disperse them. Battle casualties and disease had reduced the 9th to 423 effectives by this time.

There was more work to be done against the rebels on the island and towards the end of January 1795 a major operation was launched against the rebels in the hills. More operations during the year, both on St Lucia and on Grenada, only served to reduce the regiment further. By the time the British decided to evacuate St Lucia on 19 June 1795, Baillie, who was by now the lieutenant-colonel of the regiment, only had 105 men fit for duty and eighty sick.

Around 150 of the regiment had been sent to Grenada at the beginning of March 1795 and they too were engaged in operations against rebels. The island was a dangerous place, swarming with around 10,000 rebels. It was clear that the regiment was thoroughly worn out and much reduced. It had been operating in the West Indies for eight years. Whilst some of the men volunteered to stay in the West

Watercolour of a regular soldier, a Grenadier, and an officer of the 18th century. These are typical uniforms of men that would have seen action both on the continent and further overseas during the period.

A watercolour of the camp of the Royal Norfolk Regiment in the late 18th century

Indies, transferring to other regiments, what remained of the 9th headed home in the summer of 1796. They arrived in Norwich in September 1796 and the first set of returns the following month showed that the regiment could muster just fifteen officers, ten sergeants, fourteen drummers and eighty-nine other ranks. Although by the end of the year the regiment had risen to 205, it was still over 800 men short of establishment strength.

The regiment remained in Norwich until the end of 1797 and in January 1798 it was in Colchester, by March at Bury St Edmunds and over April and May eight companies were at Sudbury and two at Ipswich. In June eight companies with the headquarters were based at Stowmarket, with detached companies at Clacton and Colchester. In July nine companies and the headquarters were based at Great Yarmouth and one company at Needham Market. In January 1799 the regiment was sent to Guernsey, but by June it was on the Isle of Wight. The following month it was sent to the Tower of London, but by the end of July it was in Romford. By September it was clear that overseas duties were beckoning once again, this time in Holland.

The year 1799 was a significant one for the regiment; an order issued by the Adjutant-General of 30 July 1799 stated: 'I have received His Royal Highness the Commander in Chief's directions to signify to you that His Majesty has been pleased to confirm to the 9th Regiment of Foot the distinction and privilege of wearing the figure of Britannia as a badge of the regiment.'

Holland

It is important to point out at this stage that there were three battalions of the 9th and it was the 1st Battalion that had been in operations in the West Indies. This new campaign in Holland would involve the 1st and 2nd Battalions. The colonel of the regiment was now Lieutenant-General Bertie, who also commanded the 1st

Battalion. Major-General Robert Manners commanded the 2nd Battalion and Colonel Fisher the 3rd Battalion. Each battalion at this stage had eleven companies and over 1,000 officers and men each. Manners would also command the 9th Brigade of the expeditionary force, consisting of the 1st and 2nd Battalions and the 56th Foot.

The British were allied to the Russians and fighting the French and their Dutch sympathizers. The two battalions landed in Holland on 16 September 1799. In the ensuing confused battle the 9th's battalions lost around 370 men, largely as a result of the Russians having attacked prematurely. Manners's troops found themselves sorely pressed by the enemy, but when the 9th advanced with fixed bayonets the enemy faltered and withdrew. They were engaged in a desperate musketry duel and running out of ammunition and the enemy brought up artillery. By 1600, with most of the ammunition gone, the 9th began to retire and enemy Hussars swept into their rear, cutting down many men. The 9th was praised for its gallantry and was also involved in a new offensive on 29 September.

When the peace treaty was finally signed the 9th could return home, first to Norwich and then to Bagshot Heath in Surrey. The regiment was again earmarked for overseas operations, this time it would be Spain as part of an expedition of some 13,000 men and for the first time all three battalions would be involved.

Spain

The initial target was Ferrol and the expedition was off the coast on 25 August 1800. The force landed, with the 9th operating as a reserve. It was to be a frustrating expedition for the 9th and they would see little in the way of fighting. In fact by 29 November they were on their way home again, landing at Portsmouth on 21 December 1800. They were almost immediately sent to Jersey, with the 1st Battalion at Granville barracks and the other two battalions at St Helier.

In June 1801 the three battalions made for Portsmouth, with the 3rd Battalion based at Shorncliffe and the 1st and 2nd Battalions heading to Battle Barracks, via Becks Hill. The 3rd Battalion was disbanded in May 1802, after the Peace of Amiens was signed. The 2nd Battalion was disbanded in 1802. By September 1802 there was just the 1st Battalion, based at Chatham Barracks.

Ireland

At the beginning of 1803 the battalion was around 1,000 men strong and on 25 September 1803 it embarked for Ireland. There was an expectation of a French invasion of Ireland, hence the scramble to send troops. Nearly a year later, in June 1804, Lieutenant-General Peter Hunt became the colonel of the regiment. Major-General Robert Brownrigg became the new colonel on 3 October 1805. Again it was clear that the regiment was destined for overseas service.

It embarked at Cork on 10 November. The headquarters and some of the troops were on board the transport *Ariadne* when disaster struck. The vessel was caught in a storm and driven onto the coast near Calais. The colonel, his staff and 262 men were taken as prisoners of war.

The rest of the men were onboard the *Isis* or the *Harriet*. They eventually landed near the mouth of the River Weser on 7 January 1806, as part of an expedition that aimed to capture Hanover. By good fortune the regiment's colours had not been captured when the *Ariadne* had been lost, as the then Captain Gomm wrote to his sister:

> We have saved the colours by a singular good fortune. It is always customary to lodge them onboard the headquarters ship, and the *Harriet* happening to be so at Falmouth on account of Colonel de Bernierè having left the regiment for a few days, they were brought from the *Ariadne* and have remained onboard our vessel ever since.

The voyage was a waste of time: Prussia accepted that the French should continue to occupy Hanover and the expedition was withdrawn. The 9th landed at Great Yarmouth at the beginning of February 1806. The regiment would now be commanded by Colonel John Stuart, who took up his post on 26 December 1806.

Meanwhile, in 1803, Major Crawford of the 1st Battalion had left the regiment to head for Dorset to reconstitute the 2nd Battalion. He had achieved his goal by 28 October 1804. Lieutenant-Colonel Cameron took over command of the 2nd Battalion on 1 October 1807 and he would have a long association with the regiment, commanding the 2nd Battalion from 1807 to 1808 and then taking command of the 1st Battalion until 1821. His men nicknamed him 'The Devil' on account of the fact that they would follow him anywhere. Cameron was a strict disciplinarian, gallant and always willing to lead from the front. It was his strength of personality that would mould the 9th into one of the most effective fighting units of the British army. The 2nd Battalion lost some men to the 1st Battalion in June 1808, but it was destined for Portugal and glory during the Peninsular War.

A brass waist belt buckle, as worn by soldiers of the regiment between 1808 and 1813

A magnificent medal with no fewer than six battle clasps; all of the battles fought by the regiment during the Peninsular War

Portugal

The 1st Battalion, under Stuart, arrived off the coast of Portugal on 26 July 1808 as part of a force commanded by Arthur Wellesley, the future prime minister and Duke of Wellington. The 1st Battalion of the 9th was allocated to General Hill's 1st Brigade and they would fight alongside battalions of the 5th and 38th Foot. Their first major engagement would be at Roliça.

The 1st Battalion found itself on the extreme right of the British centre. They were deployed in ravines, some of which were so narrow that only three men could walk side by side. Sergeant Hale wrote: 'We found great difficulty in some places in ascending, being obliged to pull ourselves up by some bushes or tufts of grass; at the same time they [the French] continued pouring musket shot on us very sharply.' Sergeant Hale also described the fate of Lieutenant-Colonel Stuart:

> The 29th Regiment being about a quarter of a mile on our left, and having some little better road than our regiment, they ascended the heights a few minutes before us; upon which the enemy immediately attacked them with a much superior force, and caused them to fall back with the loss of their colours and about 300 men; but as soon as we made our appearance at the top of the heights, it was a great relief to them; and the first thing our colonel thought most proper to do was to show them the point of the bayonet, which we immediately did; and much to their shame and disgrace we drove them off the heights in a few minutes; at the same time the remains of the 29th Regiment gave them another grand charge, by which they retook their colours and some prisoners. But, unfortunately, in this attack, Lieutenant-Colonel Stuart, who commanded the 9th Regiment, was killed, and also the colonel of the 29th Regiment. The enemy fell back a little distance, and then turned and attacked us again; but was received most gallantly and soon repulsed.

The British in fact threw the French back three times over the space of two hours and reluctantly the French, under Delaborde, began to withdraw. The 9th was once again mentioned in dispatches, having fought with great gallantry throughout the engagement.

Wellesley's force received much welcomed reinforcement, among which was the 2nd Battalion of the 9th, as part of Anstruther's brigade. Both battalions were present at the battle of Vimeiro on 21 August 1808. The 1st Battalion was not brought into action, but the 2nd was to bear the brunt of the French attack. Led by French skirmishers, the enemy advanced in force. In the fighting the 2nd Battalion lost four rank and files, a lieutenant, a sergeant and sixteen wounded. Significantly, Colin MacLiver, the future Sir Colin Campbell, who would command expeditions in China, the Sikh Wars, the Crimea and the Indian Mutiny, was an ensign with the 9th, aged 16, and this was the first time he had ever been under fire.

By October 1808 the 1st Battalion was now a part of Beresford's brigade and would be part of the reorganized force under Sir John Moore bound for Salamanca. The men were at least five months behind in pay and a significant French force was believed to be moving toward them. By this stage the 1st Battalion had a paper strength of 945 rank and files; however its effective strength was probably little over 600.

Moore's force had been involved in a number of running battles, the weather was appalling and by 24 December it had become clear that Napoleon himself was marching northwest from Madrid, with a huge force, intent on crushing Moore. The British force would have to evacuate Spain, but the troops were spoiling for a fight. Spanish allies were deserting in their hundreds and British troops began looting and pillaging. Moore knew that if he turned to fight Napoleon his force would be destroyed.

By 12 January 1809 the retreating British army had reached Vigo. Napoleon, believing that Moore had slipped away, fell back towards Madrid. But there were still upwards of 40,000 French in pursuit. Moore turned to hold them off; he could muster around 19,000 and the leading French units amounted to some 18,000. Moore was still hoping to extract his force intact.

Battle of Corunna

The expected battle finally took place at Corunna on 16 January 1809. The French attacked at around 1400, trying to turn Moore's right flank. The attack was repulsed and a similar attack on the left was also beaten back. Tragically Sir John Moore was hit by round shot and he died just as his army gained victory in the battle. The British could now embark without being molested by the French. The 1st Battalion, forming the rearguard, dug a grave in the central position of the Corunna battlefield at around daybreak on 17 January. There was a short service and the honour of being the last unit to leave Spain was given to the 9th. On the retreat alone after the battle the battalion lost an officer and 148 men either killed or captured.

Walcheren Expedition

The 1st Battalion arrived back in Britain, landing at Portsmouth and Plymouth. The 1st Battalion was in Canterbury by 9 February and on 17 July, after receiving around 300 recruits, they marched to Deal in Kent where again they would be sent overseas. This time they were to be part of the ill-fated Walcheren expedition.

The entire British forced amounted to some 39,000 men under the command of the Earl of Chatham. The 1st Battalion now had 932 rank and files and was brigaded as part of the 2nd Division along with the 38th and 42nd Foot. The brigade was commanded by Major-General Montresor and the idea was to try to deny the French the port of Antwerp and draw French troops away from the hard-pressed Austrians. The British force began landing at the end of July 1809.

The island of Walcheren was crisscrossed by ditches and fresh water was hard to come by. The civilian inhabitants of the island invariably caught fever in the hot months and this quickly spread to the British troops. By the middle of September upwards of 10,000 officers and men were reporting sick. By this time the 9th, having been on the island for only a short period of time, was back in Canterbury, not having fired a shot. In fact the regiment had got off very lightly and although upwards of half of the regiment was on the sick list they would be the first of the regiments sent to Holland to recover and go overseas again.

Portugal

Meanwhile the 2nd Battalion had been on garrison duty in Portugal. In May 1809 the 2nd had become part of the 7th Brigade under Brigadier-General Cameron, also of the regiment. They were part of Wellesley's army that intended to force the French to withdraw from Portugal. On 10 May the 2nd Battalion was *en route* to Oporto, although it does not appear that the battalion played a particularly significant role in dislodging the French under Soult. What we do know is that the 2nd Battalion embarked at Lisbon on 18 June and landed at Gibraltar on 2 July.

After recovering from the fever that had afflicted them after their short stay in Holland, and now with a strength of around 800, the 1st Battalion embarked for Lisbon from Ramsgate on 3 March 1810. They arrived off the Portuguese coast on 27 March. The situation on the peninsula had changed once again. Portugal needed to be defended and Wellesley had established defensive lines along Torres Vedras. From here the British hoped to protect Portugal, unless of course the French attacked from two different directions at the same time. The 1st Battalion remained close to Lisbon until 10 June when it became part of the 5th Division and was brigaded with battalions of the 1st and 38th Foot, under Lieutenant-Colonel Barnes. The 1st Battalion was now commanded by Lieutenant-Colonel Cameron, who had been transferred from the 2nd Battalion in July 1809. Threatening Portugal were around 65,000 French.

The 1st Battalion, as part of the 5th Division, marched into Espinhal on 19 September 1810 and then advanced towards Foz d'Aronce. By the evening of 22 September the 1st Battalion was in place on the Busaco Ridge, awaiting the French attack. On the night of 25 September the French advance guard arrived, making for the convent there. The British could muster around 52,000 men and were facing a large and aggressive French army: 15,000 infantry, under Reynier, would attack the ridge a mile to the south of the convent and as soon as Reynier had reached his objective Ney, at the head of 22,000 men, would attack along the main road. A further 16,000 men would remain in reserve. The attack began at 0530 on 27 September and initially the 1st Battalion was not involved in the fighting, which saw the French being beaten back. But more French troops were on their way.

According to Leith, commander of the 5th Division in his report, the 9th was to play a vital role in dealing with this new threat:

> Major-General Leith accordingly resolved instantly to attack the enemy with the bayonet; he therefore ordered the 9th British Regiment, which had hitherto been moving rapidly by its left in column, to form the line, which they did with the greatest promptitude, accuracy, and coolness, under the fire of the enemy, who had just appeared formed on that part of the rocky eminence which overlooks the back of the ridge, and who had then, for the first time, also perceived the British brigade under him.

Leith went on to explain that the 9th led the decisive counterattack: 'The order, celerity, and coolness with which they attacked, panic struck the enemy, who immediately gave way on being charged with the bayonet.'

Despite being under enemy fire the 9th pressed home, switching their line of attack to deal with formed bodies of French infantry. Each time the French tried to form up, even though they outnumbered the 9th, they were forced to retire as they came under immediate attack from the battalion. Cameron, suffering from sickness, personally led the charges and even had his horse killed under him. Captain Gomm was disappointed that the 9th did not receive greater recognition for their contribution that day.

The battle of Busaco cost the French 4,500 men. The Anglo–Portuguese army lost in excess of 1,200. Despite the fact that the 9th had been in the thick of the fighting, they had only lost five killed, one officer and eighteen wounded. The French, under Foy, consisting of seven battalions, had been repulsed at a cost of 670 killed.

Throughout the rest of the month and into October the 5th Division was held in reserve and by 14 November the French had begun to retreat. They were closely shadowed by the Anglo–Portuguese army. There was little real fighting and the French seemed unwilling to turn and fight.

Gibraltar and Malaga

Meanwhile the 2nd Battalion, by July 1809, was in Gibraltar. There was a danger that the vital British base could be overrun by the French. The Light Company of the 2nd Battalion was sent to Tarifa on 14 April 1810 and seven days later the fort was attacked by 500 French troops. After a counterattack by the British the French retreated but the Light Company remained at Tarifa until the middle of September, only returning to Gibraltar on 28 September.

The rest of the battalion was sent to Malaga on 22 June, under the overall command of Major-General Bowes. The expedition was a failure; the force never landed on Malaga, finding it too heavily defended by the French. Consequently they were back in Gibraltar on 2 July.

The flank companies were reinforced with new drafts and were now up to eighty men each and these men were sent as part of a force to try to relieve Cadiz. The two flank companies became part of what became known as Browne's battalion. It was a force of some 475 men made up of flank companies from the 2nd Battalion of the 9th, the 1st Battalion of the 28th and the 2nd Battalion of the 82nd.

Lieutenant-General Thomas Graham was in overall command of a force of 5,100 men that linked up with 7,000 Spanish troops on 27 February 1811. The force was approaching Cadiz on 5 March when they ran into a sizeable French force. Browne's battalion found themselves on the hill of Barrosa, along with five Spanish battalions. As the French closed the British troops were caught unawares and before they could form a square they were charged by enemy cavalry and dispersed. The battalion reformed in woodland and was sent back to try to retake the hill. They came under tremendous fire; half of the officers and 200 of the men were lost as they tried to advance through a storm of grapeshot and musketry. As other British units joined in the attack the troops under Browne managed to reform and helped break up the French battalions holding the hill. Browne's battalion had lost 236 killed and wounded. The flank companies of the 2nd Battalion of the 9th had amounted to 160 men before the engagement; eleven of them were killed, four officers wounded, five sergeants, one drummer and seventy other ranks. Lieutenant Colin Campbell was the only unwounded officer out of the two flank companies.

On 8 March the flank companies embarked to head back to Gibraltar, rejoining the battalion on 2 April. Reunited, the battalion left Gibraltar on 20 June 1811, along with the 47th Foot and some artillery. Their goal was to relieve Tarragona, which was under siege by the French. But they arrived too late, as the fortress had surrendered on 24 June, and the battalion was back in Gibraltar by 26 July.

The 2nd Battalion remained in existence until 24 December 1815. In fact it stayed in Gibraltar until April 1812. It provided 400 men to reinforce the 1st Battalion at the beginning of 1813. By April 1813 the 2nd Battalion was in Canterbury and it sent another 141 men and six officers to the 1st Battalion. From then on the 2nd Battalion was in Chatham then Sheerness and then the Isle of Sheppey until it was disbanded.

Spain

The 1st Battalion of the regiment had spent the winter of 1810 to 1811 at Torres Vedras and Alcoentre. In January, after having received reinforcements, they were holding Sobral Fort. Neither the British nor the French dared at this stage risk an all-out offensive. The French, under Massena, suffering from a lack of food and with large numbers of men in hospital, began to retreat at the beginning of March 1811. The Anglo-Portuguese set off in cautious pursuit.

The 1st Battalion was still part of the 5th Division and by the beginning of May 1811 it had almost reached Fuentes de Oñoro. Here the French chose to turn and fight. They had approximately 47,000 men, while the Anglo-Portuguese could muster about 36,000. The 1st Battalion was not involved in the fighting here, as they were some five miles away. The battalion was, however, involved in skirmishing over the next few days, losing four or so men wounded.

Sergeant Hale was with the light companies of the 9th that were sent out on the night of 10 May to intercept the French who were retreating towards Barba del Puerco. Hale was involved in the fighting, which eventually saw the French try to escape by scaling down a cliff and crossing a river. By this stage Hale was ill with a fever and he would be absent from the regiment for seven weeks, convalescing in Lisbon.

The battalion could now be put into reserve and they had time to recuperate, but by 16 August they were part once again of the 5th Division, this time aiming to stop the French from relieving Ciudad Rodrigo, which was under siege by the Anglo-Portuguese. At this time the battalion could muster 626 rank and files. Heading toward Ciudad Rodrigo were 50,000 French and it soon became clear that the Anglo-Portuguese lacked the strength to hold them off, so the siege was raised.

The 5th Division wintered in Portugal, but in the New Year they were once again marching into battle, this time against Badajoz, the last of the French-held fortresses on the Spanish frontier

A regimental officer's uniform, dated c.1812

Uniforms as worn by the regiment just after the Napoleonic Wars

with Portugal. The 9th were not directly involved in storming the fortress, but after it fell they were given the unpleasant task of acting as policemen to prevent Anglo-Portuguese troops from plundering.

By June 1812 the battalion could muster 666 officers and men, who were to be involved in the Battle of Salamanca. Wellington had a force of some 52,000 men, just over 30,000 of whom were British. The French mustered some 43,000 infantry and 4,500 cavalry. The battalion's part in the battle took place at around 1630 on 22 July 1812. Leith Hay, the commander of the brigade, described the action:

> The general desired me to ride forward, to make our light infantry press upon the heights to cover his line of march, and bid them, if practicable, make a rush at the enemy's guns. Our light troops soon drove in those opposed to them; the canon were removed to the rear; every obstacle to the general advance of our line vanished. In front of the centre of that beautiful line rode General Leith, directing its movements. Occasionally every soldier was visible, the sun shining bright upon their arms, though at intervals all were enveloped in a dense cloud of dust, from whence at times issued the animating cheer of the British infantry.

With remarkable precision the 5th Division moved forward, instantly filling the gaps caused by casualties. Although dangerous and confused, the French failed to put up much of a fight and were soon simply a mass of disorganized men, running for their lives. Leith Hay himself was wounded. In the smoke and dust units combined and despite a spirited counterattack by French cavalry the French were routed. The 9th got off with very few casualties. Lieutenant Ackland and two sergeants were killed, forty other men were wounded. Colonel Cameron, who had led from the front throughout the entire engagement, emerged unscathed. He had actually been due to go to England on sick leave on 17 July, but had refused to leave the battalion. In all the allies lost around 5,220 men, compared to a crippling French loss of 14,000.

By 25 July the 5th Division was just six miles from Valladolid. Wellesley was determined to now deal with Joseph Bonaparte and his 14,000 men based in Madrid. These French troops had been moving up in support, but after the defeat at Salamanca they had fallen back to Madrid. By 11 August the 1st Battalion had reached Escorial and on the same day the French evacuated Madrid, leaving behind 2,000 poorly trained troops as a garrison. On 12 August the British entered Madrid.

The 1st Battalion remained at Escorial throughout August 1812 but they were up and moving, along with the 5th Division, at the beginning of September, heading again for Valladolid. They were in pursuit of the French commander, Clausel, and his troops, who were falling back towards Burgos. The battalion was assigned to cover the siege of Burgos in case Clausel's troops turned to try to save the 2,000 men in the garrison. Indeed the French were considering such a move and on 20 September Wellesley took the 1st and 5th Division to block a French force of infantry and cavalry under Maucune. But there was bad news elsewhere; considerable French forces under Soult and Joseph Bonaparte were about to retake Madrid. Wellesley had no option but to begin to retreat and give up the siege of Burgos.

On 25 September the 1st Battalion was defending a bridge and ford over the River Pisuerga, to the right rear of Wellesley's army. By this stage they could only muster around 300 men. In the face of almost insuperable odds they fought, holding onto their position, until they were finally forced to retreat, having lost seventeen killed and sixty wounded. One whole company, commanded by Lieutenant Whitley, was surrounded and captured by French cavalry. Sergeant Hale explained the situation:

> About 200 of our regiment were placed very convenient to the bridge, and the remaining part of the regiment was extended along the river. The enemy seeing so small a party left to defend the bridge, they made a grand push for that place; but fortunately, before they could make their object, the bridge blew up, which put a stop to their pursuit, so then they extended themselves along the river in about the same direction that we were, by which a sharp skirmish immediately took place and continued about four hours.

A Spanish brigade appeared to support the battalion, allowing them to retire half a mile for a rest. Around half an hour later the French were fording the river and the Spanish troops were routing. Hale picks up the story again:

> [The Spaniards] retreating in an unsoldierlike manner, in consequence of which our brigade was again ordered to stand to our arms and give them a charge, which we immediately did with great vigour, and in a few minutes we captured about 400 prisoners; there were also a great number of killed and wounded in endeavouring to make their escape back across the river; therefore they did not make any further attack that day.

The Anglo-Portuguese and their Spanish allies continued to retreat through November 1812 and the 9th wintered at Lamego. The 1st Battalion was much depleted and over the winter months received 400 men from the 2nd Battalion and then a further 147 men. They received their marching orders in May 1813, as Wellesley determined to bring the French to a decisive battle.

The 9th were part of the left column, under Sir Thomas Graham, with a strength of 52,000. By 12 June they had reached Sotresgudo, only a day's march from the Ebro, the closest point to the French border, which Wellesley had reached. The French were retiring towards Vittoria. The battalion reached La Piedra on 13 June; San Martin was reached the following day and Villarcayo on 15 June. They now began to wheel towards the east, and they soon ran into Maucune's division with the French army. Initially it appeared that the French would attack, but they thought better of it and began to retire. Gomm wrote: 'Colonel Cameron sent a battalion company to support his own light company. This being our first encounter this campaign, the men were ardent and eager. We continued the pursuit until dark, when we were relieved by light troops of the 4th Division.'

Sergeant Hale was with the light company and was involved in a two-hour firefight, after which the French retreated so quickly that they could barely keep up. The light companies followed the French for six miles, during which five of their men were wounded. It was clear, however, that a major battle would soon take place. By this stage the 5th Division was on the left of Wellesley's army. Wellesley had around 72,000 men, of whom 61,000 were either British or Portuguese, with the remainder being Spanish. Of the total force around 7,000 were cavalry and there were ninety guns. The French, under Joseph Bonaparte and Jourdon, could muster 43,000 infantry, around 7,000 cavalry and 150 guns.

Wellesley proposed to attack in four columns. The 1st Battalion of the 9th was positioned on the left, along with the 1st Division and Spanish guerrillas would operate with them. The 5th Division was under the command of General Oswald. The 1st Battalion was part of the force that was advancing on Gamarra Mayor and the bridge there. Colin Campbell was detached with the light company to cover the right flank of the brigade.

An initial attack by the force against the town was beaten back by French guns and musket fire. The second attack, led by the Royal Scots, was supported by the 1st Battalion of the 38th and the 1st Battalion of the 9th. They managed to drive the French out of the town, take the bridge and then they were beaten back by a French counterattack. The fighting in this area was brought to a stalemate, but elsewhere the situation had become serious for the French and they began to retreat in disorder. As a result they lost all of their guns; around 1,000 men were taken prisoner and upwards of 8,000 were killed or wounded. Wellesley's troops had lost 5,180 killed, wounded or missing, the majority of which were British troops. The 1st Battalion lost Ensign Saunders, nine other men killed and fifteen wounded.

Wellesley now determined to chase the French and deny them any opportunity to regroup. By 23 June 1813 the 5th Division had reached Salvatierra. It soon became clear that the French had retreated across the border into France and consequently the 1st Battalion arrived at San Sebastian on 6 July to take part in the siege. The stronghold had a garrison of 2,300 under General Rey. This was reinforced by 700 or more men who had abandoned Guetaria. The fortress itself was an impressive structure, on a promontory in the Bay of Biscay. Wellesley was keen to overwhelm the fortress and there were options; an attack could be brought in against the flank of the fortress via the banks of the River Urumea. This was fordable at low water. The other more conventional approach was directly from the mainland, but this was protected by a defensive position around a convent.

On the morning of 17 July 1813 the 1st Battalion of the 9th was selected to take part in this initial assault. They would support Portuguese troops. Three companies of the battalion would be involved in the attack on the right and the rest of the battalion, under Cameron, would be in action on the left. A pair of guns opened up at 1000 hours, firing into the convent. Two hours later the infantry began to move forward, but the Portuguese troops seemed hesitant and would not close. Cameron led the bulk of the 9th through the Portuguese allies. Meanwhile the three companies on the right, under Lieutenant-Colonel Craufurd, had advanced close to the convent. The battalion overran several of the houses close by and they pushed into the village of San Martin, coming up against French reserves.

San Sebastian

After heavy fighting, the French retired towards San Sebastian. The 9th had taken heavy casualties; in all around seventy had been killed or wounded and Cameron himself had also been injured. Wellesley set up artillery on the convent hill and opened fire on the town. Breaches were made in the defence works and Wellesley set the date for the assault; it would be 25 July. The troops would move into position at 0430. The 1st Battalion of the 9th would be involved in the storming party.

Lieutenant Colin Campbell was given command of men selected from the light companies of the three regiments in the 5th Division. They would operate ahead of the main force. The troops scrambled forward in the darkness along the banks and in the shallow water of the River Urumes. They were making for a breach in the defence works. It was tough going and as soon as the French realized the danger they opened fire with everything they had. Time and time again the troops tried to storm the breach. Campbell was wounded twice, in the hip and in the left thigh. The attack had become a disaster; eight officers and 121 men were killed, thirty officers and 142 men were wounded and six officers and 118 men had been taken prisoner.

There was now a relative lull in the siege, until fresh batteries were constructed and began firing on San Sebastian on 22 August. At 0300 on 27 August 1813 Captain Hector Cameron, Lieutenant John Chadwick and Ensign Robert Brooke led 100 men of the 9th in boats to capture the tiny island of Santa Clara. This was to the west of San Sebastian, in the Bay of San Sebastian. It was known that there was a French garrison on the island, but its capture was important as it would allow Wellesley to set up artillery there and fire at the reverse of the French defences. As the boats approached they came under fire. Chadwick and ten men of the regiment were killed, but the landing was successful and the French were rounded up and taken prisoner.

Severe damage was now being inflicted on the French defences and a new assault was planned for 31 August. The 1st Battalion of the 9th would be held in reserve, to be thrown in when and where needed. This time the assault was successful and the town itself was overrun. The French, or at least what remained of them, retreated into the citadel. Sixty artillery pieces battered the citadel and on 8 September the French finally surrendered; 1,900 men were taken prisoner and 670 allied prisoners were freed. Around half of the 1st Battalion had actually been engaged; four officers, five sergeants and forty-two men were killed, six officers, two sergeants, two drummers and ninety-eight men were wounded. Sergeant Hale was one of the wounded and he was sent to Bilbao for treatment. In all, the siege of San Sebastian had cost the regiment six officers killed and twelve wounded, and sixty-two other ranks killed and 177 wounded. There would be brief respite for the regiment, as they were heading towards the French border.

Southern France

The regiment was to march across the River Bidassoa and make for Fuentarabia; from here they would cross a ford and make for Hendaye on the French side of the river. At 0700 on 6 October 1813 they were about to cross into French territory. The 9th was leading the brigade and advancing towards Croix des Bouquets. Cameron was once again leading his men. They moved steadily forward and the French seemed unwilling to stand. Hale's brother recalled the events:

> About one mile and half distance from the river, on the other side, the enemy had formed a four gun battery, which place our regiment was

ordered to attack. We continued advancing very regularly in column of companies till we got within musket shot distance, and then we fired one volley and gave them one charge with as much vigour as the strength of our bodies would permit, by which we drove them from their battery and occupied their ground in less than fifteen minutes, and from thence we continued advancing and driving them before us for nearly two miles, when we were ordered to halt and cease firing, for we were getting very near to their main body.

Campbell was determined to be part of this action; he was still suffering badly from his wounds and had discharged himself from hospital. He was determined to lead his own light company and was badly wounded again for his pains.

During the day the 9th Regiment had lost nine men killed, ten officers, two sergeants and sixty-two other ranks wounded. In a despatch written by Wellesley on 9 October 1813 he wrote: 'I had particular satisfaction in observing the steadiness and gallantry of all the troops. The 9th British Regiment was very strongly opposed, charged with bayonets more than once and have suffered.'

The next major line of French defence was Bayonne. It had a fortress and was protected by the River Adour, which ran into the Bay of Biscay, and the River Nive to the south. Wellesley determined to cross the Nive on 9 December 1813 and on the previous night the 1st Battalion of the 9th marched up into position and approached Barouillet, on the main road to Bayonne. The 5th Division was to operate in conjunction with the 1st Division and they got under way at 0800 on 9 December and by 1300 the 1st Division had reached Anglet, more than half the distance towards Bayonne. The 5th Division was occupying the forest of Bayonne, overlooking the town itself and the River Adour. They remained in position until nightfall then fell back with the 9th acting as the rearguard. During the day one sergeant and one man had been killed and Gomm had been wounded.

On the morning of 10 December the French counterattacked with nine divisions of infantry, a division of cavalry and forty guns. The French commander, Soult, had decided to take this chance to cut off the leading elements of Wellesley's army and destroy them. As part of the 5th Division the 9th was holding positions from Barouillet to Bidart. The 9th was thrown into the fight at a crucial time; the French were advancing on Barouillet from the north and from the east. The 9th, supported by a Portuguese battalion, arrived at the head of the brigade beside the main road. The 9th was on the right and the Portuguese were on the left. They fell on the flank and rear of the attacking French columns and by 1400 the French were streaming back, but a fresh attack was being organized by the French further to the east and Soult abandoned his assault on the 5th Division. According to Napier, in his *History of the Peninsular War*:

Colonel Cameron was on the extreme left of Greville's brigade, Robinson being then shifted into the second line and towards the right, Bradford's brigade was at the mayor's house, some distance to the left of the 9th Regiment, immediately opposite the 9th was a coppice wood possessed by the enemy, whose skirmishers were continually gathering in masses and rushing out as if to assail the 9th; they were as often driven back, yet the ground was so broken that nothing could be seen beyond the flanks; and when some time had passed in this manner, Colonel Cameron, who had received no orders, heard a sudden firing along the main road to his left. His adjutant was sent to investigate the cause of the firing, and returned immediately with intelligence that there was little fighting on the road, but a French regiment, which must have passed unseen in small bodies through the Portuguese, between the 9th and the mayor's house, were rapidly filing into line in the rear.

Cameron at this stage ordered the 4th Foot to face about and march to the rear, but he marched in the wrong direction and headed towards the Portuguese. The 4th had disappeared from view but the French had nearly formed up. Napier continued the story:

Colonel Cameron, leaving fifty men of the 9th to answer the skirmishing fire, which had now increased from the coppice, immediately faced about and marched in line against the new enemy as fast as the rough nature of the ground would permit. The French fire, slow at first, increased as the distance lessened, but when the 9th, coming close up, sprang forward to the charge, the French line broke and fled to the flanks in the utmost disorder.

Calmly Cameron, despite having taken casualties, rounded up the French prisoners and then returned to their original positions. In fact the regiment had taken around 400 prisoners. Major-General Bainbrigge, in a letter to Lieutenant-Colonel Davis written in 1848, stated:

At the battle called the Nive in December 1813, the 9th was in small parties skirmishing, defending a coppice wood near the mayor's house at Basusary. A party of the enemy under an officer came round by the rear upon a party of the 9th whom Lieutenant Dale commanded, and the French officer in exultation, thinking he had surrounded them called out 'rendez vous, vous etes prisonniers!' 'no' said Dale 'I'll be dammed if we are' on which his party faced about and, after a sharp scuffle hand to hand with the bayonet, it ended in the whole French party being taken prisoners or killed.

Two officers and ten men were lost that day and nearly seventy were wounded. On the following day, at around 1000 hours, the 9th advanced towards the village of Pucho. The countryside was shrouded in fog and Wellesley needed to know the strength of the French line facing him. As the 9th moved up, with Cameron in the lead, they arrived just as the French were about to launch a counterattack. In a matter of minutes the 9th was almost surrounded but in the nick of time some Portuguese troops arrived and Cameron's men were able to retreat. At 1400 the French launched a serious counterattack. Quickly the 5th Division formed up and in the ensuing fight fourteen men were killed and seventy-two were wounded. In just three days the regiment had suffered 200 casualties.

The regiment was now withdrawn and it remained in reserve until 4 February 1814. On 14 February, along with the 5th Division, it crossed over the River Nive, as by now the French had abandoned Bayonne and were streaming back towards Toulouse. The fortress of Bayonne was still being held by 11,000 French and the 9th would remain in the area until the fortress finally surrendered. During this time the 1st Battalion received a draft of 150 men from the 2nd Battalion.

The 1st Battalion was involved in one more fight, which took place eight days after Napoleon had abdicated. On the night of 14 April 1814 the French troops in Bayonne made a sortie and in the running battle the regiment lost two killed and eight wounded.

The war was not yet over for the 1st Battalion. In May 1814 they marched from Bayonne to Bordeaux, arriving there on 22 May. They then moved down to Garonne and on 3 June they were embarked upon transports bound for Canada. The battalion arrived in Montreal on 22 August and by the October they were in Kingston, by which time they had been significantly reinforced by men from the 2nd Battalion. The regiment was not directly involved in the fighting on the Canadian frontier against the newly independent American state. However their behaviour and contribution in Canada was exemplary and Sir George Murray, the governor and commander in chief, spoke highly of the regiment when they were embarking at Kingston bound for home in June 1815.

Napoleon had landed in France in March 1815. The culmination of the Napoleonic Wars, the Battle of Waterloo, had not yet been fought and it was strongly believed that any available troops might be needed on the continent. As it was, the 1st Battalion of the 9th did not reach Spithead until 15 July and they missed their opportunity to take part in the final defeat of Napoleon's French armies. They were, however, to become part of the occupying force in France.

Occupation of France

Having been reinforced by the 2nd Battalion they landed at Ostend on 17 August 1815. They proceeded by boat to Ghent and then marched into Paris, arriving there on 5 September. They were to become part of the 16th Brigade, commanded by Major-General Sir Thomas Bradford. In the November they found themselves under the command of Sir Thomas Brisbane and over the next year they saw service as occupying troops in various parts of France. By the spring of 1817 the battalion was reduced to ten companies, with a strength of all ranks of 907. By this stage the 1st Battalion was now brigaded with the 5th and a battalion from the Rifle

Brigade under Major-General Sir J Lambert.

It would not be until June 1818 that the 1st Battalion finally left France, via Calais. They landed at Dover and Ramsgate and then marched to Winchester, now with an overall strength of 746 men. It was to be a short stay in England, as on 13 January 1819 they were given orders to head for the West Indies.

West Indies

They arrived on Barbados on 3 April 1819 and the headquarters and five companies, under Lieutenant-Colonel Campbell, were posted to St Vincent. Three companies, under Lieutenant-Colonel Peebles, went to Dominica and two companies, under Lieutenant-Colonel Lambert, went to St Lucia. Here they would remain until February 1821, when they were given orders to garrison Grenada and Trinidad. Two of the companies would also serve on Tobago.

At around this time company strength was reduced from ten to eight. They also lost the services of Colonel Cameron; he had become a major-general and after fourteen years of association with the regiment his place was taken by Colonel N Blackwell.

The following year saw disease ravage the regiment; some thirty-two recruits had been sent out to join them, but yellow fever was rampant and twenty-seven of the men, including the officer who came with them, Major Loftus, died.

The regiment continued to serve in the West Indies until the last company finally arrived in Portsmouth at the beginning of February 1827. They had spent eight years in the West Indies and many of the men had fallen ill, with eight officers and 271 men having died of disease. Colonel Campbell had become the colonel of the regiment in 1826, but he was now replaced by Major Taylor. New recruits were being trained up to bring the regiment back up to strength. If the regiment believed that they would now be spending a great deal of time in England they were mistaken. This time they would find themselves even further afield than ever before.

3

1827–1914

We now pick up the 1st Battalion at Plymouth on 25 September 1827. New colours were presented to the regiment by Lady Cameron; Major-General Sir John Cameron was in command of the Plymouth garrison. A garrison order issued on 4 October stated:

> The first division of the 9th Regiment will embark from the dockyard on Saturday morning at 7 o'clock and the baggage at 4pm on Friday. The remaining companies will be concentrated in the citadel. This regiment is naturally endeared to Major-General Sir John Cameron by long and intimate association; expressions of marked approval, which the appearance, interior system, and conduct of the corps undeniably claim for the general commanding, are therefore particularly in accordance with his private feelings. The Major-General takes leave of the 9th Regiment with sensible regret; his best wishes will ever attend the officers, non-commissions officers, and private soldiers.

Ireland

The regiment landed at Liverpool and then marched to Manchester, Stockport and Oldham. By the summer of 1828 it was in Bolton and Blackburn and in the October it headed for Belfast. In September 1830 it was transferred to Dublin and in May 1831 it was at Limerick. At the end of May Lieutenant-Colonel Custance took over command of the regiment.

A bell-topped shako dated c.1829. This would have been worn by an officer in the light company of the 9th East Norfolk Regiment. This example can be found at the Royal Norfolk Regimental Museum in Norwich.

The regiment's duties in Ireland were to quell riots, disperse meetings and protect government property. They were to embark for Gibraltar at the beginning of 1832, but this was delayed due to unrest in Ireland. Finally, on 4 November 1832 six companies made for Plymouth and four depot companies were left in Ireland.

Mauritius and India

The six companies landed in Mauritius in the Indian Ocean in April 1833 and here they were to remain until September 1835 before they moved on to Calcutta in India in the November. Meanwhile the depot companies had been sent to Chatham and they had beaten the service companies to Calcutta by a month.

On 9 June 1835 the War Office had declared:

> His Majesty has been graciously pleased to permit the 9th of Foot to bear on its colours and appointments, in addition to any other badges and devices which may have heretofore been granted, the word Corunna in commemoration of the distinguished conduct of the regiment before Corunna in January 1809.

Finally the regiment's bravery in the battle over twenty-five years before had been rewarded.

The regiment made for Chinsura in January 1836 and then on to Hararibagh, both in India, in December 1838. The regiment was now commanded by Lieutenant-Colonel McCaskill, who had taken over from Custance.

A great deal of the information regarding the regiment's activities in India was documented by Lieutenant James Slater Cumming who served with the regiment until he was killed in the Khyber Pass in 1842. The regiment arrived at Agra at the beginning of March 1840. There were enormous difficulties in this region of the British Empire and it was obvious that the 9th would be part of an expedition that would be launched into Afghanistan.

The bulk of India was under control of the British, who had expelled the French and the Dutch. However Britain was not the only empire active in the region. Tsarist Russia was rapidly expanding to the east and to the south

Mid–19th–century uniforms. These would have been worn in the 1840s to 1860s

A depiction of Britannia, as used as a cross belt badge. This was worn by officers in the period 1840–50.

A close up of an undressed officer's uniform of the mid-19th century showing the Britannia buttons

and the fear was that Afghanistan, if it fell to the Russians, would be used as the launching pad for an invasion of India. The British had tried to establish a pro-British ruler of Afghanistan but this had failed. It was therefore decided to remove the ruler of Afghanistan by force. The British occupied Kabul, along with the other major centres of population, but by November 1841 4,000 British troops were in Kabul, surrounded by hostile tribesmen. Sir Alexander Burnes, the British Envoy, had been assassinated.

The British force tried to withdraw via the Khyber Pass and, aside from a handful of officers, women and children that had been taken prisoner, only one man succeeded in reaching British India. Something now had to be done to punish the Afghans, under their ruler Dost Muhammad.

The 9th would be part of General Pollock's punitive expedition. They marched out of Firozpur on 4 January 1842. On 5 April Pollock advanced into the Khyber Pass and the 9th was the only European infantry regiment, although the 3rd Dragoons, a cavalry regiment, were also present. The rest of the force were British-trained, native infantry regiments. Pollock moved forward in three columns. The centre column was led by the Grenadier Company of the 9th, supported by seven native battalions, cavalry and artillery. Before it would be safe to force the pass the hills on either side had to be cleared of the enemy. Two companies of the 9th were deployed on the right and another two on the left. Each of these were supported by native infantry, friendly tribesmen and a reserve of one and a half companies of the 9th.

The Kabul medal, 1842, which was awarded for service during the second Afghan War.

General Pollock's own despatch described the action:

Both columns, after considerable opposition, which they overcame in a most gallant style, succeeded in routing the enemy, and gaining possession of the crest of the hills on either side. While the flanking columns were in progress on the heights, I ordered Captain Alexander of the artillery to place the guns in position, and throw shrapnels among the enemy when opportunity offered, which assisted much in their discomforture. As Lieutenant-Colonel Taylor, [colonel of the 9th] from the opposition he had met with, and the extremely difficult nature of the ground, was some time in reaching the summit of the hill on the right, I detached a party [consisting of the Grenadiers of the 9th Foot and six companies of the 33rd Native Infantry], under the command of Brigadier Wild, to assault it in front. It was however, so extremely steep near the top that, notwithstanding the undaunted gallantry of the officers and men, they were unable to gain a footing on the summit, and I regret to say the enemy were enabled to throw stones with fatal effect upon some of the leading Grenadiers of the 9th Foot.

In the end the tribesmen were swept aside, as an extract from the regimental record confirms:

The troops moved to their left to clear the redoubts commanding the entrance to the pass, which were abandoned on the approach of the British, the enemy suffering severely in their retreat. Lieutenant-Colonel Taylor finally succeeded in clearing off the enemy on the right of the road although an obstinate resistance was offered at several points, especially over the bridge, where the enemy had concentrated in force. Having been reinforced by a detachment of the 33rd Native Infantry, Captain Lushington of the 9th Foot proceeded with it and the light company of the 9th Foot to the right to take the enemy's position in reverse, while Lieutenant-Colonel Taylor attacked in front.

Captain Borton, in his own diary, wrote about the last stages of the action: 'All the officers, some sepoys [loyal native infantry], and all the 9th on the spot rushed to the attack. The fire was very hot and balls passed on every side of me; a few men fixed bayonets and rushed the position.' This final attack had been a response to seeing Lieutenant Cumming shot dead. Borton later wrote more about the death of the officer:

> Cumming was bringing his company [forward] whence he could check any advance by the enemy, when he was ordered to [another position] where his men were much exposed. Attacked in the rear, he was ordered to retire and I was sent forward to support him. As Cumming was retiring, he was shot through the head.

By being involved in the forcing of the Khyber Pass the 9th had shown their worth and Pollock's force could now advance towards Jellalabad, where the 9th arrived on 16 April 1842. Jellalabad had been under siege from the Afghans and it was now time for Pollock and his force to avenge those who had been slaughtered in the withdrawal from Kabul.

Pollock began concentrating his troops around Gandamak. In all he proposed to take 8,000 men with him to attack and seize Kabul. Immediately facing him were large numbers of tribesmen in the hills on either side of the Kabul road. Pollock determined to clear them out of the way on 24 August 1842. He split his forces into two columns, each of them preceded by four companies of the 9th. The tribesmen put up a stiff fight, but they were eventually forced to abandon their positions. Pollock's force took the fort of Mammu Khel and destroyed it before withdrawing. The 9th suffered the loss of two privates killed and nine men wounded.

By 7 September Pollock's force was ready to make their final advance on Kabul and the following day saw the regiment approaching the hills overlooking the Jagdalak Pass. It was a difficult piece of terrain to traverse and the tribesmen could fire down into the deep ravine. Captain Borton wrote in his diary:

> I can conceive few positions more formidable than that which the enemy had taken. On the crest of a lofty range to the left were situated a square fort and two extensive sungars [sangars or stone entrenchments] of rocks and bushes which literally bristled with armed men, while the right spur, thrown out from a still loftier height, was strengthened by a double and triple line of breastworks, all of which, as well as the sungar on the top, were strongly occupied. The colonel halted within range, as it proved, of the enemy's jezails [Afghan muskets], and while the men loaded and preparations were made for attack, a few shrapnel were thrown with considerable effect into the works on the right and left. To the 9th was assigned the task of driving the enemy from their position on the left. The hill was steep, but not otherwise difficult of ascent, and I reached the

summit just in time to see Ogle with three or four men peering into a sungar, which, to my great surprise, we found empty.

Just as before, the Afghans had melted away rather than face hand to hand combat with the British troops. In this fight three members of the regiment were killed and seventeen were wounded.

The advance went on until the British reached Tezeen on 11 September 1842. Here Pollock decided to halt and on the afternoon of 12 September the Afghans launched a counterattack, as Pollock described in his despatches:

> I considered it necessary to send Lieutenant-Colonel Taylor with 250 men of HM's 9th Foot to drive them back; some sharp fighting took place, and the enemy was driven up the neighbouring hills, from the crests of which they kept up a heavy fire. Lieutenant-Colonel Taylor, however, with a small party, crept up one end of the hill unperceived by the enemy, who were hotly engaged in their front, and lay concealed until joined by a few more of his men, when, rushing upon the flank of the astonished Afghans, he inflicted a severe lesson, pouring in a destructive fire upon them as they fled down the hill.

Meanwhile Captain Borton and his company, supported by native troops, had crept forward into the valley. They came up to a crest and lay down waiting for more men to come up to support them. They spotted a large number of Afghans who were clearly unaware of their presence. Borton and the mixed group of troops fixed bayonets and charged. A number of the enemy were killed and the rest put to flight.

The Afghans refused to give up throughout the night and launched several sorties. The heights still needed to be cleared and this was the job that faced the expedition on 13 September. Leaving a rearguard, including 143 men of the 9th, Pollock pushed his troops forward, including the rest of the 9th, to clear the heights either side of the pass. Again his despatches describe the role the 9th played:

> Our troops mounted the heights, and the Afghans, contrary to their general custom, advanced to meet them, and a desperate struggle ensured; indeed, their defence was so obstinate that the British bayonet alone decided the contest. The light company of Her Majesty's 9th Foot, led by Captain Lushington, who, I regret to say, was wounded in the head, ascended the hills to the left of the pass under a heavy crossfire and overthrew their opponents, leaving several horses and their riders, supposed to be chiefs, dead on the hill. The slaughter was considerable.

This area, known as the Haft Kotal, or Seven Hills, was the last stronghold and opportunity for the Afghans to prevent the British from advancing on Kabul. The British marched into the capital on 15 September.

The Afghans had not totally given up and on 20 September General McCaskill of the 9th was sent to disperse tribesmen under Aminulla Khan. The tribesmen were mustering in Kohistan, near a town called Charekar. By 28 September the British force had closed on the enemy positions. Borton, leading No. 7 Company of the 9th, was on a reconnaissance mission and was leading his troops through a garden when he saw that the village was strongly occupied. Borton's troops dispersed the tribesmen after a vicious fight.

By 12 October 1842 the force was ready to return to India, having installed a puppet ruler in Kabul. In all the total casualties for the regiment during this campaign had been twenty-eight killed, forty-eight severely wounded and fifty-four slightly wounded.

Sikh Wars

The 9th was back in Firozpur on 18 December and in Mubarikpur on 31 January 1843. Here they would stay until the April when they were sent to Sabathu. The regiment would now spend two years in hill stations before going back on active service. It was given orders to move in November 1845; another war was imminent and this time it was against the Sikh state. This was an independent kingdom, with a not inconsiderable regular army.

The Sikh army, or Khalsa, had been trained by European officers and their regular force alone amounted to 35,000 infantry and 15,000 cavalry. The major problem that had caused friction was the death of the ruler, Ranjit Singh, whose successors were strongly anti-British and they would present a formidable challenge to British India.

A diorama in the Royal Norfolk Regimental Museum in Norwich, using flat miniatures of the Battle of Ferozeshah in the first Anglo-Sikh War, 1845–6

A Sikh War medal bearing the bar Ferozeshuhur (Ferozeshah) 1845

The 9th marched to Umbala as part of the general troop movements towards the Sikh frontier. Under Lieutenant-Colonel Taylor the regiment arrived back in Firozpur on 11 December 1845. In all, the British army, including native troops, amounted to some 31,000 men. The 9th would be part of a force that would march to Moodkee.

The Sikhs had already made their move and were entrenched in a camp at Ferozeshah. Already they were probing forward and it was believed that there were a considerable number of infantry and cavalry, along with guns, now stationed just two miles from Moodkee. A battle was inevitable.

Twelve battalions of British and native troops moved up, with cavalry and horse artillery on flanks. The British artillery silenced the Sikh guns and the 9th was a part of Sir John McCaskill's division on the left, along with the 80th Foot and the 26th and 73rd Native Infantry. Sir Hugh Gough was in overall command and although his despatches do not mention the 9th specifically, Borton, in a letter to his father in January 1846, explained that the regiment had barely arrived on the battlefield at around 1600. By this time the Sikhs were already moving forward to attack. The regiment came under heavy fire and it was difficult for the troops to see very much due to the dust and smoke. Just before nightfall the regiment was deployed to see off the advancing columns of enemy infantry. They managed to do this, but Borton was wounded in the action (he was now a major). Also during the action Sir John McCaskill was killed by grapeshot fired from a Sikh gun. In the action the regiment lost two killed and fifty wounded.

The British force returned to Moodkee to reorganize and also to receive reinforcement. Gough was determined to fight a decisive action and shatter the Sikh army. Consequently, on 21 December 1845, he left two native infantry regiments at Moodkee and marched the rest of his army out at 0400 hours. He had with him 16,700 men and sixty-nine guns and facing him were up to 35,000 Sikhs, of which around a third were cavalry. The Sikhs also had around ninety guns. They were still positioned around Firozpur.

By 1330 the British force was manœuvring into position. The 9th was broadly in the centre and attached to Wallace's brigade (he had succeeded McCaskill). By 1530 Gough was ready to launch the attack and he knew that it was imperative to force the Sikhs to commit to battle, as he had little daylight left. The first of the British troops to get engaged were those on the left. After coming under devastating fire the British left began to fall back. These were the troops virtually alongside the 9th. Wallace's brigade continued their advance and now they too came under considerable pressure from the Sikhs. By the time darkness had fallen the Sikhs had only been pushed back around 300 yards and in the confused fighting Wallace had been killed.

There were skirmishes during the night and just before daylight the Sikhs began to open up with their heavy guns. Gough threw his men forward again, forcing the Sikhs out of Ferozeshah, but by now the British artillery ammunition was almost exhausted. Eventually the Sikhs gave way, having lost upwards of 2,400 men. The victory had been an expensive one; the 9th had lost 273 men killed or wounded, McCaskill was dead, as too was Lieutenant-Colonel Taylor and Borton had been wounded in the right arm. Borton had also lost one of his closest friends, a Lieutenant Sivewright, who had been wounded in the leg. When a Sikh had approached him the lieutenant thought the Sikh was going to finish him off, but instead he picked up Sivewright and carried him back to the British lines. Unfortunately Sivewright died after having his leg amputated.

By 10 January 1846 the 9th was now commanded by Lieutenant-Colonel Davis. They had moved up to watch the entrenched Sikh camp near Sobraon, which was a large bridgehead on the bank of the River Sutlej that protected a bridge of boats. It was believed that the Sikh army, under Tejsing amounted to around 20,000 men but there were also around 10,000 cavalry in the vicinity. Gough planned to bombard the camp and then send the infantry in against the left, which appeared to have the weaker entrenchments. The 9th was to be part of the reserve and had been brigaded under Brigadier Ashburnham with the 62nd Foot and the 26th Native Infantry. The main attack would be launched by General Dick's division, of which the 5th Brigade, including the 9th, was a part. The two leading brigades, the 6th and the 7th, would advance without firing and take the positions with the bayonet.

As soon as the Sikhs realized that this attack was the most dangerous one they began to reinforce, threatening to overwhelm the three brigades. The 9th was quickly involved in the fighting and by now the outer defence works had been breached. In the desperate fighting the Sikhs were finally forced back, with the British troops overrunning the guns. The Sikh army fled, trying to get back over the bridge of boats and to relative safety. The bridge almost immediately collapsed and there was a terrible slaughter as the majority of the Sikhs refused to surrender. Despite this other bloody engagement the 9th had lost just twelve killed and around thirty wounded.

This was the decisive victory in the war. The 9th marched out toward Lahore on 13 February, arriving there seven days later. They were there to witness the surrender of the Sikhs and the incorporation of the Punjab into British India. They remained at Lahore until 23 March 1846.

It was now clear that the regiment would be going home and a number of men volunteered for extended service in India with other regiments. A first draft of 175 men were lost and then another 154. The remnants of the regiment marched all the way to Dinapur and then on to Calcutta, where it embarked for England on 13 March 1847. It could now add four more battle honours, but it had been at a cost. In the period 1832 to 1847 the regiment had lost twenty officers and 195 other ranks due to combat or disease.

Malta and the Crimea

The regiment arrived at Chatham on 10 July 1847 and then headed for Winchester. On 18 February 1848 Sir James Archibald Hope became the colonel of the regiment. There would now be a period of duty once again in Ireland. The regiment received new colours in March 1848 and in June 1853 Lieutenant-Colonel Borton took command of the battalion. In December of the same year they marched to Fermoy; their destination would be Malta and the regiment arrived in two parts on 7 and 28 March 1854.

On the very same day that the balance of the battalion arrived on Malta Britain had declared war on Russia. Britain was allied with the French and the Ottoman Turks; both seeking to limit Russian expansion into the Balkans. The invasion of the Crimean Peninsula began in September 1854, however by the time the battalion arrived at Balaklava on 27 November 1854 the Battles of the Alma, Balaklava and Inkerman had already been fought.

The regiment arrived with twenty officers and 544 other ranks. Not only were they moving into a new war zone, but it was an absolute nightmare in terms of snow, mud, lack of food and water and rampant disease. The men found themselves constantly under fire; the campaign was chaotic; there was a lack of food, clothing, fuel, shelter and medicines. There was little that Borton could do to prevent his men from suffering the same fate that all of the other troops were undergoing. In his own report he wrote:

> For some days after the 9th Regiment reached camp, the sick were exposed to the same privations as the healthy, lying in bell tents on damp ground, without covering beyond that of a single blanket which was too often already wet. The weather was desperate and the duties in the trenches very severe. Cholera broke out on the third day, and in the absence of all necessary comforts, the mortality was of course very great so that ninety deaths occurred amongst 450 men. Of the 540 men who landed on November 27, 182 have died, 153 are sick absent, and thirty eight sick present.

In fact within a week of landing the regiment had lost fifty-seven men and by the end of the year a hundred were dead.

The regiment was attached to the 2nd Brigade of the 3rd Division. The division itself was commanded by Sir R England and the brigade by General Eyre. The 9th would be working alongside the other brigade regiments; the 18th, 28th, 38th and 44th.

The 9th would have to wait until 18 June 1855 before they saw action. They would be engaged in an attempt to overwhelm Sebastopol. General Eyre, in his report dated 19 June, described the action in which the 9th took part:

> I moved off yesterday morning between 1 and 2 o'clock am with my brigade, consisting of the 9th, 18th, 28th, 38th, and 44th regiments – total strength about 2,000 bayonets – and proceeded down the ravine on our left, by the French piquet house, for the purpose of attacking the enemy's ambuscades, and of making a demonstration on that side. The enemy, whose strength I could not estimate, occupied a strong position; the right rested on a mamelon [small fortified hill position], their left on a cemetery. These points were occupied by marksmen. The intervening ground was intersected and the road barricaded with stone walls, which our men were obliged to pull down, under fire, before they could advance.

Now Lieutenant-Colonel, Borton took up the story, describing precisely what the 9th were up to in this attack:

> We on the extreme left, far removed from the scene of assault, were early involved in the fight. Our brigadier is, I suspect, greedy of distinction, being little inclined to err on the side of discretion. That he failed in judgement and allowed his troops to push on too far I cannot doubt, and hence our loss was far greater than it ought to have been. My regiment, much weakened by detached parties, was at first in reserve; but it was not long before he paid me the doubtful compliment of cutting out for me a day's work which I am not likely to forget in a hurry. At about half-past-five we were moved into the cemetery, which had already been taken, and which was the only point which should have been attempted until assured that the troops on our right were advancing.

It is clear that Borton was extremely unhappy with the new orders that Eyre was about to give him. Up ahead were some houses, full of Russian riflemen and beyond that a Russian artillery battery. Eyre ordered Borton to rush forward and overwhelm the Russian position, as Borton recounted: 'Grape, canister, and round shot swept round one like hail, and for my encouragement, just as I reached the cover of the building, surprised to find myself with a whole skin, one of the latter crashed through the building as though it had been paper.'

Borton and the regiment were in a perilous position; if they retreated they would be shot to pieces, if they stayed where they were the Russian artillery would pound their cover and slaughter them, but the way forward was impossible, as he explained:

> There was nothing for it but to pack close, dodge the shots as best we might, and aggravate the enemy as little as possible. And there we spent fourteen weary hours, the enemy at one moment bringing down our houses with round shot, burying the wretched wounded beneath the ruins; then throwing shells among us which, owing to the softness of the ground, fortunately penetrated deep and in bursting only formed craters big enough for one's grave. It was most gratifying to find that my young soldiers, many of them having only landed the day before, behaved admirably. When I wanted to send a report to the General I had no difficulty in finding volunteers to take it; the knowledge that they would get a drink of water was sufficient inducement, though certain to have some fifty rifle balls fired at them during their transit both ways.

It was not until nightfall that the 9th could extricate itself and by then the wounded were in a sorry state. Everyone was covered in dust and blood. Incredibly, just one officer was killed and three officers wounded, seven other ranks were killed and forty-five wounded; it could have been much worse. Private W Cooke was recommended for the French Legion of Honour. He had picked up a live shell that had fallen among the men and threw it so that it exploded harmlessly.

In August 1855 the 9th became part of the 2nd Brigade of the 1st Division and was still engaged in the siege of Sebastopol. Luckily for the regiment it was not involved in the assault, which took place on 8 September 1855. They remained in the Crimea throughout the winter of 1855 to 1856, enduring even more losses due to wounds and disease. They finally left the scene of such carnage on 1 May 1856. It had been a challenging and ruinous time for the regiment.

On 28 April the regiment had been inspected by Lieutenant-General Lord Rokeby. He issued a divisional order two days later:

> The 9th Regiment having received orders to embark for Canada, the Lieutenant-General has great pleasure in expressing the approbation with which he regards its services whilst it formed part of the 1st Division. The accuracy with which the 9th invariably observed the regulations of the service, and the efficiency it displayed in the performance of every duty fully sustained the reputation it had acquired in the 3rd Division during the early part of the campaign.

There were no fewer than twenty-three decorations given out to the regiment. Borton was knighted and promoted to a full colonel, and Major Lister became a lieutenant-colonel.

Greece

The 1st Battalion arrived at Quebec on 8 June 1856, onboard HMS *Resolute*. In September they moved to Montreal, but incredibly they were to spend less than a month here, as they were sent home on 15 October. The regiment arrived at Portsmouth on 5 November 1857; it was sent up to Sunderland until September 1858 and then to Aldershot. It would remain in the southeast of England until February 1860, when with a strength of twenty officers and 533 other ranks it would be despatched to the Ionian islands of Greece.

Meanwhile, back in July 1857 the British government, in response to the Indian Mutiny, authorized the raising of a second battalion of the 9th East Norfolk Regiment. Lieutenant-Colonel Charles Elmhirst, who had been with the 1st Battalion, was given command of the new battalion. Other officers from the 1st Battalion were similarly transferred across to the 2nd Battalion. Recruitment commenced in Great Yarmouth in November 1857 and by this stage a number of non-commissioned officers had also been obtained from the 1st Battalion. With a strength of twenty-two officers and 210 other ranks, the 2nd Battalion moved up to Bradford in February 1858. By June, now in Sheffield, the strength was thirty-one officers and 609 other ranks. By September, in Aldershot, the battalion could boast thirty-four officers and 812 other ranks. The 2nd Battalion was destined for Corfu. They left onboard HMS *Himalaya*, arriving on the Greek island on 12 November 1858. Their strength at this stage was thirty-three officers and 867 other ranks.

Officers and men of the regiment shown in a watercolour depicting uniforms of around the 1860s

The Ionian Islands had been occupied by the British since 1815; they had been part of the Treaty of Paris, which had concluded the Napoleonic Wars. In effect, the seven islands were a protectorate. This was to be the last period of British ownership of the islands, until they were formally handed over to Greece.

Borton handed over command of the 1st Battalion on 30 December 1858 and in February 1860 the 1st Battalion arrived at Corfu. The 2nd Battalion sent a detachment to Ithaca at the beginning of August 1860 and four companies were detached to Zante. In late October the headquarters of the 2nd Battalion and six companies were transferred to Cephalonia. Over a year later, on 4 December 1861, four companies of the 2nd Battalion that had been on Zante returned to Corfu and were followed later in the month by the remainder of the battalion. In April 1863 the headquarters of the 1st Battalion moved to Cephalonia, whilst two months later, in the June, the 2nd Battalion sent a detachment to Santa Maura (now Lefkada) and then in September a second detachment to Ithaca.

The islands were formally transferred to Greece in 1864 and by the May the 1st Battalion was heading for Malta, where it would reassemble and then sail for Gibraltar. The 2nd Battalion of the 9th left Corfu on 1 June 1864; it would be many years before the two battalions would ever serve in the same theatre again.

South Africa

The 1st Battalion remained in Gibraltar until August 1865 before they were transferred to South Africa. *En route* cholera broke out and this delayed their landing at Cape Town until the November. The battalion was garrisoned in Cape Town until January 1868, when it sent detached companies to St Helena. In June 1869 it headed to East London (South Africa) but no sooner had it arrived than it was sent to King William's Town, where it would remain until July 1870. It was then bound for Dublin and then to Cork, where it arrived in September 1871.

At the end of 1871 Major-General Bates became the new colonel of the 1st Battalion. He had taken over from General Sir James Archibald Hope, who had been the battalion's commander since February 1848. The 1st Battalion left Cork in July 1872. The headquarters and five companies were to be garrisoned on Guernsey and the five other companies on Alderney. There were a series of home postings in Great Yarmouth, Pembroke, Aldershot and Colchester until in May 1877 the 1st Battalion returned once more to Dublin. It would not be until April 1882 that they returned to England and were stationed at Colchester for two years.

The 9th Foot, or the 9th East Norfolk Regiment, finally became the Norfolk Regiment in 1881. This was part of the sweeping reforms spearheaded by Edward Cardwell, who had been Secretary of State for War between 1870 and

The 1st Battalion band in 1883, taken at Colchester

C Company at Colchester in 1883

Shield with the figure of Britannia belonging to the 9th East Norfolk Regiment. Note the names of the winners and dates and battle honours. Amongst these battle honours is the Peninsular War. This photograph was taken between 1883 and 1885.

1874. Cardwell embarked on reforms of the British army, which continued well after he left political life. In 1881 regular and militia battalions of the army were amalgamated into territorial regiments and associated with local names and local depots. In effect Britain had been divided up into sixty-nine districts, each with their own country regiment that would be called by that name. The regiments had been given this local attachment to encourage recruitment.

Finally the 1st Battalion had an overseas posting, which came in 1885. They were to spend six months at Gibraltar before returning to England, based at Aldershot. Here they took part in the Great Review to celebrate the first jubilee of Queen Victoria. They were presented with new colours.

Men of the Depot B Company at Great Yarmouth in 1885

A company of the 1st Battalion in full dress uniform, taken at Aldershot in 1887

The 9th Regiment on parade with the band at Buena Vista, Gibraltar, probably during the 1880s

The men of the 9th Norfolk Regiment marching past in columns of double companies for the jubilee review held at Aldershot in 1887

Rangoon

By December 1887 they were back in Gibraltar and they stayed there until February 1889; this time they were heading for India and arrived in Bombay on 5 March 1889. Several detachments were placed, but the main base was at Wellington until December 1890, when the 1st Battalion was transferred to Rangoon. The battalion would be involved in a punitive expedition in the Chin Hills, under the overall command of Brigadier-General Palmer. Captain Baker of the 1st Battalion, Norfolk Regiment, acted as an intelligence officer during the operations and described the typical work involved:

> On November 10, 1892, a column of thirty five rifles of the Norfolk Regiment and 100 Indian infantry started to attack and destroy the village of Htanwe, about six miles north of Fort White. The village was destroyed and the crops burnt. Lieutenant Bellamy of the Norfolk Regiment took part in this expedition, which returned the same evening. On November 14th another column of one gun, seventy five of the Norfolk Regiment and 185 native troops raided Pimpi, farther off in the same direction. Starting from Kennedy Peak on the 15th, over very bad country, Pimpi was reached on the 16th and found to be burning and cleared of all property.

The battalion was involved in a number of expeditions during this campaign, the most important of which began on 3 January 1893, and it was on active patrol for the whole month. More expeditions took place throughout February to April and in all the battalion operated in the Chin Hills for some seven months. Throughout the period seven men were killed and three wounded.

Group of soldiers of the regiment standing on a road during a halt, whilst marching in India in 1894

A line of tents with kit laid out on sheeting. Members of the regiment can be seen standing beside the tents. This was taken in India in 1894.

Brigadier-General Palmer was among those who praised the battalion for their exemplary service: 'Latterly the men of the Norfolk Regiment were just as good at this work as the best Ghurkhas.'

This was not the only work that the battalion carried out in 1893; for a week they were involved in dealing with riots in Rangoon. In December they were transferred to Umbala. Service in India continued until September 1904, when the 1st

Three two-wheeled covered ambulance carts pulled by oxen and used by the regiment in India in 1894

A group of soldiers from the regiment in camp, cleaning their kit following a march in wet conditions in India around 1894

Battalion was sent to South Africa. In the following year the 1st and 2nd Battalions would be reunited for the first time in forty years.

There were other notable periods of activity during these years. In 1903 a section of the 1st Battalion was involved in operations in Somaliland and a small detachment of the battalion had accompanied Colonel Younghusband into Tibet on his expedition to Lhasa.

We will see how the 1st Battalion fared in South Africa when we look at the exploits of the 2nd Battalion, but the 1st Battalion was back in England in January 1907. They were presented with new colours in June 1909 and it was also around this time that they were authorized to use two more battle honours, Havana and Martinique, dating all the way back to 1794.

For the 1st Battalion the last few years before the outbreak of the First World War would see

Private E Rand's Tibet medal, for the expedition 1903–4

relative peace and its fair share of ceremonial duties. By November 1912 the 1st Battalion was back in Ireland and undergoing reorganization. They were headquartered at the Palace Barracks, Holywood, near Belfast, when war was declared on 4 August 1914.

China

Whilst the 1st had had to wait for several years before it got a major overseas posting, this was not the case for the 2nd Battalion. As we will recall, in June 1864, the 2nd Battalion was in Gibraltar. After weeding out any unfit men who were transferred to the 1st Battalion, the 2nd Battalion was given orders on 1 September 1 to make for China. On 3 November, onboard HMS *Tamar*, it arrived in Hong Kong on 7 February 1865. Detachments were sent to Kowloon and others to Canton. An officer and three men were also detached to drill Chinese troops.

Lieutenant-Colonel T E Knox took over command of the 2nd Battalion on 10

Men of the 2nd Battalion musketry team are holding the muskets. The Binning Challenge Shield is displayed in front of the group. This photograph was taken in India in 1911.

April, replacing Colonel Elmhirst. China was another part of the world that inflicted more casualties through disease than through combat. Many of the troops had to be invalided home. By 30 March 1866 a much depleted 2nd Battalion left Hong Kong for Japan and by March 1867 the whole of the battalion was based in Japan.

A Company posing along with items of the company's silver in India in 1912

A studio portrait of Lieutenant E P Elmhirst. This was taken in 1874.

Japan presented a difficult issue for European governments. The Japanese were mistrustful of the Europeans and unwilling to open up their ports to foreign trade. It would take a great deal of time and negotiation to force the issue and there were traditionalists who would not countenance any form of interaction. Some areas were in a virtual state of anarchy and it was feared that there would be a revolution in the country, as traditionalists attempted to prevent modernists and progressives from developing Japan. Port negotiations were in progress at Osaka but trouble was brewing. Foreign representatives withdrew to Kobe in the face of opposition.

Sir Harry Parkes was involved in the negotiations and his bodyguard was commanded by Lieutenant Bradshaw and Lieutenant Bruce and a detachment of the 2nd Battalion of the regiment. They had arrived at Kobe on 3 February 1868. A large force of traditionalists, in excess of 900, entered Kobe. The detachment of the 9th, supported by some French and American Marines, quickly saw them off in a running battle. Sir Harry Parkes later wrote:

I have much pleasure in expressing my appreciation of the exemplary conduct of the detachment of Her Majesty's troops which accompanied me. The efficiency and excellent order maintained among all the men must have attracted much attention from the Japanese authorities and people, and you will share the gratification which I felt in observing how well the detachments, as the first body of British troops seen in that city, sustained the character of the army to which they belong.

Soon, however, the regiment was bound for home. In late April 1868 it began its long voyage aboard HMS *Tamar*, passing through Hong Kong, Singapore, Mauritius, Cape Town, St Helena, St Vincent, Queenstown and finally Kingstown in Ireland.

India

The 2nd Battalion would finally return to England in September 1871. There were a number of major changes to the battalion, with new colonels coming and going until August 1874 when the battalion was entrained for Portsmouth, where it boarded HMS *Jumna*, bound for Bombay in India. It would be garrisoned at Rawal Pindi, where it arrived on 6 January 1875. This would be its base for the next three years.

One of the major expeditions that it was involved in during this time was against the Afridis, a tribe that was causing particular problems. It would be under the general command of Brigadier-General Ross and the expedition would see the 2nd Battalion as part of the 2nd Brigade, the brigade being commanded by Colonel H J Buchanan of the 9th. The expedition got under way on 3 December 1877 and their target was villages in the Bori Valley.

On 4 December the brigade moved to deal with an enemy position on a ridge in the valley. Three companies of the 14th Native Infantry and two companies of the 9th were sent forward to deal with the situation. The position was quickly taken and over the next few days the battalion was involved in destroying the villages. Throughout, however, they were under sniper fire. Over the next three days the 9th lost only two men wounded, but this was just the beginning of the operation, as the next target was the main stronghold at Pastaoni.

By now 150 men of the 9th were attached to the 1st Brigade, under Colonel Doran, along with a Native Infantry regiment and two Royal Horse Artillery guns. A further 120 men of the regiment remained with Colonel Buchanan. The initial movement forward was nothing more than a reconnaissance in force. The two columns moved forward and only encountered relatively light opposition so fell back in order that the full assault could be organized.

The attack would go in on 31 December 1877. Again the 9th was split; 100 of them were attached to Colonel Doran and 300 to Buchanan. Both of the columns advanced through the pass leading to Pastaoni. There was little opposition until Doran's column was within 600 yards of Pastaoni. The enemy was driven off without any loss and the positions were taken. The regiment remained in position until 2 January 1878.

There was just one more Afridis stronghold to deal with, at the Nara Khula defile. The advance began on 15 January 1878 with Colonel Buchanan leading the 9th, along with the 14th Native Infantry and a mountain battery. Again this was a major reconnaissance mission and all of the positions were dealt with, largely by artillery fire. Over the next few days the tribesmen continued to snipe at the British troops, but the revolt from the troublesome tribesmen was over and they came to terms with the Indian government. Throughout the expedition the 9th lost two men wounded.

On 1 May 1878 Buchanan was replaced by Brevet Lieutenant-Colonel Daunt and two days later the battalion was sent up to the Khyber Pass. There were more problems in Afghanistan and the Afridis in the pass were also causing problems. On 29 November 1878 200 men of the regiment, under Major Ridsdale, were sent up to escort a convoy through the Khyber Pass. They beat off a tribal attack and by 4

Signallers with lamps and flags, including Lieutenant Chater, at Gosport in 1884

December had returned to the rest of the battalion. The battalion remained at Peshawar until May 1879 and although there was now peace in Afghanistan this was to be short lived.

The British envoy in Kabul was murdered in September and the 2nd Battalion was warned that it was liable for active service once again. It began moving up on 21 September, but cholera was rife in the battalion. Nonetheless it passed through the Khyber Pass on 28 to 29 Sepember, reaching Dakka on 1 October 1879. At this point, with a strength of nineteen officers and 580 other ranks, it joined the 1st Brigade, commanded by Brigadier-General C J Gough. Operating with them were native cavalry and infantry, two battalions of Ghurkhas, mountain guns, sappers and a handful of Bengal lancers.

On 2 October Gough despatched part of the 2nd Battalion, along with other troops under Colonel Jenkins, to seize Gandamak. It was dangerous countryside and in the end the column only penetrated as far as Fatehabad, about halfway to Gandamak. Meanwhile other British troops had occupied Kabul.

Cholera was still a problem that added to the difficulties of the countryside and the intractable tribesmen. The British, however, were determined to deal with the Afghans once and for all and it was not to be an easy campaign. The 2nd Battalion was involved in a number of minor engagements that aimed to clear the region of enemy troops. The Afghans were persistent enemies, often sniping from distance and then simply melting away as the British closed with them. Operations were still

Portrait photographs of the non-commissioned officers of the 1st Battalion at Colchester in 1882

active throughout 1880 but by July 1880 negotiations for a peace treaty were well advanced. By the middle of August the 2nd Battalion could head back towards India. Gough's brigade was the last to leave Kabul, on 11 August 1880, with six companies of the 2nd Battalion being the last British troops to leave the city. Throughout they acted as a rearguard, but by 8 September they were back at Peshawar.

The 2nd Battalion remained in India until October 1888. There were numerous changes of personnel and additional drafts to replace men who had left the regiment and those who had died of disease and their wounds. The new colonel of the battalion was Roberts, who had replaced Daunt at the end of April 1883.

Burma

In October 1888 the 2nd Battalion was sent to Burma, arriving in Rangoon on 6 November. Sir George White was engaged in operations against the Chin. The 2nd Battalion sent 200 men, under Major Shepherd (A, C and F Companies). These arrived at the end of 1888 and in March 1889 H Company joined them followed by E Company in the July. The situation was awkward for Sir George, as the British had, in the past, launched a major punitive expedition. His orders were simply to blockade and harass the tribesmen. However, it was decided to destroy two villages that had been rebuilt by the tribesmen. Major Shepherd, at the head of 100 men of the Norfolk Regiment, along with 100 men from the 42nd Ghurkhas, set off on 30 April 1888. They managed to burn the first village, but the second one proved to be a more difficult prospect. Taking sixty-five Norfolks and sixty Ghurkhas, Captain Otway Mayne headed for the place on 4 May. The tribesmen were dug in and had built two stockades. They resisted rifle fire and a bayonet charge. Lieutenant Michel and two other men from the regiment were killed close to the stockade and several others were wounded. Major Otway Mayne wrote:

> Michel was killed about ten to fifteen yards away from me in a ravine close against a concealed stockade; in fact, I was going down to fetch him when I got knocked over and [surgeon-captain] Le Quesne went down and bound him up and brought him out. Le Quesne was later tying up my right arm for me when a bullet passed between us and got him in the left arm. I was with young Michel when he died, about ten minutes later, having been shot high up in the femoral artery. On this occasion also Corporal Stephenson distinguished himself. He was killed and died at the same time as Michel from a spear wound in the throat.

Subsequently, Le Quesne was awarded the Victoria Cross for his gallantry. At this point Mayne decided that discretion was the better part of valour and pulled back. A week later the tribesmen had abandoned the stockades and they were burned down. There were further decorations for the action that had taken place

Men of the Norfolk Regiment on parade at Dagshai in 1895. Dagshai was originally built as a sanatorium for tuberculosis patients and it became a cantonment town. It is now in the Solan District in the state of Himachal Pradesh in India.

on 4 May; Major Shepherd was awarded the Distinguished Service Order and Corporal Harwood and Private Crampion given the Distinguished Service Medal.

By 10 January 1890 the 2nd Battalion had left Rangoon and was heading for Bombay. It was to be a short visit, as on 3 February they set out for England, landing at Portsmouth on 5 March and then travelled by rail to Colchester.

By 30 April 1893 Lieutenant-Colonel C R Shepherd, who had won the DSO, was now in command of the battalion. Five companies of the battalion were stationed at the Tower of London until the September. There was sad news that month, as on 7 September 1893, Arthur Borton, now a well decorated, knighted man, died in London and was buried in Kent. Lieutenant-General Charles Elmhirst became the new colonel of the regiment and when he died in the December was replaced by Lieutenant-General T E Knox.

A small detachment of thirty-one men of the 2nd Battalion, under Lieutenant Hare, embarked at Southampton on 2 May 1896. They were to serve as part of No. 6 Company Mounted Infantry in South Africa. Their first taste of battle took place on 30 September 1896. They were part of an action against a rebel chief, Mashongombi. They attacked the south side of his stronghold under heavy fire and managed to break into the position but one of the soldiers was shot, later dying of his wounds. After being complimented for their service in South Africa, they were sent back to England, reaching there on 23 June 1897.

As for the rest of the battalion, some five companies under Major Phillips had left for Ireland on 10 November 1896. The commanding general at Aldershot

Men of the 2nd Battalion on parade in front of Fermoy Barracks buildings in Ireland in 1898

before they left said of his 'Holy Boys': 'Smart in the field, champions on the range, well behaved in barracks and camp, twice the winners of the Evelyn Wood [shooting competition] and other trophies, they leave behind them a record which will be long spoken of in the 3rd brigade.'

Lieutenant-Colonel Phillips, Major Beecher and Captain de B Bell of the 2nd Battalion in Ireland at Fermoy Barracks in 1898

Display of regimental silver and colours held by the 2nd Battalion from their tour of Ireland in 1898

Group portrait of officers of the 2nd Battalion in Ireland at the Fermoy Barracks in 1898

South Africa

On 30 April 1898 Lieutenant-Colonel L H Phillips took over the battalion from Shepherd and a year and a half later they received orders to make for Aldershot and then to prepare for embarkation to South Africa. With a strength of twenty-six officers, 984 other ranks, five horses and a machinegun they arrived at Cape Town on 22 January 1900. They were to become part of the 14th Infantry Brigade of the 7th Division. The brigade commander was Major-General H Chermside. The Norfolks had arrived in a theatre of war that presented them with as dangerous a foe as they had ever faced. It was also an incredibly confused situation.

Effectively this was a war that would expose many grave problems in the British army, in command, organization, weapons and tactics. However it was to be a lesson that would not be learned; the Boers, their enemy in South Africa, were unlike anything that they had faced before. This was not a conventional war, but a vicious hit-and-run conflict, where casualties in a matter of minutes would exceed those that the battalion had suffered in a whole campaign in the past.

The British had appointed a new commander in chief to deal with the rapidly deteriorating situation in South Africa. Lord Roberts had landed on 10 January 1900, along with his new chief of staff, Lord Kitchener. Roberts's plan was to make a determined thrust into the Boers' Orange Free State and seize Bloemfontein and Pretoria. But first they would have to relieve several towns and positions that were under siege from the Boers.

Lord Roberts and his staff watch the action from Fort Wonderboom in South Africa, c.1900. This was a fort that the Boers had built to defend Pretoria. Its ruins were taken by the British.

Officers of the 2nd Battalion in South Africa in 1900

Crucial to the plan was the use of the railway line between the Orange River and the Modder River. The British would have to outflank the Boers to allow the mounted infantry to pass around them and relieve Kimberley. It would be the job of the infantry to seize the fords. The troops got under way on 11 February and by the following evening the lead cavalry units had taken the fords across the Riet River.

The next target was the fords across the Modder River. As the horsemen surged forward the infantry, in intense heat and on half rations, moved forward. By late evening on 15 February Kimberley was relieved, but on the same day Andries Croje's Boer troops, in danger of being cornered by the 7th Division, had moved west. They managed to pass between two British divisions and reached the Modder River at Paardeberg Drift on 17 February. They were in the process of crossing the river when 1,500 mounted British infantry caught up with them. The Boers decided to dig in.

The British 6th Division moved up to deal with the Boers. Lord Roberts, having fallen ill, passed overall command to Kitchener, who ordered Lieutenant-General Thomas Kelly-Kenny to launch a series of frontal assaults against the Boer

A photograph of Pretoria, South Africa in June 1900, which was part of an album of photographs of the 2nd Battalion covering the period 1893–1938

entrenchments. The result, which became known as 'Bloody Sunday', saw twenty-four officers and 279 other ranks killed and fifty-nine officers and 847 men wounded. The bombardment from the British artillery had inflicted over 350 casualties on the Boers. Many of the horses had been killed and the wagons destroyed.

Roberts finally arrived on the scene and at 1600 on 18 February orders were received to send the 14th Brigade up to Paardeberg. The 2nd Battalion received their orders at 1700 and marched without eating at 2000.

One of the key positions overlooking the Boer entrenchments was Signal Hill and it was here that the 2nd Battalion took up position. The two sides settled down to snipe at one another and to improve their

Another version of the 9th Regimental badge featuring Britannia. Around Britannia is written honi soit qui mal y pense, which is literally translated as either 'shame be to him who thinks evil of it' or 'evil be to him who evil thinks'. This artefact, from the Royal Norfolk Regimental Museum, has links to the Royal Canadian Regiment, which uses this motto. The Royal Norfolk Regiment operated with them during the Boer War.

A watercolour of officers and men of the late 19th century. This would have been one of the last versions of the uniforms worn before the adoption of khaki.

defences. The deadlock was finally broken on the night of 26 to 27 February. The Royal Canadian Regiment advanced toward the Boer camp and dug trenches on high ground less than seventy yards from the Boer lines. When the Boers woke up the following morning their positions were entirely overlooked. They had no option but to surrender. The British bagged over 4,000 prisoners.

So far the 2nd Battalion had been lucky and had only suffered a handful of casualties. By 7 March 1900, however, they were on the road again, heading for Bloemfontein. By daybreak they were on the left bank of the Modder River and at 0930 they moved southeast towards Table Mountain, reaching Poplar Grove at 1500. Without serious incident they reached Bloemfontein on 16 March.

Three days later there was news that the Boers had blown up the bridge at Glen, some fourteen miles to the north. The bridge needed to be reinstated and it was decided to send a force to clear the Boers away. General French left on 28 March with an advance force. The rest of the 7th Division followed, including the 2nd Battalion. The target was Karee Siding, a station to the north of Glen. The Boer force was astride the railway and they had a strong position; on their right was Houdenbeck Hill. The idea was to work around the Boers, and try to cut them off and meanwhile the 14th Brigade would move against Houdenbeck Hill. By around noon on 29 March the 14th Brigade was approaching the hills to the east of the railway. Three-quarters of an hour later they came under fire and the leading companies began to deploy. The artillery opened up on Houdenbeck Hill. The 2nd Battalion was leading on the right, pushing forwards and seeing the enemy falling back. They got to some hills about a mile and a half to the east of the station and waited for reinforcement. They were under continual fire from the Boers, who had entrenched themselves along a ridge.

By 1400 it was clear that the Boers were being reinforced and the fire was getting more intense. The task of taking Houdenbeck Hill was given to the East Lancashire Battalion, with the 2nd Battalion protecting their right. During the action Colour Sergeant Hendry was killed, two officers and seventeen other ranks were wounded. On 4 April half of the battalion, under Major Becker, were sent to garrison Glen.

The regiment remained in the thick of the fighting, which recommenced on 3 May 1900, as the British advanced towards Pretoria. By 10 May the battalion could muster just 660 men but on 22 May 105 men of the Norfolk Volunteers arrived to reinforce them. The battalion was once again involved in heavy fighting on 4 June 1900, as the Boers made their last desperate attempt to protect Pretoria. The battalion was engaged against a heavily defended ridge to the southwest of Pretoria. In the ensuing fighting the 2nd Battalion did not lose a single man and Pretoria surrendered unconditionally at 0500 on 5 June 1900.

The 2nd Battalion was now entrusted with the occupation of Pretoria. There was very little fighting, but there was an incident at the beginning of January 1901; part of the 2nd Battalion's duties were to occupy outposts. One such post, at Zuurfontein station, between Johannesburg and Pretoria, was being garrisoned by

Officers of the Royal Norfolk Regiment in South Africa around 1900, enjoying an impromptu meal

Officers and men of the Royal Norfolk Regiment at Fort Wonderboom near Pretoria in South Africa

a detachment of the 2nd Battalion and some troops from the Lincolnshire Regiment. The Boers crept toward the post through the wire entanglements and attacked the station for two hours. The enemy was finally beaten off, but not before the 2nd Battalion had lost two killed and two wounded. This was a typical example of the kind of guerrilla warfare that British troops would have to face into 1902.

Lieutenant-Colonel C E Borton had taken over command of the 2nd Battalion from Phillips in January 1901 and from April to October the bulk of the 2nd Battalion was based at Rustenburg, some eighty miles from Pretoria. Boer guerrillas were active in the region and on several occasions members of the 2nd Battalion were involved in raids and counter raids. Detachments of the battalion also operated as part of the columns commanded by General Kekewich and Lord Methuen. In April 1902 at Rooiwal a detachment of the 2nd Battalion was operating as part of the column commanded by Kekewich. In fact several British columns were operating in the region, trying to corner Boer guerrillas. One of the columns blundered into 2,700 mounted Boers and as soon as the Boers realized that strong British columns were closing in on them they retired, but not before the 2nd Battalion had suffered six men being wounded.

A peace treaty was finally signed on 31 May and although the 2nd Battalion, who had taken part in long and arduous operations, had not suffered particularly

Officers of the regiment at Lichtenburg, now in the northwest province of South Africa, in 1902

high casualties, they had performed miracles. For five and a half months with General Kekewich they were the only infantry battalion to operate with otherwise exclusively mounted troops.

It is important to remember that throughout all of these months a detached mounted infantry company, under Lieutenant G B Orr, had been operating in South Africa. It had been H Company of the 2nd Battalion, under Captain Ross, with four officers and 164 other ranks that had been earmarked for mounted duties. The company was attached to the 7th Battalion Mounted Infantry, under the command of Colonel Bainbridge. The entire battalion initially amounted to some 450 men. Their first taste of action was in early February 1900 when they were involved in operations around Volvekraal. Later in the month, on 15 February, they were engaged in the campaign that culminated in the battle at Paadeberg. The Norfolk company was actually separated from the other three companies of the 7th Mounted Infantry. The company had been detached to escort a battery on 18 February.

Captain Ross was told by Lord Kitchener to cross a drift three miles upstream and attack the Boer positions as soon as he could. The company, at around 1300, dismounted close to the north bank and attacked a small white house two or three miles to the west. There were around twenty Norfolk men with Captain Ross and a dozen or so other mounted infantry. One of the officers with him was Lieutenant Cramer Roberts (he was later to be taken prisoner by the Turks in 1916). Ross's men advanced to within 1,000 yards in skirmish order when they came under fire. Suddenly fire came from behind Ross, but the shots were not aimed at his men;

they were aimed at Colonel Hannay, who was leading the whole of the mounted infantry force. This volley killed Hannay and Ross moved forward once again, now being only about 700 yards from the building. His men were virtually pinned down and Roberts was wounded. Ross and the men were in a very difficult position; they were not only under fire from the Boers, but there were also British shells exploding as close as 200 yards from them. As if this were not enough, British rifles were striking the ground no more than 50 yards away. Darkness fell and Ross had around half a dozen wounded men to worry about. He managed to get to the drift to collect ammunition, but there was no food to be had, so they dug in on a knoll before they were ordered to withdraw to the drift at first light. Roberts and some of the other wounded were too injured to be moved, so they had to be left and became Boer prisoners of war.

After this point it is difficult to disentangle precisely what Ross and his men did as distinct from the 7th Mounted Infantry. We know they were in Bloemfontein and that they were involved in operations in the Free State throughout October and November 1900. The last operations of the 7th Mounted Infantry, in March and April 1902, were effectively police duties in the northwest of the Free State.

There were other Norfolk battalions activated in 1900, largely as a result of the crisis in South Africa. The 3rd Battalion of the Norfolk Regiment was created on 26 January 1900 and it remained active until 11 April 1902. It had been decided on 9 January 1900 that seven militia battalions, chosen from those that had volunteered for overseas service, would be sent to South Africa. These units would be primarily defence and communication troops. In actual fact Lord Roberts wanted more than seven; he needed fifteen but had to settle for thirteen. Public opinion was in his favour and by 2 April 1900 no fewer than thirty-six militia battalions had left England, all but six of them for South Africa.

The militia battalions would enable regular, frontline battalions to be freed from the arduous duty of covering lines of communication. Roberts distributed twenty-three battalions along the three railways that made their way through the Cape colony.

The 3rd Battalion of the Norfolk Regiment left Britain on 25 February 1900. They had a strength of twenty-two officers and 503 other ranks. They initially made landfall at Cape Town, but were then sent up to East London, disembarking on 21 March. The battalion was scattered across innumerable detachments, protecting bridges, culverts and crossings, running from Cape Town to Bloemfontein. The headquarters of the battalion moved to a railway crossing midway between Edenburg and Bloemfontein on 13 July 1900. Detachments of men covered a fifty-mile section of railway in blockhouses up and down the length of the track. The commander of the battalion was Colonel Custance and he knew that the Kaffir River was a hotspot for enemy activity.

The 3rd Battalion remained in position for a year and was then moved up to Norval's Pont, where the railway crossed the Orange River. This was the frontier between the Cape colony and the Free State. The battalion was responsible for thirty miles of track; twelve miles south of the river and eighteen miles to the north. With a combination of blockhouses, barbed wire, trenches and good communications the Boers found it impossible to cross this section of the railway or to cause any meaningful damage. During this period eleven men were killed or died of diseases and the 3rd Battalion remained in position until the war ended in 1902. It was then sent home and discharged.

The 4th and Volunteer Battalions

There was also a 4th Battalion, which was commanded by Colonel Kerrison. It had been mobilized on 1 May 1900 at Norwich and then moved down to Colchester. This battalion also volunteered for service overseas but this was refused. They tried again in 1901 and received an overseas posting of sorts on Guernsey. They arrived there on 29 April but it was only a short posting, as on 16 July 1901 they were back in England and disbanded. However a company of mounted rifles was extracted from the battalion and sent out to South Africa. The battalion did not cease to exist, however; it did a month's training in Colchester in 1903 and was at Mousehold in Norwich in 1904.

In addition to these battalions were the volunteer battalions. There were four Norfolk Volunteer Battalions and the army was keen to invite volunteers for service in South Africa. One of the ideas was to draw enough men from the volunteer battalions to replace the company that had been detached from the regular battalions as mounted infantry. As a result, the 1st Service Company left for South Africa onboard the *Doune Castle* in February 1900. The 2nd Service Company left on the *Kildonan Castle* on 16 March, with a third detachment of some six men going out in March 1902, but these returned in the August. The two service companies consisted of three officers and 115 other ranks each.

The two companies served with the 2nd Battalion. Unfortunately, for one of the companies their stay in South Africa was very short. In April 1901 it was decided to send twenty-three of the volunteer companies home. The 1st Service Company left Cape Town on 22 April 1901. Despite their relatively short stay in the theatre of war they received a hero's welcome in Norwich on 16 May. They marched to the marketplace, were warmly greeted by the mayor and given silver medals. They were then entertained in the Agricultural Hall. The unit was commanded by Captain Diver, who had replaced the unfortunate Captain Archdale of the 3rd Volunteer Battalion, who had fallen ill just before the company was sent abroad.

The 2nd Service Company remained operational with the 2nd Battalion and finally left Cape Town on 7 May 1902. They too were warmly greeted in Norwich on 27 May and treated to a celebratory meal at the Maid's Head Hotel by the Sheriff of Norwich. The third small detachment, along with 100 reservists, returned to Norwich in August 1902 and was similarly lauded for their efforts.

The presentation of King's South African Medals to soldiers of the 2nd Battalion in 1903. The medals are being presented by Major-General H J Buchanan. This took place at Colchester barracks.

The 2nd Battalion itself finally reached Colchester on 10 February 1903. Here it received its colours and medals were given out to the men. The battalion was invited to Norwich on 16 February and they too marched through the city and were entertained at St Andrew's Hall at the expense of the city.

Members of a Boer operational commando, near Ladysmith in South Africa, c.1900–3

*portrait of Sergeant-Major A D
emmence, taken in India in 1912*

*portrait of Lieutenant-Colonel A J
Luard, taken in India in 1912*

On 9 April 1903 the regiment was presented a gold cup in commemoration of the Norwich visit and their service in South Africa. The cup had been bought from donations given by people across Norfolk. A bronze figure of peace, 9ft high and standing on a granite pedestal, was unveiled on 17 November 1904 on Castle Meadow. On it were engraved the 300 names of men of the Norfolk Regiment and Norfolk men serving in other units that had been killed during the Boer War. In addition, two windows in Norwich Cathedral were given over to a list of names of the officers and men of the Norfolk Regiment who had lost their lives.

Colonel C E Borton was replaced by Lieutenant-Colonel Wintour in 1904 and in the following year the 2nd Battalion returned to South Africa. In 1906 a monument was erected at the old cemetery to commemorate the lives of officers and men lost from the regiment during the Boer War. In October 1908 the 2nd Battalion was transferred to Gibraltar and in February 1911 it embarked for Bombay. By this time the new colonel of the battalion was A H Luard and the

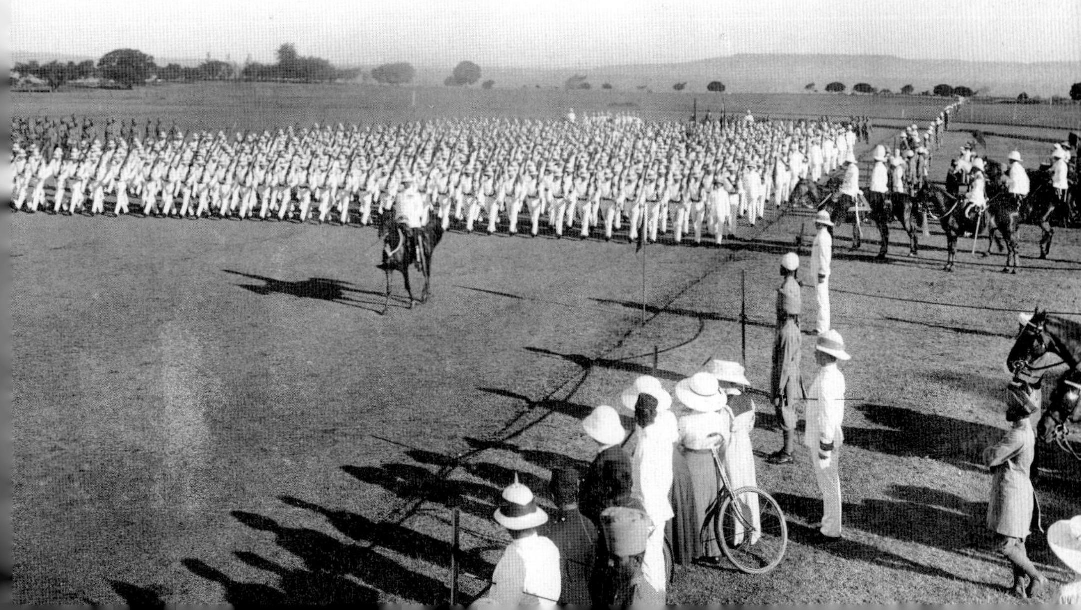

*Men of the 2nd Battalion marching on a parade ground
at Belgaum, India, in 1912*

battalion would be stationed at Balgaum, some 300 miles from Bombay. It temporarily returned to Bombay on 25 November 1911 to act as a guard of honour for King George V (who was the colonel-in-chief of the regiment) and Queen Mary. With the festivities over the battalion returned to Balgaum on 6 December and remained here until 3 November 1914. Lieutenant-Colonel E C Peebles, DSO, replaced Luard on 1 September 1912 and it would be Peebles that would lead the 2nd Battalion into the First World War.

4th, 5th and 6th Battalions

It is also worth considering the fortunes of the 4th, 5th and 6th Battalions in the period 1909 to 1914. Back in 1908 it had been decided that militia battalions, as they then were, would cease to exist, but the ones that were already in operation would become reserve battalions. The 3rd Battalion, having offered to operate anywhere in the world, became part of the first line of the army reserve. Henceforth the 3rd Battalion would have its own distinct colours, rather like the 1st and 2nd Battalions. In effect, the 3rd Battalion would supply a regular reserve to the two leading battalions of the Norfolk Regiment. Volunteer battalions would also disappear and they would become territorial battalions of the regiments to which they were attached. In effect these were second-line army reserves and their jobs would be, at least on paper, limited. They would supply garrisons at home, be part of the defence force if Britain were invaded and under special agreement they could volunteer for overseas duty.

As part of the reorganization Norfolk was asked to contribute two eight-company territorial battalions. The paper strength would be 1,009 men of all ranks. This meant that the Norfolk Volunteers needed to be reorganized, as there were four battalions of them. The 1st and 4th Volunteer Battalions became the 4th Territorial Battalion of the Norfolk Regiment. The 2nd and 3rd Volunteer Battalions became the 5th Territorial Battalion.

There was one other complication, as there was a sixth territorial battalion of cyclists. A cyclist company had been organized out of the 1st Volunteer Battalion between 1891 and 1895. These were under the command of Colonel Dawson. It had proved to be a good idea and the other three volunteer battalions followed suit. In fact from 1900 the four

A close up of a badge belonging to the 3rd Norfolk Rifle Volunteer Corps. The unit existed for just over 100 years, from around 1800 and this badge would have been used as a helmet plate.

Officers and men of the Royal Norfolk Regiment as they would have appeared around 1891

companies were formed into a composite battalion and received special training. It was recognized that cyclists would be quite useful in the event of an invasion as they were more mobile than foot troops. As a result, across the country eleven cyclist battalions would initially be created. The 6th Norfolk Battalion was one of these early units. It began with a strength of four officers and 176 other ranks, however it was to grow to twenty-one officers and 480 other ranks. The new commanding officer of the battalion was Lieutenant-Colonel Prior. Companies were formed at Ditchingham, Fakenham, Great Yarmouth, King's Lynn, Norwich and Thetford.

The 6th Battalion, through regular drill and training, had a good reputation. In the event of an invasion they would cover the coast from the Wash to Southwold.

This meant that by 1908 there were in effect six battalions of the Norfolk Regiment; two frontline battalions, one reserve battalion, two standard territorial battalions and the cyclist battalion. The whole of the territorial force was reviewed by King Edward VII in October 1909. Colours were presented to the 4th, 5th and 6th Battalions. There were combined manœuvres involving these three battalions around Sheringham in July 1910.

For the first time, in August 1911, the East Anglian Territorial Division encamped at Thetford. They were under the command of Major-General J H Byng and 8,000 strong. Some of the men, including the 6th Battalion, were actually on training manœuvres in mid-July 1914. The men had barely got home when they received their mobilization orders on 29 July. For most of the men in the six battalions war was just beyond the horizon.

The militia and volunteer battalions had been in existence for many years but to a large extent they had been separate entities. Back in 1662 and amended by a further act of parliament in 1663, organized militias were authorized. They were first called out in 1690 in response to a possible French invasion and were called out again during the Jacobite risings of 1715 and 1745. On these occasions the mustering of the militia had been disorganized and, as a result, in 1757, a new act regulated the militia and called for an ordered and well disciplined force. The act in 1757 demanded a certain number of men to be called up and Norfolk had to produce 960.

Initially these units were known as the 1st Battalion Western Regiment of the Norfolk Militia and the 2nd Battalion Eastern Regiment of the Norfolk Militia. They were allotted numbers 39 and 40. The two battalions were called up during the Seven Years' War, being required for service between June 1759 and December 1762. They were called up again at the beginning of the Napoleonic Wars and during the American War of Independence, between 1778 and 1783.

The 1st Battalion was reviewed on Mousehold Heath in May 1778. It was despatched to Ipswich and in November 1780 was in winter quarters at Hull. We also know that in May 1782 it was at Swaffham and Dereham, but it was marching to a camp at Caister-on-Sea, near Great Yarmouth. The regiment was reviewed by General Conway at Herringfleet in September 1782 but by March 1783 the 1st Battalion was demobbed at King's Lynn and the 2nd Battalion at Wymondham. Up until this point the commander of the two militia battalions had been Lord Orford, but on 31 March 1792 this position was taken over by Horatio Walpole.

Both of the battalions were recalled to duty in 1793. We know that the West Norfolk Militia was at Danbury in Essex and, although the records are incomplete, the unit may have been at Shorncliffe in 1796. At around this time a new unit was created, known as the Supplementary Norfolk Militia. There were to be six divisions that would serve in various parts of the county. We also know that the 4th Division of this unit, consisting of 316 men, was in training at King's Lynn. There was a considerable reward for men wishing to join up to these supplementary militia units; the princely sum of 8 guineas. It was a short-lived experiment, as the supplementary militia units were absorbed into the regular militia in 1799.

With peace in 1802 the militia was disbanded, only to be recalled the following year. They remained technically in service until 1814. Once again there were the western and eastern militias and both of them were at Dungeness in September 1805. The Duke of York inspected the Western Norfolk Militia at Canterbury on 7 August 1806.

Obviously some counties were finding it difficult to recruit men into their militia, largely because other counties were poaching their potential recruits. As a result, in 1809, another act of parliament was passed that outlawed the enlistment of militiamen into a regiment's unit if they did not live in that county.

The Western Militia was in Norwich in August 1809; in May 1811 they were in King's Lynn and in December at Woodbridge. In April 1813 they were at Berwick-upon-Tweed and then were posted to Edinburgh Castle. Almost no sooner had the Western Militia been disbanded in 1814 than they were called up again after Napoleon escaped from Elba and was at large for 100 days, which culminated at his defeat in the Battle of Waterloo. The Western Militia volunteered for service in Ireland and they remained there until April 1816 before being disbanded once more.

As for the Eastern Norfolk Militia, we know that during the period 1778 to 1783 they were at Colchester, Harwich and Manningtree. When they were called up again between 1793 and 1802 they seemed to travel far and wide and were in Chelmsford, Chatham, Gravesend, Rochester, Hithe, Deal, Dover and by 1797 were back in Norwich.

In February 1798 the commanding officer of the Eastern Norfolk Militia was given an order from Westminster:

> You are to permit such apportion of the officers and non-commissioned officers under your command as you shall judge expedient to march to the places in the county of Norfolk in which you may think your influence most likely to promote the enlistment of supplementary militia into the 9th Regiment of Foot, at which place or places they may be allowed to remain until it shall be necessary for them to march so as to assemble at Norwich prior to the day which may be appointed for assembling the supplementary militia there.

As for the rest of their period of enlistment, until 1802, we know that in 1798 they were back in Ipswich. They then served for a time in Yorkshire and then at Nottingham, Derby and Manchester. They were in Colchester when they were finally disbanded. Called up again in 1803, they were sent to Beccles, Lowestoft and Colchester.

In a document that was once housed at the Royal United Service Institution a particularly humorous event is recorded, which probably took place in 1803:

> Major George Wyndham of the East Norfolk Militia, previous to their being reviewed by HM King George III, took considerable pains with his officers, all of whom were country gentlemen, to teach them to salute in a graceful manner. When they rehearsed their parts, on the morning of the inspection, he prided himself on the success of his efforts. At length His Majesty appeared on the parade ground, preceded by one of his yeomen of the guard, and upon this official an unfortunate captain of a company threw away the major's carefully rehearsed salute, strutting past the King without making any return even to His Majesty's courteous salutation. On Major Wyndham remonstrating with his captain for this blunder the latter replied 'Fudge! Dost think I doesn't know the King? Why he had GR in large gold letters on his breast.'

Many of the men in the Eastern Norfolk Militia volunteered to provide drafts for the regulars. In fact they provided 233 privates and eleven corporals. The Eastern Militia remained active in 1806 at Hastings and Colchester, they were in Chatham and Rochester in 1809, and they too served in Ireland between 1811 and 1812. They returned to Great Yarmouth in June 1814 and this time they would not be recalled until 1820.

Both of the militia battalions were called out for the Crimean War and mustered on 27 December 1854. Both were to serve for around eighteen months. The Eastern Militia was largely in Essex and the Western Militia was in Ireland. Only the Western Militia was called up for the Indian Mutiny and they were recalled on 10 November 1857 at Norwich. At this stage there were about 700 officers and men and they remained in service until April 1858.

There were major changes to the militia battalions in 1881; new rules came into force on 15 July. Each regiment would now be organized into four battalions. The 1st and 2nd Battalions would be line units and the 3rd and 4th Battalions would be militia units. Consequently, the Western Militia became the 3rd Battalion of the Norfolk Regiment and the Eastern Militia became their 4th Battalion. It was very difficult to tell the difference between the line and the militia units, except that the militia battalions would have the letter M on their shoulder strap.

Colonel J R Harvey, in a history of the 4th Battalion Norfolk Regiment, explained the origins of the volunteer battalions and the militia:

> An enquiry into the origin of the volunteer is beset with considerable difficulty. It is necessary, on the one hand, to guard against the inclusion under the term volunteer of such bodies of men as were from time to time raised for the purposes of defence, but who, being in receipt of pay and uniform, and subject, from the date of their enrolment, to military discipline, were indistinguishable from the regular militia. On the other hand, it must be borne in mind that all branches of the military service are connected by a common bond of affinity – the militia with the standing

Regimental uniforms, as worn by men and officers in the mid-19th century. Note that the yellow cuffs are still present.

Helmet plates belonging to the 4th and 1st Norfolk Volunteer Battalions.

army, of which it was once the backbone; the volunteers with the militia, onto which, at first, they were grafted, and so with the regular army and the old constitutional force which lay at the root of both.

From time to Britain had been threatened with invasion, but after the Napoleonic Wars until the Crimean War the volunteer forces were sadly neglected. When the Indian Mutiny broke out in 1857 all available troops at home were sent abroad either direct to India or to replace regiments in far flung parts of the British Empire that were already *en route* to India. This meant that the volunteer corps was needed once again.

The major difference between the volunteers who had served at the beginning part of the nineteenth century and those who would serve in the 1850s was that the former were only ever expected to operate in their own military district. The new volunteers could be expected to serve anywhere in the British Isles.

In 1859 meetings were held all across Norfolk to discuss exactly how a volunteer corps could be raised. Expenses were a difficult issue, as the men had to provide their own uniforms. They would wear a grey tunic and trousers, a grey shako, a black leather belt and ammunition pouches. The first three companies were created in Norwich, with their headquarters at St Catherine's Close. A fourth company was raised in November 1859, and a fifth in January 1860. Major Brett commanded the five companies.

Elsewhere, across the county, eight more companies were raised, at Great Yarmouth, King's Lynn, Aylsham, Harleston, Diss, Loddon, Fakenham and Holkham. A new rifle range was created for the Norwich volunteers at Mousehold

Officers of the 2nd Battalion in India, probably in 1881

in 1860. In March of the following year the Norwich battalion mustered a sixth company, which would be known as the 1st Norfolk Mounted Rifle Volunteers.

In 1877 the grey uniform was replaced with a scarlet tunic for the 1st Norfolk Volunteers and collectively the Norfolk volunteer battalions became known as the Norfolk Volunteer Infantry Brigade. By 1881 there were four battalions of Norfolk Volunteers and by this stage the bulk of them had ten companies.

A group portrait of the Adjutant and Orderly Room Staff of the 1st Battalion in India in 1894

4

Mesopotamia and Gallipoli 1914–1917

Such was the need for manpower in the First World War that some regiments which had never had more than four regular battalions grew to the size of a division, or even a corps. The Norfolk Regiment would end up with twelve battalions; a mixture of regular, territorial and service battalions. It was not necessarily expected for anyone other than the regular battalions to see service abroad and in fact this was the case for the 1st and 2nd Battalions until 1915. At that point out went the 4th and 5th Territorial Battalions and so too did the 12th Yeomanry Battalion. All of these units would see service in Gallipoli, Egypt and Palestine. In fact the 12th Yeomanry Battalion would also see service in France. The 1st Battalion, along with the 7th, 8th and 9th, all fought in France and Belgium. The other four battalions, the 3rd, 6th, 10th and 11th, would primarily serve as recruitment and training battalions and be required to provide drafts of men to replace casualties for the other battalions.

A watercolour of officers and men of the regiment advancing against Turkish positions in Gallipoli in 1915

Typical uniforms as worn by the regiment during the First World War. Khaki had been introduced from the end of the 19th century.

2nd Battalion in Palestine

It seems sensible to consider the Norfolk Regiment by theatre and rather than the 1st Battalion we actually begin with the 2nd, which was already abroad when war broke out in August 1914. The battalion had been in Belgium since 1911 and on 3 November 1914 they headed for Bombay, ultimately bound for the Persian Gulf. The battalion sailed on the transport *Elephanta* and on 11 November they disembarked and became part of the 18th (Indian) Brigade, commanded by Major-General C I Fry. They would be working in cooperation with the 7th Rajputs, the 110th Mahratta Light Infantry and the 120th Rajputana Infantry. Along with the 16th (Indian) Brigade they would form the 6th (Indian) Division.

They began their advance on 17 November at 0600 hours, marching along the right bank of the Shatt-al-Arab, where the River Tigress and the River Euphrates meet. The battalion had advanced around six miles when scouts reported that Turkish troops had taken up positions around an old fort and a police station. The battalion was sent forward, along with the 7th Rajputs, to engage. Under enemy artillery fire it was decided to reinforce them and consequently both of the brigades moved up in force and drove the Turks from the trenches. This baptism of fire saw seven killed and forty-eight wounded. The pursuit was called off at 1600 and in

Officers of the 2nd Battalion in a formal pose in India in 1912

dreadful weather the battalion bedded down for the night near the old fort. The men lacked greatcoats and blankets and were constantly being sniped at by the Turks.

By 21 November the battalion was on board the SS *Medjidieh*, bound for Basra. They arrived there at 1000 on 22 November. The city had been evacuated by the Turks and there was a huge amount of looting. For a time the battalion was involved in policing operations, collecting up rifles from local Arab villages.

On 3 December 1914 D Company, consisting of four officers and 183 other ranks, headed for Kurna. Along with other units they were to engage the Turkish troops dug in around there. The advance began early on 4 December and by 1100 they were advancing on an enemy-held village. Three hours later the village had been cleared but it was now clear that the force was not strong enough to capture Kurna. Consequently reinforcements were brought up, including the rest of the battalion. The Turks had advanced and taken up their old positions, with a force of around 2,000 men and four guns. The 2nd Battalion was launched against the village of Mazera, supported by other units from the brigade. They came under tremendous fire and the Norfolk battalion cleared the village with the bayonet. Luckily casualties were relatively low; four men died and fewer than forty had been wounded, but this victory led to the surrender of the garrison at Kurna.

The battalion had a fairly quiet time of it during January 1915. They had occupied trenches and forts around Mazera and occasionally had been under artillery fire. By the middle of February the battalion was back in Basra and they spent the March there. A small number of them were engaged in an operation on 11 March to stop sailing barges from supplying the Turkish camp at Nakailah. This Turkish camp had become the mustering point for enemy forces in the region and it was clear that they were building up for a major offensive against Basra, only eight miles to the east.

On 22 March it was decided to reorganize the Mesopotamian Expeditionary Force as a proper army corps. The command was given to General Sir J Nixon. By the beginning of April 1915 it was decided to move against the Turks.

The Norfolk battalion marched out of camp at 0645 on 5 April 1915; they were bound for Shaiba, some twenty miles south of the Turkish camp. They reached there at 0730 and took up positions in a fortified and entrenched camp around an old fort. The total British force consisted of three regiments of cavalry, eight battalions of infantry and four batteries of guns.

The Turks began their advance on the British position at around 0515 on the morning of 12 April. There were upwards of 12,000 enemy troops. Here the Norfolks would remain under constant rifle and artillery fire until it was decided that the Turks had to be forced out of their trench works, which they had dug in order to besiege the camp. The battalion was involved in a number of attacks, culminating in a charge on the afternoon of 14 April 1915. The battalion launched a bayonet charge over 200 yards of open ground. After they had swept over the Turkish trenches there were hundreds of enemy dead. The battalion had also lost heavily, with four officers and twenty-nine other ranks killed, seven officers wounded along with ninety other ranks. The next few days were taken up with collecting and burying the dead.

By 22 April the battalion was back in Basra. By now the weather had turned and it was extremely hot, but conditions were tolerable in the city and the battalion remained there until 28 May. On that day they began a campaign that would take nearly a year to complete.

The battalion disembarked at Amara at 0640 on 4 June 1915. The town is on the left bank of the River Tigress and the idea was for British and Commonwealth troops to advance up the Tigress and make for Kut and Baghdad. The battalion was involved in a number of small-scale operations throughout June and into early July. But progress was incredibly slow. It was, however, becoming clear that the Turks and their German allies were in considerable force in the region. The battalion was involved in a major operation on 24 July 1915, which saw them capture a number of enemy prisoners.

By the beginning of September the British and Commonwealth troops were now ready to begin their advance against Kut. The battalion started out on 7 September 1915 and halted at Ali-al-Gharbi until 13 September. They would now fight in very difficult terrain around the vast Suwada marsh and the Suwaikieh swamp. On 27 September they attacked heavily fortified Turkish positions; this was simply a feint, as more British troops had turned the Turkish positions and were heading towards Kut itself. When the battalion made its final advance at 0530 on 29 September 1915 the Turks had abandoned their positions. So far casualties had been relatively low, but a major battle was looming as the Turkish troops who had been forced out of Kut had halted at Ctesiphon. They probably had as many men as the combined British force.

By the end of September it was becoming clear that the dreadful conditions were beginning to decimate the battalion. There had been 611 officers and men fit for duty on 29 September, by 8 October ninety-two had reported sick; around half of them should have been in hospital. Poor food was a major problem and beriberi was rife.

Nonetheless towards the end of October the battalion was involved in operations against the Turks at El Kutunie, but the men were not directly engaged in the fighting. Even with the threat of a Turkish concentration of troops the British resolved to continue their advance on Baghdad.

The 6th Division, along with elements of the 12th Division, amounted to some 14,000 men. The force was divided into four columns, with the Norfolks in B Column under Brigadier-General Hamilton. They were the first to move and they began making for Zeur, where an advance guard of enemy cavalry was beaten off.

By 20 November 1915 the 18th Brigade was again the advance guard. They had covered about seven miles and were at the village of Lajj. The Turkish positions at Ctesiphon were about eight miles away and the enemy was in strongly fortified positions, covering the bend of the River Tigress and then extending some six miles to two fortified mounds that the British would nickname 'Vital Point'. The Turks had taken up positions in the old Roman fortified city and at some points the wall was 40ft high. There was a second Turkish line extending from a camp and bridge over the river in parallel to Vital Point.

The Norfolks would be involved in a turning manœuvre around the north of Vital Point, which would then fall on the second Turkish line. This would be achieved while the other columns kept the Turks' attention. The Norfolk battalion was some three miles to the northeast of Vital Point by around 0100 hours on 22 November 1915. The 18th Brigade's ultimate objective was the village of Qusabah, on the River Tigress and behind the Turkish second line. They began to advance at around 0800, coming under heavy rifle and artillery fire. Casualties were beginning to mount, but by 1130 the two advance trenches in front of the Turkish second line had been overrun. They now came under such ferocious fire that it was impossible to advance further. The battalion was reinforced and they managed to push forward about another 150 yards, but they were still 1,000 yards short of the Turkish secondline trenches.

The Turks now launched a counterattack and the 18th Brigade was compelled to fall back. The casualties had been enormous; half of the machinegun section had been wiped out, all of the officers from D Company were either killed or wounded.

In fact by the end of the day twenty-seven had been killed, two were missing and 225 had been wounded. The battalion spent the night near Vital Point.

By the end of this engagement just seven officers and 250 men were fit for duty. Ration carts arrived early in the morning of 23 November and it was the first proper meal the men had had since the evening of 21 November. The battalion was shifted to the far left of the British positions but they were still under enemy artillery fire.

The situation was becoming quite desperate and it had been decided that the whole force would retreat towards Lajj and await reinforcements. In addition to this, by 1630 on 24 November it was clear that at least 10,000 Turkish reinforcements were about to arrive.

A further retreat was necessary on 27 November, with the 2nd Battalion operating as a rearguard. They covered the retreat for all of the twenty-one miles to Azizieh. Still the Turks continued to advance and once again the British fell back, this time towards Umm-at-Tabul.

On 1 December 1915 it was decided to launch a counterattack against the pursuing Turks. The Norfolk battalion deployed at around 0630, supported by the 7th Rajputs. They took up position in a large dry water course. As dawn broke to their astonishment they saw an enormous camp had sprung up in the darkness. British artillery opened up on it and two companies of the battalion advanced 200 yards; the other two remained in reserve. There were simply too many of the enemy however, with at least around 12,000 men. There was only one option and that was to retreat once again.

The battalion was in Kut by the morning of 3 December. Over the past thirty-three hours they had marched for forty-six miles. Order again had to be restored to Kut as there was widespread looting. At the time Kut was simply a ramshackle collection of houses with a population of around 6,000. It had a large, covered bazaar and a river frontage of about a mile and a half. The battalion would now form part of the garrison, digging trenches and gun pits and awaiting the inevitable Turkish attacks. They followed the same routine for days and on Christmas Eve the Turks launched the heaviest bombardment so far.

The battalion was assigned the protection of the northeastern bastion of the fort. A and C companies relieved B and D and vice versa. As the days passed with sniping, bombardment and fatigue duties the Turkish troops dug their trenches closer and closer to Kut. Supplies were running short by the end of January 1916 and the situation was even worse by the beginning of February. All attempts to break through to Kut with reinforcements had amounted to nothing. Casualties continued to mount and the British came under daily attacks from enemy aircraft. The garrison was reduced to eating horses and mules; rations shrank as the fighting spirit of the men shrivelled. Men were so tired that even when they were on sentry duty they had to lean against walls to prevent themselves from fainting.

Major-General Sir C Townsend, by now the new commander of the 6th

Division, wrote: 'Such was the state of weakness of the troops that men fainted on sentry duty and could not work at any fatigue. The garrison was now absolutely done. Men were dying at an average rate of fifteen a day, dysentery and scurvy claiming many victims.'

General Hamilton, commanding the brigade in which the Norfolk battalion served, added:

> In spite of all the trying conditions of the prolonged siege, the discipline, good order, and soldierly bearing of the battalion were maintained to the end. The daily guard mounting in the street at the entrance to the serai [billets] was in itself a soul stirring revelation to the unquenchable spirit of the Norfolk Regiment. Though worn to shadows of their former selves with starvation, constant duty, and frequent sickness, though their clothing was grimed and ragged, the men were still steady under arms, their drill punctiliously correct.

Continued attempts to bring in supplies to the garrison were all largely ineffective and negotiations began for a surrender. The garrison unconditionally surrendered on 29 April 1916, after a siege of 146 days. We know that seven officers and 303 other ranks were fit for duty a month earlier, but beyond that date it is impossible to know how many of the Norfolk battalion marched into captivity.

One of the officers, Captain A J Shakeshaft kept a diary during the captivity. The diary recounts the dreadful conditions and the brutality of many of the guards. It seemed clear that very little would be done to protect the men from dysentery, neglect and starvation. They were forced to march miles in the searing heat, often they were stoned by local civilians. When men died on the march they were buried with as much dignity as possible, only for the corpses to be dug up and the blankets stolen. By the time they reached Aleppo the men were emaciated and could barely march; some were carried in carts.

This was not, however, the end of the 2nd Battalion. Drafts from other battalions and the recovered sick or wounded were brought together with members of the 2nd Dorset Battalion to create a new composite battalion. This was formed on 4 February 1916 and attached to the 21st Brigade of the 7th (Meerut) Division. The battalion mustered some forty-five officers and 853 other ranks. They were known as the Norsets, as two of the companies were Norfolk men and two from Dorset. They went into action on 8 February, facing the Turks at Umm-el-Hannah. It was part of the operation that was aiming to relieve Kut.

Throughout the rest of February and March and into early April they occupied trenches facing the enemy. At 0600 on 6 April 1916 the men began digging in just 1500 yards from the enemy positions. On 7 April they were involved in the attack on Sannaiyat. They ran into heavy machinegun and rifle fire and were still 900 yards short of the enemy positions. Falling back, they dug in and they remained in entrenchments until 22 April.

C Company of the Norsets on parade in Mesopotamia in 1917. This was a composite unit made up of members of the Norfolk Regiment and the Dorset Regiment.

At 0700 on 22 April 1916 they moved up in support of an advance by the 19th Brigade. They had to advance across flooded trenches and swampy ground. The enemy strongly resisted the advance and the troops were forced to fall back. For a short time just before noon there was an armistice for the two sides to collect their dead and wounded. During the day the Norsets had lost thirteen officers wounded, twenty-two other ranks had been killed, 146 wounded and twenty-two were missing.

The offensive actions were no longer worth the cost after 29 April, when Kut surrendered. But the Norsets remained at the front through June and into July 1916. They were then sent down to join a newly formed provisional battalion of the Norfolk Regiment, which had been created at Basra on 16 July 1916. This now meant that the new provisional battalion, or the reconstituted 2nd Battalion, was once again a truly Norfolk Regiment entity.

There was a huge amount of sickness, with diarrhoea, cholera and other diseases. In fact by the end of August the effective strength of the battalion was only 498 men. Training and drill were the order of the day throughout August and the first half of September and by the time the battalion was ready to move it had fifteen officers and 488 men. However by 2 October 1916 only 266 of the men were fit for duty.

The battalion spent until early January 1917 around Sodom Point. They were then marked to go into action once again. The battalion was heading for the River Tigress. They marched towards Kut, aiming to be part of the attack on the Turkish positions at Dahra. They crossed the Tigress in the early hours of 23 February 1917, crossing its 340 yards of water in pontoons and rowing boats. Lieutenant

Horner was the first to cross and single-handedly he dealt with a Turkish machinegun post, winning himself the DSO. Together with Sergeant Williams, Horner captured a trench and thirty-five prisoners. Williams was awarded the DCM.

The battalion was working in cooperation with the 2nd and 9th Ghurkha Rifles. They now had a line established facing a Turkish strongpoint. The battalion got under way at around 1030, trying to work their way through the enemy dugouts and entrenchments. By 1220 they had overrun many of the Turkish positions and the fort was carried at bayonet point. But this had to be abandoned due to heavy machinegun fire. During the day six officers were wounded and six other ranks killed, forty-one wounded and three were missing.

The advance on the Dahra Ridge began again at 0600 on 24 February 1917. The Norfolks were in the centre of the advance, flanked by Ghurkhas and Punjabis. The troops advanced rapidly and the ridge was captured. This allowed the battalion a brief respite and they were relieved.

The march towards Baghdad began on 25 February. The Norfolk battalion led the 37th Brigade. As they marched towards their target they passed enormous amounts of Turkish equipment abandoned everywhere. It was clear that the Turks were in desperate retreat. The battalion was strong and could boast twenty officers and 271 other ranks on 28 February.

By 3 March 1917 they were at Azizieh, three days later they crossed the battlefield at Ctesiphon and by 10 March Baghdad had been occupied. The Norfolks were at Diala and enjoying a brief rest and the opportunity to throw grenades into the river to catch fish. Between 20 and 23 March they marched up to Bakubah and here they were split up and sent on different duties to cover outposts.

Men of the Norfolk Regiment marching through the desert in Palestine, dated 1917 to 1918.

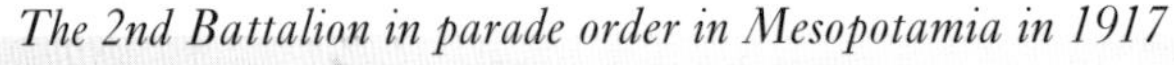

Norfolk Regiment soldiers sitting in a dugout at the Kurduraz camp in Palestine 1917 to 1918

The battalion operated as an escort for motor vehicles on 5 April 1917 and they came under heavy artillery fire, but fought their way through and drove on to advance posts of Russian troops from Persia. The battalion spent between May and September 1917 garrisoning Bakubah. It was an important link for the troops between Baghdad and the supply bases. Additional troops in the form of 200 draftees arrived to reinforce the battalion in the June.

Throughout the rest of the year the battalion was involved in garrison and patrol duties, although on the morning of 3 December 1917 they forced a bridge half a

The 2nd Battalion in parade order in Mesopotamia in 1917

The presentation of the new colours to the 2nd Battalion by King George V at Buckingham Palace in 1919

mile from Kizil Robat, supported by Ghurkha and Punjabi units. Casualties during this period had been relatively low and at the end of the year they had thirty-one officers and 1,013 other ranks.

Between January and mid-April 1918 they continued operating as garrison troops, even though operations were still being directed against the Turks, who were slowly retiring. On 26 June 1918 elements of the Lewis gun detachments were operating with Kurdish irregulars. In August and September the battalion was building railways. By the time the armistice was announced in the November the battalion was at Imam Abbas and by the end of 1918 they were at Shahraban.

Lieutenant-General Sir R G Egerton relinquished his command of III Indian Corps on 3 February 1919 and was full of praise for the battalion:

A W Archer's Waziristan 1919 to 1921 campaign medal

> The great feat of arms performed by you in the clearance of Dahra Bend was followed by the magnificent achievement at Shumran, when you forced the passage of the Tigress in full flood in the face of a determined enemy – a performance which will, I believe, live in history as you unique in the annals of any army in the world. And in connection with this I raise my hand to salute the gallant Norfolk Regiment in particular.

1/4th and 1/5th in Gallipoli, Egypt and Palestine

The 1/4th and 1/5th Territorial Battalions were brigaded together and fought at Gallipoli, in Egypt and in Palestine. They were also for some short period of time a composite battalion. The 1/4th Battalion assembled at the Drill Hall in Chapelfield, Norwich, on the morning of 5 August 1914. The 1/5th Battalion mobilized at Dereham on the same day. On 11 August 1914 the 1/4th headed for Essex, followed by the 1/5th on 17 August. In Essex they drilled and practised and by April 1915 they were both in Bury St Edmunds. In May they became part of the 54th Infantry Division and together with the 1/5th Suffolks and the 1/8th Hampshires became part of the 163rd Infantry Brigade.

With a strength of around 1,000 officers and men each they embarked on SS *Aquitania* bound for the Dardanelles. They landed at Suvla Bay on 10 August 1915. The 1/4th Battalion was commanded by Colonel Harvey and on landing he wrote:

> On the left Suvla Point with Nebrunessi Point to the right formed a small bay, known as Suvla Bay, some mile and a half across. To the right of Nebrunessi Point a long, gently curving sandy beach, some four or five miles in extent, terminated where the Australian position at Anzac rose steeply to the Sari Bair range. Inside and immediately in front was a large, flat, sandy plain covered with scrub, while the dry salt lake showed dazzlingly white in the hot morning sun. Immediately beyond was Chocolate Hill, and behind this lay the village of Anafarta some four miles from the shore. As a background the Anafarta Ridge ran from the village practically parallel with the sea, where it gradually sloped down to the coast.

The plain was dotted with stunted trees and scrub; perfect for Turkish snipers. Day after day men were picked off. Water was also a major problem; it was difficult and challenging countryside.

On 12 August 1915 the 1/4th was assigned to the duty of trying to clear the area of enemy snipers. The advance got under way at 1645. Also involved in the operation was the 1/5th. Sir Ian Hamilton, the commander in chief of operations in the region, wrote a despatch on 11 December 1915, in which he described 'a very mysterious thing':

> The 1/5th Norfolk were on the right of the line and found themselves for a moment less strongly

Colonel Arnold Allen Cecil Keppel, 8th Earl of Albemarle. He was Brigadier-General of the Norfolk Volunteer Infantry Brigade between 1901 and 1906. Prior to this and, presumably when this photograph was taken, he was an honorary colonel of 5th Battalion of the Norfolk Regiment

opposed than the rest of the brigade. Against the yielding forces of the enemy Colonel Sir Horace Beauchamp [the 5th Battalion's commanding officer], a bold, self-confident officer, eagerly pressed forward, followed by the best part of the battalion. The fighting grew hotter, and the ground became more wooded and broken. At this stage many men were wounded, or grew exhausted with thirst. These found their way back to camp during the night. But the colonel, with sixteen officers and 250 men, still kept pushing on, driving all the enemy before them. Nothing more was ever seen or heard of any of them. They charged into the forest and were lost to sight or sound. Not one of them ever came back.

This is the tale of the so-called vanishing Norfolks. It was the subject of a BBC film, *All the King's Men*, starring David Jason. Jason took on the role of Captain F R Beck of C Company of the 1/5th Norfolks. The story of the missing men has at times led to ludicrous assumptions, including alien abduction or them being swallowed up by a low-lying cloud. The truth, although tragic, is probably far more mundane and commonplace in a confused and brutal action such as this. Undoubtedly many of the men were either killed or wounded by Turkish snipers during the advance. Undoubtedly, many of the men probably fell into Turkish hands. Consequently, the accusation has often been that the Turks executed the men. The focus has often been on C Company, which was dubbed the Sandringham Company of the battalion. Many of the men had been drawn from the Sandringham Estate and were led by Beck, who was the estate land agent and a close personal friend of the royal family. The royal family was deeply distressed that there was no clear explanation as to what had happened to so many of the estate workers. But they were not the only men to have literally disappeared during this engagement. On 9 August seven officers and 140 men of the 6th East Yorks were missing in action after a Turkish counterattack. They may well have been trapped in a gulley and shot.

There is confusion as to the figures; the original war diary claimed that in this action the 1/5th Norfolks lost twenty-two officers and around 350 men. In fact fourteen officers and around 142 men were killed or missing in action. One officer and sixteen of the men were from the Sandringham Estate. Whatever their actual fate, it is likely that they are buried as unidentified soldiers in Azmak cemetery, on the Suvla plain.

Some of the men took as many as four days to find their way back to the British lines. It had been a chaotic advance and certainly knots of the men had become isolated and overwhelmed by the Turks. A number of the bodies were found in 1919 scattered over an area of a square mile, around 800 yards beyond the Turkish frontline. A local Turkish farmer claimed that when he came back to his farm it was covered with the decomposing bodies of British soldiers. These he said he had thrown into a ravine.

Certainly, as far as the men of the 1/4th Battalion were concerned, it had been a disastrous engagement. Throughout the night of 12 August men who had lost their units gingerly approached the British frontline. Around 200 men from various units were with the 1/4th by the following morning. 1/4th was holding a ridge, under continuous fire and exhausted. Eventually they were relieved and by 16 August both of the battalions were holding a ridge running northeast from Suvla Point. By the following day the battalions were holding Jephson's post on Saddle Ridge, as Captain M B Buxton (of the 1/5th Battalion) explained:

> The trenches here consisted, when the Norfolk battalions first reached the line, only of rifle pits, and the first thing that was done was to make a strong line of trenches and to build dugouts. During all this time the troops had been very short of water. The 5th Battalion sank several small wells in the hope of finding water, but these produced nothing more than brackish and muddy puddles.

Buxton went on to explain the harsh conditions: there was a shortage of food and water, it was difficult for the men to find blankets, they had no change of clothes and it was hot during the day and so cold at night that it was difficult to sleep. Nonetheless they continued to improve their positions. Occasionally they came under heavy artillery fire and it was difficult for them to bring up food and ammunition. Finally, on 20 August 1915, they were relieved for a short time. But they were to spend the remainder of August protecting this position, until they were moved further down the Gallipoli peninsula.

By the end of the first week of September both battalions had been ravaged with disease and wounds. In fact when Colonel Harvey of the 1/4th was sent home due to illness on 4 December he left behind him ten officers and 170 men fit for duty. The 1/5th had a similarly tough time. By 1 November 1915 their numbers had been so reduced that they had to be reorganized into two companies.

On 31 October Captain Balme had led a patrol, as Captain Buxton explained:

> The Turks had been in the habit of posting a listening post at night on a steep spur which led down from their line, but which could only be approached from our lines by climbing up, one at a time, a precipitous ridge which led up to it. Captain Balme of the 3rd Essex Regiment, who was attached to the 5th Norfolk, took a small party one evening before dusk to attack this. They succeeded in climbing the steep sides of the ridge without attracting the attention of the Turks, and were able to get into the post before the Turkish outpost took up their position for the night. When the Turks put in an appearance they were most successfully ambushed, and Captain Balme was able to bring the whole of his party back without a casualty. For this he was awarded the MC. Captain Balme was, later, invalided from Egypt but rejoined his own regiment in France, where he was afterwards killed.

Both of the battalions spent August to November at the Anzac sector of the front. After manning the front trenches the 5th Battalion was finally withdrawn on 30 November 1915. By now the weather had deteriorated and there were blizzards. The 5th finally left the peninsula on the night of 4 December and by this time there were only two officers of the original 5th Battalion left.

The 4th Battalion, reduced to eleven officers and 199 other ranks, was also withdrawn on 7 to 8 December 1915. Both battalions found themselves in Egypt and were together again at Mena camp, near Cairo, in February 1916. They were literally at the foot of the Great Pyramid.

Over the next six weeks or so new drafts of troops arrived from England and the two battalions were later deployed to defend the Suez Canal. Here they would remain until June 1916. It was to be a relatively uneventful year, but 1917 would see them both engaged in operations in Palestine.

In February 1917 they were marching across the Sinai Desert, towards Gaza, where the front had now established itself. Lieutenant-Colonel de Falbe, formerly of the Hertfordshire Yeomanry, had temporarily taken over command of the 5th Battalion, but after being invalided home was replaced by Lieutenant-Colonel Grissell, DCO. Grissell had been with the 2nd Battalion of the Norfolk Regiment for many years.

As part of the 163rd Brigade the Norfolks had come up to relieve the 156th Brigade, based at El Arish. The 4th Battalion took over from the 8th Scottish Rifles, based on Mount Murray and the 5th Battalion replaced the 4th Royal Scots, covering Mount Dobel, Bushy Knoll and the Step. The battalions remained here until 20 March, when they moved to El Burj. They reached Rafa on 25 March and then on to Beni Sela the following day. They were moving up as part of the operations for the main attack against Gaza.

Writing on 27 March 1917, Captain Buxton described the situation:

> The brigade (163rd) marched the eight miles to Sheikh Abbas in artillery formation, arriving there about 10 o'clock without firing a shot, and took up their position along the ridge. The Turks had much larger forces in Gaza than we expected, and large reinforcements were marched from Beersheba and other places round, and so the attack was not so successful as we hoped. In the afternoon we received orders to take up a position during the night west of Sheikh Abbas on the Mansura Ridge. The brigadier sent me down on my horse to find out the way, and I then came back and guided the columns to Mansura Ridge during the night. Directly it was light we saw a large force of Turks advancing on the ridge and they shelled us rather heavily. The 5th Norfolk were ordered to go forward and take up a line about 500 yards in front of the ridge. After a good deal of machinegun and rifle fire the Turkish attack was broken up and then never got much nearer than 400 or 500 yards.

The situation, however, was still quite dangerous and by the late afternoon it was clear that even more Turkish reinforcements were about to attack the British positions. The attack came in at dusk, but was broken up with machinegun and artillery fire. It was obvious that Gaza was going to be harder to take than had been anticipated and there was now a lull in the fighting.

On the night of 16 April 1917 the 163rd Brigade was once again given orders to take the Sheikh Abbas ridge at dawn. This they managed to achieve the following morning. The attack was led by the 8th Hants and the 8th Suffolk, with two tanks and supported by the two Norfolk battalions.

Orders were now given for a general attack to take place at first light on 19 April. The four battalions of the brigade began to advance at around 0730. Although the British artillery had pounded the Turkish positions the infantry still came under tremendous fire. Each of the battalions had to cover a front of around 900 yards and both of the Norfolk battalions found themselves facing Turkish redoubts. Again Buxton explained the situation:

> It was quite obvious what had happened. The advance had been held up just below the Turkish line, and one could see our men lying out in lines, killed or wounded. The 1/5th Norfolk B Company, under Captain Blyth, had captured Tank Redoubt and had held it for some time, till all ammunition was spent.

The outlying Turkish trenches were taken, but the brigade was under tremendous pressure and under continuous fire. More localized attacks were launched by the brigade, but they only succeeded in increasing the number of casualties. The 4th Battalion lost a total of eighteen officers and 460 other ranks killed, wounded or missing and the 5th lost nineteen officers and 643 other ranks. Among those was Grissell – originally posted as 'wounded and missing', but afterwards found to have been killed. Consequently both of the Norfolk battalions were brought together as a single composite battalion. What remained of the 4th made up the 1st and 2nd Companies and the 5th, the 3rd and 4th Companies. The battalion was given over to Lieutenant-Colonel Torkington of the Scottish Rifles. Unsurprisingly, the composite battalion was put into reserve and major reorganization was needed. It was not until 1 June 1917 that the two battalions became separate again. Torkington took command of the 4th and Major G M de L Dayrell of the 5th Bedfords took command of the 5th. During June the 4th Battalion received reinforcements of two officers and 140 other ranks and the 5th 242 other ranks. Additional reinforcements arrived in the July, with 175 men for the 4th and 245 for the 5th.

The situation was pretty uneventful until it was decided in November 1917 that there would another attempt to overwhelm the Turkish positions at Gaza. On 1 November the 163rd Brigade moved up into position. They would try to turn the Turkish left. The main attack got under way at 0230 on 2 November. The 5th

Suffolk, along with D Company of the 4th Norfolk Battalion was selected as assault units. They advanced to a position known as Halfway House. The Turkish defenders thought they were just a patrol and paid little attention to them. By 0300 the whole of the 4th Norfolk Battalion was moving up in support and it ran into enemy artillery fire. Again they took heavy casualties. There was vicious hand-to-hand fighting shortly before 0400 around the El Arish position.

Meanwhile, the 5th Battalion having lost contact with other units due to the darkness and the confusion was caught in a barrage and was out of position. Although the brigade had failed to reach its main objectives, they had taken a number of Turkish trench lines, but it had been at a heavy cost. The 4th Battalion had lost two officers and twenty-three dead, three officers and 102 other ranks wounded and four were missing. The 5th Battalion's casualties are not listed in the war diary, but it is believed that their losses were at least the same as those of the 4th.

In the captured trenches the Norfolk battalions found themselves under continual barrage and rifle fire. But it was largely ineffective; the Turks were jittery and it was soon clear why – they had begun to retreat. Once again the British force could move forward with relative impunity, but they were still running into Turkish patrols and strongpoints that needed to be overwhelmed.

Jerusalem fell on 9 December 1917, but the fighting was by no means over. The Turks were still holding positions in the surrounding hills. A patrol of the 4th Battalion ran into Turkish positions on Cistern Hill at 0530 on 11 December. The patrol ascertained that the Turks were building up to attack Zephiziyeh Hill, which was held by C Company of the 4th. A heavy Turkish attack came in at 0800 and within an hour 300–400 Turks had got to within grenade distance of the positions. B Company, however, was on its way, under Captain Flatt. They charged with fixed bayonets and chased the Turks out of their advanced positions all the way towards Cistern Hill. A number of the 4th Battalion were killed or wounded in this engagement; Captain Flatt was one of those wounded.

Both of the battalions were in action again on 15 December 1917; their target was Stone Heap Hill, a rocky feature that overlooked the plain. The 4th Battalion launched their attack at 0800 and they would have to cover 1600 yards. The Turks were routed from the position, as the Norfolks literally charged all the way to the summit. More attacks were planned that day; two companies of the 5th Norfolks were ordered to take a small, round hill about 800 yards to the north of Stone Heap Hill. The target was plastered with artillery fire and consequently just two were killed and seven wounded in exchange for its capture.

The two battalions remained in the main British lines throughout the first five months of 1918. They were, however, involved in two major raids, the first of which took place on the night of 8 to 9 June 1918. Under the command of Captain Jewson, MC, C and D Companies of the 4th were to advance along a ridge and overwhelm any enemy defences. It was a long and dangerous mission, which lasted for three hours, but fortunately there were no losses. A second raid was launched on the night of 18 to 19 June, again by the 4th Battalion, but this time involving A Company, under Captain Steel and Second-Lieutenants Camilleri and Funnell. They were tasked with raiding the enemy positions at Kayak Tepe and Jevis Tepe. They were quickly discovered and came under fire, but they pushed forward and overwhelmed the first set of Turkish positions, bayoneting fifteen of the enemy. Lance-Corporal Duke alone killed five. They now came under machinegun fire from Jevis Tepe. Funnell was the only unwounded officer left and he ordered the men to start moving down the slope. Colour Sergeant-Major Covell led the party to cover the retreat and Sergeant Rickwood, MM, went out three times to pick up the wounded. Steel and another man were killed, Camilleri was wounded, as were fourteen other ranks, and two of the men were missing.

The battalions would be involved in the final advance on 19 September 1918. The 163rd Brigade was now a part of the XXI Corps and the brigade was tasked with capturing the enemy's defences between the foothills and the sea and then to advance eastward into the hills. There were now considerable numbers of reinforcements, including French battalions. The 5th Battalion led the attack at 0200 on 19 September and the 4th Battalion moved up in support. As they advanced, although the artillery fire was heavy, Turkish resistance was light and by 1145 the brigade was ordered to take the high ground. Captain James, along with A Company and two platoons from D Company of the 5th Battalion, attacked around fifty Turks dug in around a hill. Second-Lieutenant Lovell, with a Lewis gun team, was tasked with keeping the Turks' heads down. They managed to take the hill, during which James was wounded. The brigade, supported by French troops, began advancing east and they continued until darkness fell. Many of the Turks melted away rather than face death or capture and for the two battalions combat duties were over.

By the beginning of November they were in Beirut and they stayed there until 28 November 1918, when they headed for Egypt. They reached Kantara on 30 November and then entrained for Cairo.

On 31 December 1918 the 4th Battalion had an effective strength of forty officers and 923 other ranks. The 5th had thirty-three officers and 755 other ranks. Both of these strengths had been considerably increased by nearly 350 for the 4th and nearly 300 for the 5th in the space of a month.

Norfolk Yeomanry

The other Norfolk battalion that was operational in the Middle East during the First World War was the Norfolk Yeomanry Regiment. It sailed out of Liverpool, bound for Gallipoli, on 25 September 1915 and was commanded by Lieutenant-Colonel A F Morse. It would not become the 12th (Yeomanry) Battalion of the Norfolk Regiment until February 1917. Strictly speaking, it did not become part of the Norfolk Regiment until it became the 12th Battalion, but nonetheless its history is inextricably linked to the regiment.

The battalion disembarked from the *Olympic* at Walker's Pier in Anzac Bay on the night of 10 to 11 October 1915. They marched three miles to Dixon's Gully and dug in. The regiment was attached to the 54th East Anglian Division then commanded by Brigadier-General Hodgson. Initially casualties did not come from Turkish gunfire, but from dysentery.

On 21 October 1915 the regiment came into contact with the 4th Norfolk Battalion and for the next two months they would alternate with the 4th Battalion in manning the trenches to the right of Hill 60. This position overlooked the Suvla plain and the salt lake. When the regiment had left Liverpool it had twenty-six officers and 504 other ranks. However by 27 November it had been whittled down to fourteen officers and 301 other ranks. On the night of 6 to 7 December, while repairing trenches, one man was killed but an ex-policeman carried out the body oblivious to the dangers.

While the 4th and 5th Battalions of the Norfolk Regiment left the peninsula relatively early, the 12th would remain for much longer. They were told that their evacuation would not take place until 23 December. Over the course of December troops were evacuated from Anzac and Suvla Bays. This began from 13 December and by this stage the regiment had been divided into three different groups; the smallest group, of twenty-one men, remained in the trenches, laying down fire as if the whole regiment were still in position. The other two parties were embarked, but the twenty-one men remained in the trenches until 0140 on 20 December. They in fact got off three days sooner than they thought, in three groups at five-minute intervals. The evacuation was just in the nick of time, as the Turks were probing and suspicious of the reduced activity on the peninsula.

The regiment embarked for Egypt with just thirteen officers and 221 men fit for duty. In the period 11 October to 20 December 1915 six had been killed and twenty wounded. All of the others had succumbed to disease and exposure. What remained of the regiment arrived in Alexandria at 0800 on Christmas Day.

The regiment spent the whole of January 1916 at Sidibishr, about five miles from Alexandria. They became part of the 1/1st Eastern Mounted Brigade and were desperately in need of equipment and, of course, reinforcement. On 22 February they were transferred to the 3rd Dismounted Brigade, under the command of Brigadier-General H W Hodgson. The total strength of the brigade was 149 officers and 2,398 other ranks. The brigade, of course, was not just Norfolk men, but those from Suffolk, east and west Kent, Sussex and the Welsh Horse. They spent the first part of March 1916 training in their new role as dismounted units. Finally, on 14 March, they were attached to the 42nd Division.

They arrived at El Kubri, near Suez, on 17 March 1916. The Norfolk Yeomanry were detached on 21 March to cover the defences at Crewe's Post, beyond the Suez Canal and in the desert. The defences here needed to be improved but it was a fairly uneventful period.

On 29 July 1916 the regiment was shipped to Sollum to become part of the Western Coastal Force. Their job was to keep an eye on the Senussi. These were a group in Libya, which had been encouraged by the Turks to fight a guerrilla war against the allies. In 1916 the British had sent this expeditionary force against them, led by Major-General William Peyton. The Senussi were based at the Siwa Oasis, 150 miles away, and although there would be difficulties with this tribe, the regiment saw no action.

By October 1916 the regiment had begun training as a mobile force and on 26 December the whole brigade was to be reformed as an infantry brigade. Henceforth the Norfolk Yeomanry was to become one battalion, known as the Yeomanry Battalion of the Norfolk Regiment. Each of the three squadrons became a company and a troop was taken out of each of the squadrons to form D Company. On 14 January 1917 the 3rd Dismounted Brigade became the 230th Infantry Brigade and on 11 February the battalion officially became the 12th (Yeomanry) Battalion, Norfolk Regiment. It was assigned to the 74th Infantry Division. The brigade, of which it was now a part, comprised of the 10th Buffs, the 15th Suffolk and the 16th Royal Sussex Yeomanry Battalion.

By the beginning of March 1917 the 12th was in Alexandria and they received a large draft of reinforcements. Their new brigade commander was Brigadier-General McNeill and the commander of the 74th Division was Major-General E S Girdwood. The 12th, now with thirty-eight officers and 972 other ranks, entrained for El Kantara on 10 April, bound for Palestine. It finally was put into the line east of Wadi Ghuzze, near Gaza, on 15 April.

At 0100 on 17 April 1917 the battalion marched to entrench itself at Wadi Ghuzze, near Raspberry Hill. Initially the battalion was held in reserve; it was a frustrating time as they could see the fighting, but took no part in it. They were held in reserve throughout the rest of the month and into May. So far, the battalion had avoided many casualties although there were some cases of sores, septic throats, scarlet fever and diphtheria. Plans, however, were afoot to be more aggressive in this theatre, with the arrival of General Sir Edmund Allenby as the new commander in Palestine, on 28 June. The 12th had not been idle, however, as by the end of the July they had 177 fully trained Lewis gunners, eighty-eight bombers and forty-three snipers. They had even allowed the band instruments to be brought up, which cheered the men. By the end of July 1917 the strength was thirty officers and 900 other ranks. Colonel Morse was evacuated due to sickness on 1 September and replaced by Major M E Barclay. Morse was only expected to be absent for a short period of time, but he would not rejoin them until 1918, by which time the 12th were in France.

Finally the 12th would get their taste of action in operations against Beersheba and Sheria. On the night of 30 to 31 October 1917 they marched up to their assigned positions near Wadi Saba. The enemy was close and on the following day they would assault the Turkish trenches and redoubts. The bulk of the 12th was sent forward to overwhelm a Turkish position designated as Z5. It was tough going, as the ground was stony and broken. The battalion took the position and a number of prisoners, leaving behind some machine-gunners and snipers to cover the retreat.

On 3 November the 12th were marching north and Major M E Barclay went forward with a handful of men to reconnoitre towards Sheria. This position needed to be captured, as water was at a premium. The attack on Sheria was to be led by the Sussex and Suffolk battalions, with the 12th in support and started at daybreak on 6 November. The outlying Turkish positions were overwhelmed and the final approach to Sheria was made at dawn on 7 November, with Sheria being taken at 0630.

The battalion now was put in reserve, largely due to the lack of transport available, but by 25 November it was to the east of Gaza and marching on the Gaza to Jerusalem road to rejoin the main army. The men kept up their spirits on the long and exhausting march, largely due to the band. The 12th had also acquired a regimental mascot, Abdul, a small donkey that they had found standing forlornly beside its dead mother back in the May. It became the battalion pet and remained with the 12th through their operations in Palestine and in France. In fact when it got to France it was presented with a collar of bells and a saddle cloth bearing the regimental colours and badge. Abdul survived the war and was brought back to England, along with Major M E Barclay and paraded in Norwich.

By 30 November 1917 the 12th was in the second line around nine miles to the west of Jerusalem. It spent the following week building roads. It was planned that Jerusalem would be attacked on 8 December. The 230th Brigade moved up into the front line and the 12th was on the left, the 10th Buffs on the right and the 15th Suffolk in support. The Norfolks advanced up a stony slope; the enemy fell back and the 12th took its first objective, a line of trenches, at 0500. As the 12th advanced over the crest of the hill they could see the Turks lining up behind rocks and walls. Nonetheless the 12th continued its advance, fighting through the gardens and through a village for one and a quarter miles to reach their second objective, Khirbet El Burj. It was decided that they would hold, as not only was there a deep gulley ahead of them, but also the Turkish machinegun and artillery fire had stiffened. The next target would have to wait until the following morning.

When the 12th got under way at first light they discovered that the Turks had abandoned the positions. They would now play a supporting role in the continued advance and from time to time they would also have to repair roads. The weather conditions were appalling and often the men's overcoats and blankets had to be left far behind in the rear, making the nights uncomfortably cold.

The 12th were brought up for a fresh attack to be carried out between 9 and 12 March 1918. The objective was Abu-el-Auf. The 12th would follow up behind the 15th Suffolk and the 16th Sussex. By 1400 A and B Companies were now leading and they reached the top of Burj Bardawille, where they encountered heavy machinegun fire. At dusk they were withdrawn, but at 0230 the following day the advance continued. In the darkness at around 0300 they thought they were close to the Turkish positions and charged, only to find the area largely empty. But Captain J Harbord, ahead of most of the men, ran into seven Turks. He promptly shot four of them and captured one officer and two other men. For his gallantry he was awarded the Military Cross. Eventually the 12th reached the top of the hill, under the cover of Lewis gun fire. They charged, but the Turks fled. The 12th continued their advance. Captain Fenwick Owen was now in command of the battalion and he was wounded, forcing Harbord to take over. Turkish machine-gunners and snipers contested every inch of the advance. By that night Lieutenant-Colonel J F Barclay took over command of the battalion. On 11 March the 12th began to advance once again, at around noon and they came under artillery fire near the high ground close to Khirbet Sahlat. Here they paused and built roads.

Lieutenant-Colonel J F Barclay led a raid against the Turkish trenches at 1930 on 22 March. He chose a squad of rifle bombers and at 2100 A Company and the rifle bombers advanced under the command of Harbord. B Company, along with a Lewis gun section, guarded the right. A second platoon guarded the left and the two remaining platoons of B Company followed up. At a range of around 200 yards the rifle grenades were fired off. The Turks replied by throwing hand grenades, believing the British to be closer than they were. This betrayed their positions and at 2130 the Turkish positions were stormed. Eight Turks were bayoneted and one was taken prisoner.

If the 12th thought for one moment that their war was coming to an end they were sadly mistaken. By 29 April 1918 they were near the Suez Canal; they then headed for Alexandria and sailed for France on 1 May 1918, onboard the SS *Caledonia*. They were reunited with Colonel Morse on 9 May, having arrived in Marseilles two days before. Major-General Girdwood, the commander of the 74th Division, was extremely disappointed to have lost the 12th. In a letter to Morse, dated 21 June 1918, he had said:

> The whole Yeomanry Division, and in particular myself, suffer an irreparable loss by the transfer of your gallant battalion to another division. No man has ever been better served than I have by the Norfolk Yeomanry, or could wish to have under his command a finer battalion.

The 12th had now become part of the 31st Division. They were moved up into the line on the Nieppe Forest front on 25 June 1918. The 12th was not deployed in the attack by the 31st Division on 28 June but remained in reserve. This did not mean that they did not suffer casualties and in fact on 5 July Colonel Morse was wounded and did not return to the battalion until after the war. Captain J Harbord died of wounds that were received at the same time.

On the night of 8 July a platoon from each of A and D Companies was sent out to try to blow up a pair of bridges over the River Becque. Second-Lieutenant Wagner's platoon from D Company managed to blow up his target, but Second-Lieutenant Knox, with the platoon of A Company ran into stiff opposition and was unable to carry out his mission. He had come up against a strongly held farm and on the night of 9 July he went out again to take the farm and blow up the bridge. He stormed the farm and set up a post, leaving an NCO and six other ranks. He then tried to deal with the bridge but once again ran into heavy opposition.

On the night of 10 July the 12th went into divisional reserve for the next six days and returned to the front on 16 July. Ten days later Major Birkbeck led a raid with two platoons of A Company against German positions to the east of the River Becque. The men advanced behind a barrage at 2330 and they managed to force the Germans to abandon their positions, but five of the Norfolks had been wounded and two were missing.

A patrol led by Second-Lieutenant W Stone had managed to get behind the German frontline on 15 August 1918, but unfortunately the following day he was killed. Also on 15 August, at around 1430, Second-Lieutenant E P Smith took a platoon of D Company to attack German strongpoints. Smith found a trench held by up to sixty Germans. His section charged and only Smith and Corporal Neve managed to reach the trench and they were forced to retreat. Elsewhere, another raiding platoon, under Sergeant Walker, had been forced to retire under heavy fire and Second-Lieutenant Heading, commanding a support platoon, had managed to give covering fire. A Lewis gun section had also crawled up to deal with a German

Officers and men of the 1st Battalion in France in 1918

listening post in a ditch. They saw eight Germans running, but twelve were heading towards them. All twelve of the Germans were hit and Sergeant Tannard picked off Germans as they stood up to throw hand grenades at them.

On 19 August the 12th was detailed to move forward to assist in the capture of the road running between Outtersteen and Vieux Berquin. There were two farms on this road and the 12th was only to advance once one of the farms had been taken. Confusingly, Major J F Barclay had gone on leave and command of the 12th was now with Major M E Barclay. The 12th got under way at 1700 on 19 August 1918 and they came under heavy fire, but managed to overrun a number of German strongpoints. Part of B Company had reached the final objective, Labis Farm, but was coming under stiff opposition. The company was commanded by Lieutenant Richards, who was to win the Military Cross for his actions during the day. The company took the farm at 1923, having inflicted enormous casualties on the enemy. A large number of prisoners had also been taken: sixty, along with twelve machineguns. But the cost over the last few days had been heavy; eight officers and thirty-eight other ranks killed and one officer and 100 other ranks wounded.

Although they were still under heavy German artillery fire they began to consolidate the new frontline. Patrols continued to operate, running into German opposition. By 30 August the Germans had evacuated the town of Bailleul, but had taken up positions 1,000 yards further on. The 12th was praised for their fighting spirit and skill over the past few days in a letter received from Divisional Headquarters.

The 12th would go back into action on 29 September 1918. The British had crossed the Messines Ridge and were advancing on the railway between Comines and Warneton. By dawn the battalion had reached all of its objectives, the Germans had evacuated their trenches and at 0950 the battalion was about to advance once again when they were ordered to move to the rear.

There had been some changes in command and by 11 October 1918 the battalion was now commanded by Major Birkbeck. But Lieutenant-Colonel J Sherwood Kelly, VC, returned to command the battalion on 19 October. The 12th was in the frontlines, launching patrols and raids throughout the rest of October. There was interesting news of part of C Company, which had launched a patrol around Ploegsteert that month, but from captured German regimental orders:

> The prisoners belong to a big patrol ordered to make good the occupation of a farm [Hof Osternelle, near Ploegsteert] to put out of action the machineguns conjectured to be there. The twenty one prisoners, among whom were four NCOs, had all taken off their badges and could not, or would not, give a satisfactory reason for having done so. The great majority of the prisoners belonged to the workman class. They make a good military impression, but in their statements are so extraordinarily reticent that one

must assume that their superior officers have instructed them clearly, and warned them how to behave when taken prisoners.

The 12th would see no combat after the end of October. They were moved back into reserve for rest and recuperation. On 22 November 1918 a number of medals were awarded to the battalion and in the December Colonel Morse sent them a personal message:

> I shall be very grateful if you will convey to all ranks of the battalion, at any rate those with whom I served, how sorry I was to leave them in July and to have to say goodbye now. Also how much I appreciate their good work all through the war, and their invariable loyalty and good fellowship. I look upon them all as personal friends; no man ever had better; and I shall always be delighted to hear from any and to see any of them who come back to Norwich or anywhere near to have a chat about old times.

Here we must leave the four battalions that served against the Turks and return to the four battalions that served on the western front.

5

France 1914 to 1918

The 1st Battalion was given orders to mobilize on 4 August 1914. Six days later it was ready and on 14 August the battalion had left Belfast and had embarked on two transports bound for France. They were to become part of the 15th Infantry Brigade, commanded by Brigadier-General Count Gleichen. They would have a long association with some of the other battalions in the same brigade. The 1st Battalions of the Bedfords and the Cheshires would remain with them until the end of the war. Initially the other battalion was the 1st Dorsets, which was later replaced by the 6th Cheshires and the 6th Liverpool and ultimately the Royal Warwick Regiment. Together with the 13th and 14th Brigades, the 1st Battalion of the Norfolk Regiment made up the 5th Infantry Division, under Major-General Sir Charles Fergusson.

The battalion arrived in Le Havre and made for rest camp number 8, some six miles away. It was to be a short visit, as on 17 August the brigade clambered aboard trains and headed for the front. They arrived at Le Câteau-Cambrésis on 18 August. By 22 August they had marched to Dour and then on to Bois de Bossu.

The 5th Division represented the left of the British army and the Norfolks brigade would support the other two brigades in the division. The brigade first came under fire on 23 August 1914, while they were digging trenches, but they suffered no casualties.

The Battle of Mons

The Battle of Mons was the first major action of the British Expeditionary Force in the war. The British were attempting to hold the line of the Mons–Condé Canal. The German 1st Army was advancing. Although the 1st Norfolks were not engaged during the first day of the battle, which opened at dawn, they would be involved on the following day, 24 August 1914. They had been relieved by the 1st Suffolks at 0430 and they had marched to Dour as the divisional reserve. However by around 1100 both the 13th and the 14th Brigade had begun to retreat. This had been forced by the sudden withdrawal of the French 5th Army. The 15th Brigade was on the left of the other two brigades and by 1145 it had become apparent that the retreat was in serious threat, as a large German force was approaching. The British 19th Infantry Brigade and some cavalry had fallen back. The 1st Norfolks and the 1st Cheshire battalions, together with a squadron of the 19th Hussars and the 119th Artillery Battery, were placed on the left and began counterattacking to hold the Germans back. They were around 1,000 metres to the west of Elouges, close to the railway that ran from there to Quiévrain. The position appeared to be good, but the situation began to deteriorate just three-quarters of an hour later.

German artillery forced the 9th Lancers and some of the 4th Dragoon Guards to fall back. They began reforming in the sunken road that was being held by the reserve Norfolk company. As the Germans closed the 119th battery came into action. The German batteries retaliated and many of the shells fell amongst the Norfolks. The whole force, under Colonel Ballard, seemed still to be in a good position and Ballard was sure that the Germans would not risk a frontal attack. However the northern flank of the force was now threatened and he had to order a retreat.

The Norfolks had already suffered quite high casualties; one platoon, in an advanced position, never received the orders to retire and neither did the Cheshire battalion. As a consequence, they were cut off and fought bravely until their ammunition ran out. By this time they were completely surrounded and were forced to surrender. The Cheshires had been hit the worst and by the following day just two officers and 200 men remained. As for the Norfolks, four officers had been killed and 250 ranks killed, wounded or missing. About 100 wounded men had had to be left in Elouges.

The following morning they continued their retreat toward Troisvilles, some three miles to the west of Le Câteau-Cambrésis. Initial orders had been to continue the retreat on 26 August, but it was now obvious that the entire British II Corps would now have to stand and fight. The 1st Battalion was allotted a position in the second line along a sunken road running east from Troisvilles. Standing the ground with them was the 1st Bedfordshires, about 1,000 metres to the north. The 1st Dorsets covered Troisvilles itself and to the right of the Bedfords were the 2nd King's Own Scottish Borderers. By 1315, with both flanks of the force under threat, the Norfolks fell back toward Reumont, about 2,000 metres to the south. They received orders at 1530 to continue to retreat.

The bulk of the battalion occupied a spur that ran southeast from Reumont. However, one and a half companies of the battalion were in a quarry to the southwest of the village. It was these men who first encountered the advancing Germans. In conjunction with the Royal Welsh Fusiliers they operated as the rearguard. The rest of the battalion continued to retreat until they reached Honnechy. The Germans were advancing towards them and the Norfolks' fire stopped the German advance dead about 1500 metres from their positions.

The battalion was still operating essentially as a rearguard for the rest of the division. That night the retreat was continued. By 27 August they had reached

St Quentin. The brigade was praised for their actions over recent days. In fact their brave stand had saved the French army from disaster.

The Norfolks, still operating as a rearguard, began to retreat towards the Somme Canal. They marched through Noyon, Pontoise and on 29 August were at Carlepont. By 2 September 1914 the battalion was almost in sight of Paris, but they were still retreating. By the time that they reached Tournans on 5 September they were just 20 miles to the southeast of the French capital and here the retreat ended. The battalion began to advance.

By 9 September they had reached the River Marne. Once over this obstacle they began to run into heavy German opposition. At Hill 189, to the southeast of Montreuil Aux Lions the Germans opened fire on them with artillery, killing one and wounding thirteen. Supported by the 1st Dorsets and the 1st Bedfords, the Norfolks attacked the hill under heavy artillery fire. They got to a point to within 120m of the German entrenched positions and dug in. By the following morning the Germans had retreated; their field battery had been abandoned and there were dead German artillerymen everywhere.

By 13 September 1914 the Norfolks were close to the River Aisne. They had been given orders to cross it by rafts at night and this they achieved before marching into the village of Ste Marguerite. They were under heavy fire and three companies of the battalion, along with four from the Bedfords, three from the East Surreys, two from the Cheshires and elements of the Duke of Cornwall's Light Infantry, were ordered to assault the German positions on a spur above Condé. The attack was an unmitigated disaster; it had quickly fallen into confusion and chaos, added to which British artillery shells were falling amongst their own troops. Captains C E Luard and T R Bowlby, along with twenty-five other men from the battalion who were operating too far in advance, got into grave difficulty. Both of the officers were killed and the rest of the men were either killed or taken prisoner. These were men of C Company.

On 15 September another attack was ordered; this time the Norfolks would lead at 0800, with the Bedfords and Cheshires in support. The Norfolks penetrated the woodland and then ran into a belt of barbed wire. Unable to penetrate it they fell back.

La Bassée Front

After having been withdrawn from the front the brigade made its way north by train on 7 October 1914. They reached the La Bassée front on 11 October. They were kept in divisional reserve until 19 October and then given responsibility for holding the front between Festubert and Givenchy. After digging in they beat off a major German attack on 25 October, losing one officer and twenty men killed and a further thirty wounded.

For a time the battalion shared their trenches with men from the Indian

Lahore Division, as well as some French troops. A heavy German attack was launched against the Devonshires on 29 October and a company of the Norfolks was sent to help them. Ultimately the fighting became so intense that three more companies of the battalion, along with some French infantry, were sent to help. The Lahore Division replaced the brigade on 30 October, but the Norfolks stayed behind to help teach the Indian troops how to handle trench warfare.

Ypres

By 13 November the battalion was heading north towards the Ypres front. They were temporarily attached to the 14th Brigade. On 18 November 1914 they took over the French trenches at Kemmel, just to the east of Kemmel Hill. They remained there for ten days and then rejoined the 15th Brigade on 29 November.

The battalion occupied trenches around Messines and Ploegsteert during the winter of 1914 to 1915. They supplied working parties, carried out training and learned how to make best use of Lewis guns. It was a freezing cold winter and some days they would suffer no casualties despite the constant German shelling, but on others as many as fourteen or fifteen would be lost.

By the end of February 1915 the brigade had been sent up to the southern face of the Ypres salient. They took over from a position held by the 84th Brigade, around St Eloi. If anything the trenches were even worse here. Since November the battalion had lost four officers killed and another four wounded, nineteen other ranks had been killed and forty-seven wounded.

The new trenches were occupied from 3 March 1915 and at first the area was relatively quiet. On 14 March the Germans opened up a huge artillery bombardment and the enemy stormed St Eloi, exposing the right flank of the 15th Brigade. The Norfolks had been incredibly lucky; they were moving back up to the front on that very day and missed the worst of the enemy shelling, although Lieutenant McUrdy and six other men were killed, with nineteen being wounded.

The Germans had blown up a position known as The Mound. This had been recaptured by the 27th Division and by the beginning of April 1915 the Norfolks were holding part of the line from The Mound, running northeast and then southwest. One of the key positions in the area was Hill 60 (really only a pile of earth that had been excavated by the French when they built the Ypres to Comines railway). To the south of Hill 60 was another mound and because of its shape it was called Caterpillar. Close to that was a smaller one, known as The Dump.

The 1st Norfolks were involved in supporting a successful attack on Hill 60 on 17 April. The Germans responded with their usual vigour and their artillery for the first time used gas. The Norfolks had no masks and there were a number of casualties. Despite this, at 0300 on 18 April, they held off a major German counterattack. In the two days one officer was killed and another wounded, eleven other ranks killed and forty-six wounded. The battalion was engaged once again on 20 April; this time two officers were wounded, seven other ranks killed and thirty-one wounded. Grimly, the Norfolks held their positions. There was a major gas attack on 5 May, causing seventy-five casualties. They were finally relieved on 6 May.

Throughout June 1915 they were in trenches at Verbrande Molen, suffering twenty-two deaths and 123 wounded. In the first thirteen days of June an officer was killed, along with seven other ranks and thirty-nine men were wounded. They were taken out of the line for a much-needed rest until 29 July.

The 15th Brigade also received a new commander, Brigadier-General M N Turner and similarly the divisional commander was replaced by Major-General C T Kavanagh. The 5th Division would now head towards the Somme front.

Fricourt

After travelling overnight they relieved the French 119th Regiment in their trenches at Fricourt, to the east of Albert, on 2 August 1915. Although the period until 22 August was relatively quiet, the Norfolks still lost six killed and eleven wounded.

Throughout September 1915 the Norfolks held a number of trench sections in the same area and in fact by the standards that they had become used to, apart from the bombardments, it was a relatively quiet period of time. There were of course notable exceptions. On 1 December the battalion had just got into its trenches when the Germans exploded a mine. Several of the men were buried. Lieutenant Burlton was awarded the Military Cross and Sergeant Dunbabin and Private Doughty received the Distinguished Conduct Medal.

Arras

By the beginning of February 1916 the division was on the move once again. They had been shifted to the north of Amiens and into the Cavillon area. They had hoped to have a rest here, but they were to be sadly mistaken. The German launched a major operation against Verdun on 21 February and the 5th Division was moved up so that French troops could be shifted from the Arras region to be sent as reinforcements. In appalling weather, with heavy snow and impassable roads, the battalion tried to move up towards Verdun; all the way it was blocked by French troops moving in the opposite direction. The 1st Battalion clambered into trenches to the west of Arras and then, on 9 March, frontline trenches to the northeast of the city. The weather did not improve until mid-March.

April 1916 dawned and proved to be comparatively quiet, but not so the following month. On 7 May the Germans started destroying the barbed wire in front of the battalion's positions, with artillery fire. It was necessary for the battalion to send out night patrols to mend the wire and check for the buildup of German troops in case of an attack. On 20 May Lieutenant Hoare and stretcher bearers from the battalion managed to save an officer and an NCO from the 15th Warwickshires, who had been buried in a crater in no-man's land. The following night Hoare, along with Lieutenant Hall and a handful of men, covered a trench raid and were attacked by a German patrol.

German shelling destroyed the left trench being held by the Norfolks on 1 June 1916. The Germans turned their attention to the trenches on the right on 2 and 3 June, killing four and wounding eight. At 2117 on 4 June three large mines were set off by the Germans. Two of the mines were right under the Norfolks' front. The Germans followed it up with a large-scale infantry attack along the road from Bailleul to Arras. The Norfolks opened up and held off the Germans, at a cost of twenty-one killed, twenty-five wounded and nineteen missing. After this encounter the battalion was retired.

General Stephens, now commanding the 5th Division, presented a number of military medals and Distinguished Conduct Medals on 12 June. On 25 June the VI Corps commander, General Keir, awarded four military medals to two NCOs and two privates of the battalion. All of these awards related to events that had taken place on 4 June 1916.

The Somme

The 5th Division was earmarked to take part in the offensive on the Somme, which was to begin on 1 July 1916. The battalion was moved up on 16 July and by the 19th it was holding the line around Longueval. One of the key positions in the area was known as High Wood and on 21 July they were brought up to reinforce the 13th Brigade for its attack. The assault, as far as the Norfolks were concerned, got under way at 0600 on 23 July 1916. D Company advanced in four waves and occupied the frontline on the southwest corner of High Wood. C Company took a trench to the north of Bazentin Le Grand. A and B Company occupied the old German frontline trench. The 1st West Kents relieved the battalion at 0845, under heavy fire. Originally the battalion was to fully be relieved on 24 July, but due to the heavy German shelling this was postponed until the early hours of 25 July. By this time they had come under heavy fire from the Germans, including gas shells.

The battalion was in position at the Pommiers redoubt until 2245 on 26 July 1916 when they moved forward to launch an attack the following morning. For five hours, with their gas masks on, they endured heavy German shelling. Incredibly, they were still able to take part in the assault on Longueval just a few hours later.

Longueval was barely visible under a dense cloud of debris, smoke and dust. There was heavy fighting and the battalion reached Longueval at 0230 on 27

July 1916, occupying trenches around the village. Throughout they were under heavy artillery fire. The British responded at 0510 on 27 July and the Germans replied once again at 0650. For the Norfolks it had been much more than a simple test of endurance; A Company was down to one platoon, B Company had barely any cover left. Many of the men from A Company had been buried.

Still the battalion was urged to push forward, storming shallow trenches and German strongpoints. German reinforcements were moving up and in the thick of the fighting A Company could not muster a single officer. C Company was down to one officer, Second-Lieutenant Windham, who found himself in command of all of the Norfolks to the west of North Street in the village. B Company made their assault at 0720 and passed the church, advancing another 75 metres before running into a German strongpoint. Men from B and D Company managed to work around its flanks and they took around 100 German prisoners, bringing their total so far to 150.

Again the battalion pressed on, capturing more German prisoners, and taking more redoubts. The final objective was supposed to have been 300m to the north of the village, but in the event it was impossible to advance beyond the village itself. There were still pockets of Germans holding up in the cellars and the Norfolks knew that any further advance would be suicidal, as the British barrage had passed. On this day alone two officers had been killed, nine wounded or gassed, fifty other ranks killed, 157 wounded or gassed and fifty were missing, believed dead. In one week of fighting 429 members of the battalion had been killed, wounded, gassed or were missing. At times the battalion had had to clear German positions with the bayonet, harking back to earlier conflicts where cold steel had settled the day.

The battalion was temporarily withdrawn, but by 31 July 1916, until 1 August, they were again in Longueval, enduring a heavy bombardment. The 5th Division was withdrawn to the southeast of Abbeville by 3 August and they received a large draft of men from the 2/6th Battalion. The vast majority of the men had never seen combat before and required intensive training.

The whole division was sent back to the Somme front on 24 August. In the meantime the front line had shifted forward and the Norfolk Regiment was allotted a position around Falfemont Farm. The capture of this farm was vital in order to allow the French to advance along the valley and take Combles. An initial attack by other British troops had failed on 3 to 4 September, but at 0800 on 4 September the Norfolks were moved up to launch an attack on the farm themselves.

A and B Company got the assault under way at 1510. A handful of A Company broke into the southwest corner of the farm, under Captain Francis, but they were dislodged by the German defenders. The rest of the force was pinned down by German machinegun fire. While the Germans concentrated on the Norfolks, the Bedfords and Cheshires managed to storm a trench line to the north of the farm. This now allowed A and B Company of the Norfolks to surge forward. By 1600 the Norfolks were within 50 metres of the farm on the left, but their right-hand side was pinned down by the machineguns. The British were determined to take the farm and at 1840 the Norfolks were urged to launch another assault, this time with assistance from the 16th Warwickshires and the 1st Bedfords. The attack went in five minutes later and again it fell short and the Norfolks dug in, waiting for darkness to fall. At 2030 elements of A Company tried to rush the southwest edge of the farm. By 0300 A and C Companies had succeeded in pushing the Germans out of the farm and they were pushing patrols forward to overwhelm the German trenches and link up with the French. By 0730 the link up had been established, but they now came under artillery fire, which did not cease until 1030. The Norfolks and the French had come under fire from their own artillery.

By 1515 on 15 September 1916 the Norfolk battalion was down to two officers and 100 men. Six officers had been killed, seven had been wounded, fifty other ranks had been killed, 212 wounded, ninety-four were missing believed dead. This was a staggering total of 369.

Although seriously depleted in numbers, the action was not over for the Norfolks. On the night of 24 September they moved up into the trench works, preparing to attack German positions to the west of Morval. This was a village some 2,000 metres to the northeast of Combles. The assault got under way at 1235 on 25 September, with the Norfolk battalion leading. So reduced were the numbers that Colonel Stone, the battalion commander, led the attack himself. He went over the top ahead of the centre company.

The German trenches were plastered with artillery fire and by the time the barrage lifted the Norfolks were already in the German positions. The Germans had fled, trying to get into shell holes, but most of them had been so traumatized by the bombardment that they were happy to surrender to the Norfolks; 150 were taken prisoner. The Norfolks' part of the attack was now over; other units would press on to their left and right, but the action had cost them six officers wounded, seven other ranks killed and seventy wounded. Despite the casualties Colonel Stone was overwhelmed by the gallantry of the battalion:

> I cannot sufficiently express my admiration of your gallantry and splendid conduct throughout. You came to the Somme battlefield with a very high reputation, which you had rightly earned during twenty three months of strenuous warfare – you leave the Somme with the highest reputation in the British Army.

On 29 September 1916 Colour Sergeant-Major Pryer was awarded the Military Cross, Lieutenant Ambrose and Corporal Cook the Distinguished Conduct Medal and Privates Leggatt and Lark the Military Medal, all for their gallantry at Falfemont and Morval.

Béthune Front

By 1 October 1916 the battalion was heading back to the Béthune front, where it had last been in action in October 1914. They were in the frontline by 4 October, near Quinque Rue, between the Bois du Biez and the Givenchy Ridge.

At 1800 on 14 October Second-Lieutenant C F Harrison led a raid against a farm called Cour d'Avoué. The assault party consisted of twenty men with a pair of Lewis gun detachments. They crawled forward for 150m and then headed left towards the moat around the farm. Harrison left the bulk of the men to complete the wire cutting and leading just three men he rushed the German position at bayonet point. They captured two Germans from the 6th Bavarian Regiment.

The battalion had a period of training between 3 and 20 December 1916 and as the snow began to fall once again they were heading back towards the trenches, returning on 24 December. The battalion held a position either side of the La Bassée Canal. Although they came under trench mortar fire from time to time, it was a relatively calm period. They had nine days rest towards the end of January 1917. On 12 January Stone, having been promoted to command the 17th Brigade, was replaced by Major R W Patteson.

The battalion launched three raiding parties under the command of Captain Kelly on the night of 26 to 27 February 1917. The raiders were quickly spotted but under the cover of the barrage Kelly's men managed to kill two of the enemy. The battalion was also involved in fighting off a German raid on 10 March at Cambrin. Just under a month later, on 7 April, they began moving towards the infamous Vimy Ridge.

The ridge ran southeast from the River Souchez to Givenchy en Gohell. The ridge itself was stormed by Canadian troops on 9 April 1917 and the Norfolks were sent up along with the 15th Brigade to relieve the Canadians on 14 April.

On 23 April, under the command of Lieutenant-Colonel Carroll, the battalion began advancing towards La Coulotte: the German frontline. The attack went in at dawn. The British artillery barrage opened up at 0445 and the 1st Norfolks were in the frontline of the attack, with a total strength of twenty-four officers and 745 men. It had been reported that the German barbed wire had been destroyed, but they soon found this to be incorrect. Nonetheless, the four companies of the battalion pressed on, coming under heavy machinegun fire from a railway cutting. Men from A and D Companies worked their way into the German trenches and wiped out four machinegun positions. The battalion pushed on, but still came under fire from machineguns near the railway and in neighbouring houses. For nine dreadful hours, from 1000, the battalion was plastered with artillery fire. Total casualties were fifteen officers and 178 other ranks.

From 24 April 1917 through to 7 May they were withdrawn to the corps reserve area. The 5th Division was attached to XIII Corps and, as a consequence, the Norfolks were to counterattack in support of the 95th Brigade against Fresnoy, which had just been lost to the Germans. The attack was due to get under way at 1900 on 8 May, but it was postponed until shortly before 0200 on 9 May. The British artillery opened fire and the Norfolks surged forward, led by C and D Companies. They came under tremendous machinegun fire and although some parts of the battalion managed to get into woods near the village, the attack had failed. By the time the battalion reached safety just thirty-six men and five Lewis guns remained. Six officers had been wounded, six other ranks killed, 103 wounded and eleven more were missing.

Captain Kelly, along with Lieutenant Chapman, was instrumental in a vicious fight on the night of 24 May 1917. The battalion was occupying the frontline trenches at Willerval and was in the process of being relieved by the Highland Light Infantry. Suddenly, at 2300 the German artillery opened up, hitting the trench line. Eighty-five men of the 13th Bavarian Regiment stormed part of the trench works held by three officers and fifty men of the 1st Battalion's B Company. Kelly rallied his men and counterattacked with bombs and bayonets. The Bavarians were forced to retreat. Kelly, along with Chapman, now brought down fire on more German units moving up. In the confused melee the 1st Battalion lost twenty killed, twenty wounded and two men were taken prisoner.

By the end of June 1917 the British were ready to launch their own attack on the German positions. The 15th Brigade would be led by the 1st Norfolk Battalion, supported by the 1st Cheshires and the 1st Bedfords. The attack got under way at 1910 on 28 June under a creeping barrage. The German frontline trench was taken despite some stubborn opposition from thirty or more Germans in a concrete bunker. The major target was Oppy Wood and by 2100 the 1st Battalion had managed to establish a line some 80m into the woods and in some places had pushed forward another 75m. Over seventy Germans had been captured. Lieutenant Chapman had been seriously wounded and another officer less seriously. Fifteen other ranks had been killed and a further forty-six had been wounded.

July saw the 1st Battalion back in reserve and there was very little of note during the August. There had been a few attempts by the Germans to penetrate the trench line with patrols, but in each case the 1st Battalion had driven them off.

Ypres

By 25 September the 1st Battalion was sent to the Ypres area. The third battle for Ypres had been under way since the end of July 1917. The 1st Battalion was bussed up to the frontline on 1 October. The conditions were appalling, with heavy rain that flooded the trenches, shell holes and craters. The 5th Division was now attached to X Corps and earmarked for an attack close to the Menin Road. The 1st Battalion took up positions facing the German-held Polderhoek Château. This was a strongly held German position, with machinegun nests and concrete bunkers. Every time the British attempted to close in on the German position they faced counterattacks and lost the ground.

On the evening of 8 October the 1st Battalion was given orders to prepare for an attack the following morning. The battalion started assembling, under the command of Major Lambton, at 0400 on 9 October. A and C Companies were to lead the attack. B Company would back them up and D Company would be held in reserve. In torrential rain the men assembled and watched the barrage lift at 0520. Supported by the 16th Warwickshires the 1st Battalion began to advance. The rain and darkness caused A and C Companies to move too far to the right and they found themselves right in front of the château, instead of to the left of it. By the time the mistake had been realized the Germans had opened up with their machineguns and the British barrage had moved beyond the German frontline positions. The casualties were enormous and by the time the battalion had returned to its start positions at 2100 three officers had been killed, four wounded, thirty-eight other ranks killed, 144 wounded and 112 were missing. Some of the stragglers would continue to make their way back throughout 10 and 11 October.

The battalion received a new draft of close to 150 men on 17 October and a second one of 144 on 18 October. By now the battalion was out of the line, reorganizing and retraining. On 1 November the battalion was back facing the château. Conditions had not improved and the trenches were waterlogged, with the men under continual fire. Eventually the battalion was taken out of the line again, on 11 November, and there was a period of rest, refitting and training until 26 November.

Italy

The 5th Division was about to be redeployed to the Italian front. The Austrians and their German allies had launched a major offensive against the Italians. To bolster their ally the French and the British snatched divisions from the western front to reinforce them. Some seven French and five British divisions, including the 5th Division, were to be redeployed in the Piave sector of the Italian front. The 1st Battalion set off by train on 1 December 1917, arriving at Montagnana, near Padua, on 6 December. They were not immediately thrown in and in fact only began moving up towards the front on 23 January 1918.

The whole of the 5th Division was allocated the right bank of the River Piave. The 1st Battalion was responsible for a front around 800m long and they were flanked by the 16th Warwickshires and the 12th Gloucesters. February was comparatively quiet. In the March a number of raids and attacks were planned, but all of these were cancelled. On 17 March the 1st Battalion was put into reserve and settled down around Padua, grateful for the rest and chance to enjoy conditions that were not dominated by mud and blood.

Neuve Chapelle

The respite, however, was brief. The Germans had launched a massive offensive on the western front in March 1918. The 1st Battalion was heading back to France. They left Vicenza at 0230 on 5 April. The battalion's trains could not pass through Amiens as the Germans were now within ten miles. The 1st Battalion was supposed to relieve Canadian troops to the south of Arras, but these orders were cancelled and consequently they were instead diverted to Neuve Chapelle on 11 April.

The Germans were very active in this area and as the battalion moved into position on the afternoon of 12 April they had no real idea where the Germans were. In fact, as the battalion moved into St Venant, to the south of Nieppe Forest, they got there just in time to prevent the Germans from taking the village. The Germans were close, at Merville, and it seemed that it would only be a short time before they would collide with the German troops once again. But, in the event, the front in this sector would remain relatively stable for some time.

By this stage the commander of the regiment was Lieutenant-Colonel E W Montgomerie and the 15th Brigade itself was commanded by Brigadier-General Oldman, also of the Norfolk Regiment. Although the frontlines were fairly static until the August this period was not without incident for the 1st Battalion. At 0200 on 11 May 1918 B Company's No. 6 Platoon, under Captain Taylor and Second-Lieutenants West and Howe, seized the opportunity of a barrage to raid a pair of houses concealing German machineguns. West, with a Lewis gun, was on the left and Howe on the right. Howe moved along the canal bank towards Merville, dealing with Germans hiding behind a hedge with grenades. He then sent Corporal Burton, with a Lewis gun, to rake a German trench that they had found. By the time Howe reached his objective only three men were with him; then Burton and another man arrived and they began to search the houses, but were unable to find the machineguns. In the attack they had killed six Germans, taken six prisoners and seized one machinegun from the trench.

There were other successful trench raids during this time. On 16 June 1918 Lieutenant Bowstead and men from D Company crawled forward to deal with a German forward position. They found it to be empty and continued forward another 50m. They still found nothing, but as they returned they encountered a short trench occupied by three or four Germans. In the encounter a German officer was wounded and Bowstead shot another. Bowstead was later to be awarded the Military Cross for his gallantry that day.

By July 1918 the 15th Brigade and indeed the whole of the 5th Division was attached to IV Corps. Rumours and speculation were rife about the demoralization of the Germans and the prospect of one more major push that would end the war. After a period of rest in August orders came through for an advance on 21 August 1918.

The 5th Division set off at 0455 and the men of the 1st Battalion advanced through dense mist, passing the first objective of the corps, the heights to the east of Beugny, which had been taken by the 37th Division. Shortly afterwards the second objective was taken and that night and the following day were taken up with consolidating the newly won ground. Casualties had been relatively light, but by the time the battalion began digging in the casualties mounted from German artillery fire. Lieutenant-Colonel Humphries, who was by now commander of the battalion, died from his wounds and Major G de Grey, DSO, became the new commander.

The 1st Battalion would now take part in the general advance towards the Arras to Albert railway, on 23 August 1918. Two companies of the battalion cooperated with the 1st Bedfords, breaking through German barbed wire and overrunning machinegun posts. By 25 August the battalion was in trenches near Achiet le Grand and here they came under heavy artillery fire, wounding Major de Grey, who was succeeded by Major H S Walker of the 1st Cheshires. On the same day two of the battalion were killed and fifteen more wounded.

The 15th Brigade pushed forward again at 0445 on 30 August and this time they were heading for the road connecting Sapignies and Bapaume. By 1430 most of their objectives had been taken, but on the following day they came under heavy gas and high-explosive attack from German artillery. There were a number of casualties.

Hopes that the German resolve had been broken seemed so far to be premature and more attacks were inevitable. On the night of 1 to 2 September the battalion moved up to launch an assault at 0515. They were to attack Beugny and take the ground to the south of it. In the attack twenty-one were killed and eighty-five wounded, but the objectives were taken, along with 250 German prisoners.

Battalion orders summarized the situation for the 1st Battalion during this time:

> The divisional commander has asked the commanding officer to inform all ranks of the 1st Battalion of the Norfolk Regiment how much he appreciated the extraordinary good work carried out by the battalion during the operations from August 21 to September 2. During this time the division has recaptured a depth of over 15 miles of enemy territory, which is more than any other division in the whole army has been able to accomplish in the same time, and has captured an enormous amount of

booty and prisoners. During the operations near Beugny village on September 2 the 1st Battalion of the Norfolk Regiment was the only battalion, out of three divisions, that reached the final objective in its entirety, and it was only due to the fact that the battalion held on throughout the night to the high ground south of the village that the village became untenable to the enemy, and he was forced to retire.

The 15th Brigade pushed on, on the morning of 3 September, overrunning more German positions. They were rejoined by Major de Grey but the division had taken 4,300 casualties and was due for relief from the 37th Division. The 1st Battalion found themselves back for rest and recuperation, but once again it was short-lived and they were in assembly positions for another advance to be launched at 1000 hours on 28 September 1918. Their target was the railway running from Gouzeaucourt to Cambrai. C and D Companies took the objective, with A and B Companies in support.

In the early hours of 29 September they were once again advancing. Desperately the Germans threw gas and high-explosive shells at them, killing nine and wounding forty. Undeterred, the advance continued the following day, reaching the village of Banteux. They could see the enemy withdrawing in front of them. The battalion took 200 prisoners, one of the battalion's officers was killed and five other ranks were wounded.

The 1st Battalion had another period of rest and retraining until 22 October 1918 when they were moved up to the support lines and then, on the following day, they took over the front line at Beaurain. For once it would be a short stint in the frontline trenches, as they were relieved the same evening. Throughout October the battalion had only suffered two deaths and three men wounded; a huge difference from some of the more disastrous months.

Crossing the River Sambre

The 1st Battalion was pushed back into line for the last time on 3 November 1918. They would be involved in the attack on the forest of Mormal. The attack got under way at 0530 on 5 November. The troops advanced in torrential rain and by 0730 they were well within the forest, at their first objective, having encountered no opposition.

On the following day they were sent to the eastern edge of the forest to launch another attack. They were to advance at 1730 against a bridge crossing the River Sambre. Two hours later it was discovered that the Germans had blown up the bridge. Engineering parties tried to rebuild the bridge overnight, but by 0600 on 7 November this had to be abandoned due to heavy enemy fire. By 0730 an attack was launched across the river using a pontoon bridge. The railway was captured by the Cheshire Battalion and a platoon from B Company of the 1st Battalion of the Norfolk Regiment. The 95th Brigade now took over and pushed on and the 1st Battalion was withdrawn to the railway and then back into reserve, which is where they were when news of the armistice broke.

The 1st Battalion had fought unceasingly for four and a half years. Of the men that had left Belfast in August 1914 only one officer and fifty other ranks remained. Certainly some of the others had been transferred or promoted, but the vast majority had either been killed in action or died of wounds and disease. A fair number of the men had also fallen into enemy hands.

Private R Sheldrake had been taken prisoner as early as 14 September 1914 and he kept a private diary, which he managed to smuggle home after the war. He had suffered dreadful conditions and lack of food, but generally the Germans had treated him fairly well. Initially he had been mistaken for a wounded German soldier and had received preferential treatment. Sheldrake survived the experience and due to the damage to his left arm and back was repatriated at the end of 1915.

The 7th (Service) Battalion

The 7th (Service) Battalion of the Norfolk Regiment was formed at Shorncliffe by 22 August 1914, at a full strength of 1,000 men. It was one of the so-called Kitchener Battalions, or Pals Battalions, named as a result of the enormous number of volunteer recruits that wished to sign up. In fact in some places there had been queues of up to a mile outside recruitment offices and 2.5 million men volunteered for these units. Each of these battalions was to form a complete unit under existing British army regiments.

The 7th, however, was not made up of entirely Norfolk men. D Company and half of C Company were Londoners and some of the others came from Lancashire or further afield. But around half of the battalion were indeed from Norfolk. Initially they were quartered in barracks along with the 7th Suffolk Regiment. Conditions were poor, equipment was short and for several months the men did not even have rifles. They were placed under the command of Lieutenant-Colonel J W V Carroll.

The men were under training until they finally received their embarkation orders and entrained for Folkestone, bound for Boulogne, on the *Invicta*, on 30 May 1915. Their initial strength was thirty officers and 954 other ranks. They were to become part of the 35th Brigade of the 12th Division and would operate alongside the 7th Suffolks, the 9th Essex and the 5th Royal Berkshires.

The 7th Battalion took up their positions at Ploegsteert Wood, occupying trenches 113 to 120, on 4 July 1915. For the remainder of the month the 7th took it in turns with the 5th Royal Berkshires to cover the trench works. Throughout the period they were under mining, shelling and sniping attacks, during which five men were killed and one officer wounded, along with twenty-two other ranks. August saw similar duties, with two officers and five other ranks killed and twenty other ranks wounded. Carroll was promoted to command the brigade and Major J C Atkinson took over command of the 7th until 8 October, when he was succeeded by Major F E Walter.

By the end of September 1915, however, the 7th was now occupying shallow trenches near Philosophe and under heavy German artillery fire. Between 1 and 4 October the 7th lost eleven men killed and fifty-seven wounded. Thirteen more from D Company were wounded on 8 October.

The 7th's first assault was to take place on 13 October. The British bombardment lasted between noon and 1345 and it was supposed to be accompanied by a smoke screen. Due to some error the smoke screen had stopped and the men of the 7th could see the Germans scrambling into their trenches, ready to defend themselves when they went over the top at 1400. As a consequence, when the 7th began its advance it came under tremendous fire. One group of fifty took 200m of the German trenches and grimly held on until they were reinforced. Elsewhere, under Second-Lieutenant Franklin, another part of the main German trench and communication trench had been taken. But as reinforcements moved up to support the success they were cut down by German machineguns. The 7th's casualties were huge; five officers were killed, six were wounded, sixty-six other ranks killed, 196 were wounded and 160 were missing. Despite the fact that they were moved back into reserve on 14 October, they still came under heavy shell fire.

A draft of 263 men had arrived by 17 October. On 26 October the 7th were shifted to Vermelles and back into the frontline on 31 October. By the end of the month the 7th could muster twenty-four officers and 863 other ranks.

On 15 December 1915 the 7th were in the trenches on the frontline near Givenchy church. They remained in this area throughout January and February 1916 and by 29 February they were in the frontline trenches to the south of the Hohenzollern redoubt. This was a major German fortification that had been assaulted by the British throughout September and October 1915 and enormous casualties had been inflicted on the waves of British troops. But it had stubbornly remained in German hands. Here the 7th would remain until 24 April 1916. In twelve days in the frontline two officers had been wounded, seven other ranks killed and twenty wounded.

The 7th on the Somme

The 7th spent a period in reserve, but at midnight on 16 to 17 June 1916 they boarded trains bound for Amiens and then began training for a massive offensive on the Somme. On 1 July the battalion marched up to Hennencourt Wood and at 1850 they headed for trenches to the southwest of Albert. They would attack Martinpuich the following day. The 7th's attack was dependent on the British 8th and 34th Divisions breaking through the German frontlines. The attack had failed and consequently the 7th found itself back in reserve until 2315 on 2 July, when they moved up into trenches for an attack on Ovillers.

The troops were in position at 0200 on 3 July; the order to attack came at 0315. The 35th Brigade was on the right-hand side of the assault, the Berkshires were in the lead, with the Suffolks on the left, the Essex in support and the Norfolks in reserve. They advanced through mist and darkness, coming under heavy German artillery fire. Over 100 of the 7th were killed or wounded. As the leading battalions' attacks petered out the 7th moved up to occupy a whole brigade front, as the casualties in the other battalions had been so enormous. They dug in as best they could, still under heavy German artillery fire. They were pounded at 1000 and 1530 on 4 July and received the same treatment the following day. Casualties were beginning to mount and in fact during this short operation one officer and eleven other ranks were killed, ninety or more were wounded and twenty were missing.

The 7th had several days of training and rest until 7 August 1916, when they took over part of the front at Ovillers. They were in a dangerous part of the front; the trench areas had been nicknamed after avenues. The main German frontline was Sixth Avenue and the 7th's B Company held Fifth Avenue, C Company Fourth Avenue, D Company Third Avenue and A Company were in Ovillers. Preparations were under way for an assault on Sixth Avenue and the area of trenches on its right, referred to as Ridge Trench.

The attack went in on the night of 12 to 13 August 1916. A and D Companies led, followed by B and C Companies. The attack was preceded by a heavy bombardment and as it lifted the 7th was already in the German trench, capturing a number of prisoners. By dawn, having secured the strongpoints, each of which each had a Lewis gun, a machinegun and forty men, the 7th withdrew. They had lost at least nine men killed, over 100 wounded and eighteen were missing.

The 7th was put back into reserve on 13 August and they headed for Arras, now a part of VI Corps of the 3rd Army. August had been a dreadful month; twenty-three men had been killed, 193 wounded and twenty-one missing.

September saw a number of raids on German positions launched by the 7th. Second-Lieutenant Ketteringham, with eighteen men of C Company, had raided the German trenches at 0200 on 9 September 1916. In half an hour they did enormous damage and killed several Germans. Ketteringham had also killed a number of Germans on a patrol a week earlier and for his efforts he had been awarded the Military Cross.

Colonel Walter had been promoted to command the brigade and Colonel Prior had been transferred to command the 9th (Service) Battalion of the Norfolks. Captain Gielgud took over command of the 7th for a period.

The 7th's next major engagement was an attack on what was known as Bayonet Trench. The battalion assembled at 0500 on 12 October 1916 and all

P 93 - 117

BOLTS, MAYES & PARTNERS (Accountants)

With Compliments

40A Woodgrange Road,
Forest Gate,
London E7 0QH

Telephone :
01-534 1884 / 3505

four companies surged forward. Their initial objectives were to capture Bayonet and Scabbard Trenches, in the Longueval region of the front. If possible they were to push on and capture a farm beyond. The 7th managed to advance around 50m before they came under heavy machinegun fire. When they reached the objective trenches they found that the wire was uncut and the men were pinned down by the machineguns. On the left the 7th Suffolks had broken through into the trench but were quickly pushed out. The 7th, meanwhile, were still around 100m short of their target. They tried to close in and were still making their attempts as darkness fell. By the time they got back to their own lines three officers had been killed, four wounded, and two missing believed killed. Thirty-six other ranks had also been killed, 125 wounded and fifty-one were missing.

By 25 October 1916 the 7th were back in the positions that they had occupied the previous August, near Arras. Here they would remain throughout November and until the end of 1916. They spent January 1917 training and they were still in reserve in the February. By the beginning of March, however, they had returned to the Arras area and were involved in raiding and dealing with German patrols.

The 7th were told to prepare for an attack on German trenches on 9 April 1917. They moved out to their positions at 0300 and the objective was a number of gun pits and trenches. Orders did not arrive until 1005 and as they advanced towards the German positions they came under fire. The full attack got under way just after noon and the 7th charged forward, silencing machineguns and overrunning German positions. The Germans were surrendering everywhere and delays were caused due to the number of prisoners. They pressed on, capturing more German positions and scooping up more prisoners. In this short engagement around Feuchy Chapel the battalion took 250 German prisoners, seven artillery guns and six machineguns. They had lost two officers and twenty-one other ranks killed, three officers and 135 other ranks wounded and six more men were missing. As the Suffolk and Essex battalions took over the attack they came under intense fire and the 7th was sent up to support them.

This attack petered out and on 10 April the 7th was launched against the German positions on the right-hand side of the Cambrai Road. A single German sniper caused at least thirty casualties, including several non-commissioned officers. By the time the attack got under way, at around 1230, the Germans had evacuated their positions. After a short rest the battalion was given another attack order on 28 April 1917. They attacked at 0425 and took their first objective, a series of German trenches. Once again casualties were high and in the past five days 228 men had either been killed or wounded.

The same grim circumstances continued throughout the summer months of 1917, with more casualties and short periods of respite. There was disaster, however, in late October 1917. It was the 30th, at 0630. The whole of the front around Villers Guislain came under tremendous bombardment from the Germans. It was followed by a mass German infantry attack. The Germans began overrunning allied positions and the 7th was forced to withdraw, leaving behind several men who had got cut off. There is no clear account of precisely what happened, but Lieutenant-Colonel Gielgud, MC, was amongst the twenty-seven killed, eighty-nine wounded and 217 missing. Lieutenant-Colonel E T Rees took over command of what remained of the battalion.

After a relatively long period of reinforcement and reorganization the 7th was back on the front by March 1918. This coincided with a major German offensive. The 7th was involved in tough fighting at Ancre, between Albert and Aveluy, attacking, counterattacking and withdrawing with great skill, as the German pressure mounted. Again it was going to be a ruinous period and by the time the 7th was relieved on 28 March the battalion had suffered another 282 casualties.

Once the frontlines had been re-established the 7th were in and out of the trenches until new British offensives were launched in late August 1918. By now the war had turned decisively against the Germans but they had not given up the fight. Throughout August the battalion had advanced around eleven miles, at a cost of forty-seven killed and 313 wounded or gassed.

The battalion was thrown at Vaux Wood, on the Somme, on 5 September 1918 at 0645. Casualties were ruinous, with over 100 killed or wounded. Another 120 were lost the following day. This was to be the last combat engagement of the 7th. They were involved in a skirmish on 10 October, but by the time that the armistice was declared they were to the rear, where they remained until the end of the year.

The 8th (Service) Battalion

Rather like the 7th (Service) Battalion, the 8th began life at Shorncliffe. By 20 September 1914 it was up to strength of twenty officers and 1,300 men. Over the winter of 1914 to 1915 the battalion was gradually outfitted and undertook training around Colchester. On 25 July 1915 thirty-four officers and 997 other ranks left Folkestone bound for the Continent.

The 8th was part of the 53rd Brigade of the 18th Infantry Division. They would operate with battalions from Essex, Berkshire and Suffolk and were first shipped to the north of Amiens where they spent some time digging trenches in the second line. They were moved up on 4 September 1915 to take over trenches near the Mametz to Carnoy Road.

Initially the battalion was commanded by Brevet-Colonel F C Briggs, but on 14 October 1915 Major H D de L Ferguson, DSO, took over. Throughout October the 8th suffered five killed and fifteen wounded, mainly due to artillery fire and snipers.

The battalion's first major operation was to be in the huge Anglo-French offensive on the Somme in the summer of 1916. By 26 June they were at Carnoy and their objective was the enemy trenches to the southwest of Montauban. The British guns opened up at 0720 and after the Germans returned fire the battalion attacked. The German trench, known as Mine Trench, was quickly overwhelmed and by 0740 the support trench had also been taken. Now the advance became trickier, as they came under fire from supporting German trench works. They pressed on, reaching Pommiers Trench, but in other places parts of the battalion were held up by German strongpoints. The fighting petered out at around 1800, but the men were not safe from a prolonged bombardment by the Germans. The first major battle had cost the 8th dearly; eleven officers and 331 other ranks had either been killed, wounded or were missing. More casualties were inflicted the following day, until the 8th was finally relieved.

They received reinforcement, but by 19 July they were back in position and ready to launch a counterattack. The idea was to drive the Germans out of Delville Wood. The battalion was supported by the 10th Essex and 6th Berkshire battalions. The attack was launched at 0715 and initially all went well, but in the difficult terrain the action became fragmented; successful at some points and less so in others. The 8th dug in and tried to hold the ground that they had taken at such a fearful cost; seventy-eight had been killed, 174 wounded and thirty were missing.

On 22 July the 8th was taken out of the line and they returned to take part in the fighting to seize Thiépval. Initially the battalion operated as a support unit, mopping up groups of Germans who had been isolated by the advance of the Suffolk and Essex Battalions. Nonetheless the casualties were high and day by day they mounted.

The offensive now switched to try to seize the Schwaben redoubt. There had been desperate fighting in the area since 28 September and the 8th would be part of a new attack, scheduled for 5 October 1916. Seizing the redoubt cost the 18th Division nearly 2,000 casualties, of which nearly 100 belonged to the 8th. Even after the seizing of the redoubt the fighting was still intense. The 18th Division's historian wrote about one typical encounter:

> A party of Landwehr [effectively the German equivalent of Kitchener battalions] put up a good fight, however, against the company of 8th Norfolks that was led by Captain Morgan, DSO. Only most aggressive bombing caused them to give in. Afterwards Captain Morgan took sixteen prisoners in very easy fashion. He was superintending the clearing up of the trench, when he noticed a waterproof sheet hanging from the parapet. Lifting it, he found that it screened the entrance to a dug out eight steps deep. On each step sat a couple of Germans, their

backs to the entrance. When Captain Morgan called them to come out,
they came unarmed.

The area clearly still needed to be consolidated, leading to even more casualties and in fact from 21 to 23 October another 136 men were killed or wounded from the 8th.

After a period in reserve the 8th returned to the front line near Maraumont towards the end of January 1917. In the freezing weather conditions the battalion remained until 17 February. The weather had now broken and everywhere there was mud, which sapped the stamina of the battalion even more. Nonetheless they were earmarked to attack at 0545 on 17 February. The first objectives were overrun at 0600. They were aiming to seize the railway line close to the River Ancre and this was achieved by 0700. The Germans still stubbornly resisted, launching counterattacks when they could, sapping the strength and the manpower of the battalion.

After this there was another period of rest until 4 March 1917 when the 8th came up to take part in the attack on Grevillers and the village of Irles, to the east of Maraumont. The 8th was to take the Grevillers trench itself and D Company had penetrated the German trenches by 0521. Elsewhere other elements of the battalion had succeeded in reaching their objectives and capturing several prisoners. By the time the 8th had reached Grevillers trench it was almost unrecognizable, as it had been hammered by British artillery. They continued to advance, making for the village but running into uncut German barbed wire, which impeded their advance. By noon the village itself had been cleared and upwards of 130 prisoners taken, along with a huge amount of weapons and equipment. Incredibly, the battalion had only suffered thirty-four casualties.

By July 1917 the 18th Division had rejoined II Corps and were therefore to be part of the Third Battle of Ypres. The idea was that the 18th Division would move up on the left of the 30th Division when it had taken Glencorse Wood. There had been an unfortunate mistake, however, and instead of attacking Glencorse Wood the 30th Division had instead attacked Château Wood. As a consequence, as the 53rd Brigade moved up, it thought it was heading towards positions that were already in British hands, but they were not; they were still strongly held by the Germans. A, B and D Companies were fortunate, as shortly after they had begun their advance they were told the truth. C Company, however, commanded by Captain Patten, was less fortunate, but he received sufficient intelligence to make him wary. C Company approached Glencorse Wood, opening fire with all of their weapons. For the whole of the afternoon they kept up a steady fire, supported by scattered elements from the Berkshires and the Lincolns. C Company, nonetheless, suffered forty-three casualties.

On 10 August 1917 the 8th was told that they would be involved in an attack at around 1900 against Inverness Copse. The troops moved up, heading for a part of the line that was held by the 7th Bedford Battalion. They arrived just at the time when the Germans had launched a significant raid. A counterattack, led by Captain Morgan, across 600m of difficult terrain, broke up the German attack and helped to recover a lost strongpoint.

Brigadier-General H W Higginson, in command of the 53rd Brigade, wrote:

> Captain J D Crosthwaite, brigade Major, was an eye witness of the attack, which he describes as having been carried out in a most dashing and gallant manner. The assaulting troops advanced by rushes, under the cover fire from Lewis guns and rifles. The enemy losses were heavy; I myself saw a considerable number of dead Huns when I visited the strong point afterwards. The leadership of the officers and non-commissioned officers and the gallantry of all ranks in the assaulting companies are worthy of the highest praise.

They remained in the frontline and under constant artillery fire and gas attacks until they were relieved and sent into reserve on 18 September.

Although the battalion was not to know it at the time, their existence was coming to an end. But there would be one last opportunity towards the end of October 1917 to prove their worth. On 22 October the battalion formed up at 0200, aiming to capture the village of Poelcappelle. To actually call it a village is inaccurate, as hardly a single building remained intact. It was a wasteland of shattered brick, studded by German pillboxes and shell holes. The 8th was to lead off, supported by the Essex battalion.

At 0535 the artillery opened up and the battalion dashed forward under the cover of the barrage. They overran the outlying German defences and began mopping up before pushing on towards three farms straddling the road to Langemarck. It was a triumph, but at a cost of 224 killed, wounded or missing. Major Berney-Finklin, who had been a captain, an adjutant in the 8th, when they had left for France in 1915, wrote:

> On November the 5th Lieutenant-Colonel E N Snepp was seriously wounded by long-range gunfire, when the battalion was resting in huts some considerable distance from the firing line. On November 22nd Lieutenant-Colonel J D Crossthwaite, MC (London Regiment), assumed command. During November and December the battalion held the line in the vicinity of Poelcappelle resting usually in the Herzeele area, and quitting trenches for the last time about the middle of December.

On 29 January 1918 the battalion paraded for the last time. Only one officer and a handful of other ranks remained from the original men who had paraded on St Martin's Plain in Folkestone on the evening of 4 September 1914. Some 770 men from the battalion had been killed, but the war was not over for the other men; fifteen officers and 300 other ranks joined the 9th (Service) Battalion on 6 February 1918 and five officers and 100 other ranks joined the 7th (Service) Battalion. Officially, the 8th ceased to exist on 20 February 1918 when the last of the men were drafted into corps reinforcement camps and into entrenching battalions.

The 9th (Service) Battalion

The 9th (Service) Battalion mustered at Norwich on 9 September 1914, with a strength of 900 men under Major E Orams. After a period of training it was in Boulogne on 30 August 1915, now under the command of Colonel Mansel Shewen, who became a brigade commander on 21 September, when the battalion was taken over by Lieutenant-Colonel E Stracey. The battalion was attached to the 71st Brigade of the 24th Division. Its sister battalions were the 8th Bedfords, the 9th Suffolks and the 11th Essex.

Their first taste of action was on 26 September 1915 near the La Bassée Canal. The 71st Brigade would attack Vendin-le-Vieil and the assault was launched at 0645, when they immediately ran into heavy enemy sniper fire. The attack petered out and by the time they were relieved by the Grenadier Guards that evening the casualties had been 209 killed, wounded or missing. In late September the 71st Brigade was transferred to the 6th Division and the makeup of the brigade was altered.

January 1916 saw the battalion in the St Jean sector, taking it in turns with the 9th Suffolk and the 1st Leicesters to hold the frontline trenches. By March they were on the south side of the Ypres salient and towards the end of the month, after snow, there was a thaw and the

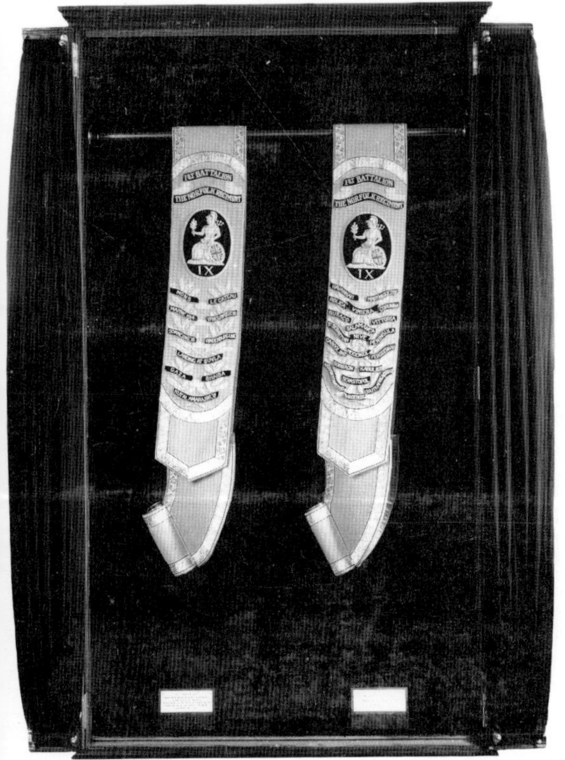

The King's Colour Belt presented to the regiment by Major H Berney-Ficklin, MC, on occasion of his transfer to the Highland Light Infantry after serving with the regiment for twenty years

conditions were appalling. After a period of training from 5 April they were once again in the trenches on 23 April 1916 and remained there throughout May.

As August 1916 dawned the battalion headed for the Somme front, reaching Villers Candas on the morning of 3 August and on the 14th they relieved the Coldstream Guards. The 9th would take a leading role in the offensive that would be launched on 15 September.

They would advance against Ginchy and Leuze Wood on a 250m front. A British tank arrived at 0550 and at 0620 they got under way. This was to be the first time that tanks were used operationally. By 0700 the tank had reached the German frontline, but the 9th was lagging behind. There was insufficient artillery support and the ground was difficult. The men were scattered in shell holes and at 1255 it was decided to try to consolidate what had been gained. The battalion, however, had lost heavily, with over 400 being killed, wounded or missing. Unsurprisingly, the battalion was put into reserve for recuperation.

Lieutenant-Colonel Prior took over command of the battalion on 1 October and found that the majority of the men were new draftees. Nonetheless the 9th would soon be back in action once again; this time their target was a German-held ridge, to the east of Gueudecourt. The attack was preceded by a heavy bombardment and the troops got under way at 0340 on 18 October 1916. It was still dark and understandably, given the lack of experience of the officers and men, it quickly descended into chaos. Colonel Prior recounted what had happened:

> I determined to go up the line and see for myself what had happened. Just as I was starting I met a runner from Second-Lieutenant Cubitt, of B Company, with a report that he had gained his objective, and, though counterattacked, had driven the Bosche out of the trench and had been holding it since. I saw Blackwell (D Company) and told him to organise a party from his company, reinforce Cubitt, and take command of the position. I then went along the line, and here the news was not so good. The right of B and A Companies had apparently failed. There were stragglers of both companies who had got back to our original front line, but they could say very little beyond the fact that, in the darkness, they had missed their direction, got caught in the Bosche barrage, and those who were not killed or wounded had eventually got back to their own line.

Cubitt at the time was only 21 and for his conduct in the action he was awarded the Military Cross. He had seen conspicuous acts of gallantry amongst his men in the most trying of circumstances. Once again the 9th had been battered: 239 casualties.

Again the battalion was put into reserve. They received a draft of 140 men and on 10 December Colonel Prior, coming back from a reconnaissance for a proposed raid, was shot through the arm by a sniper. He would be absent from the battalion for three months and temporarily Lieutenant-Colonel R S Dyer-Bennett took over.

Command of the battalion went to Lieutenant-Colonel J B O Trimble on 27 January 1917. Colonel Stracey then took over until Colonel Prior's return on 24 February. The battalion had had a steady trickle of losses, mainly down to snipers, trench raids and gas attacks. Prior wrote of the appalling conditions in which the men now found themselves:

> It is only those who have been there, who know the effect of a cold thaw on the liquid mud of Flanders, and its paralysing effects, who know what it is to stand silent and motionless for their tour of duty, legs and arms completely numbed, and with no chance to restore the circulation. On relief from sentry duty the man was but little better off, his sole chance of restoring circulation being to try and clean his trench of some of the liquid mud.

This indeed was a period of intense cold, great discomfort and the ever-present danger of a violent death. Raid and counter raid were launched and such was the life of the battalion until it was earmarked for the First Battle of Cambrai in November 1917.

The plan was to try to storm the German Hindenburg line. There had been extensive reconnaissance, but in order for the attack to be a complete surprise there would be no preliminary bombardment. The ultimate target was the village of Ribécourt. Incredibly, although the German resistance was significant and A and D Companies had to resort to hand-to-hand fighting in clearing the villag, all of the objectives were taken with the help of tanks, at a cost of twenty-nine killed and fifty-eight wounded.

The Germans, however, were not done and at the end of October they launched a massive counteroffensive. By this time the 9th was in Nine Wood, to the southwest of Noyelles. So vicious was the German attack that the entire 6th Division was in danger of being cut off. As it was, despite heavy shelling, the 9th was not engaged and they were extremely fortunate to be withdrawn on 14 December until 31 December, allowing them to enjoy a Christmas dinner in relative safety around Lens.

They were back at the front on 17 January 1918, taking over trench works at Le Bucquière, on the Bapaume to Cambrai railway. At the beginning of February they received a considerable draft from the 8th Battalion, which was in the process of being disbanded. By this time they were holding trench works in the Dénicourt area. On 13 February they were transferred to the Quéant-Pronville sector and they would remain here until 21 March, when the Germans launched their offensive.

Colonel Prior had been gassed in late January, but he returned to the battalion in time for the German attack. He described the incredible experience that day:

> I spent the whole night [20 to 21 March 1918] in going round the front line post with Cutbill of B Company and Sprott of D. It took me a very long time, as I had to make a good number of alterations, and it was very nearly dawn when I got back to battalion headquarters. During the course of my tour I went some way out into no-man's land, and obtained the impression that this was no longer a false alarm. I don't quite know what gave me this impression. In the Bosche lines there was a stillness which, at the same time, was not a complete silence, just as if a large number of men were already in position, waiting in intense excitement, and speaking to each other in whispers. A few minutes later the crash came. All over the front the sky was lit by the flash of enemy guns, and shells began to drop. The bombardment all over the whole of our front was terrific. Shells were bursting everywhere, and the noise was frightful.

In the Lagnicourt sector of the front, part of which was held by the 9th and the 2nd Sherwood Foresters, the Germans were unsuccessful. It was the only part of the front that did not collapse. One of the Norfolk companies alone had cut down 2,000 German infantry. They fired their rifles at such a rate that they were literally too hot to hold. The Lewis guns had to be cooled down before they could risk slotting in another magazine. Finally the Norfolks and the Sherwood Foresters were told to pull back. The 9th had been decimated; a total of seventeen officers and 347 other ranks were killed, wounded or missing. A large majority of these men had been cut off, but it had been a heroic and stubborn resistance.

In desperate times Prior scratched together men from the 1st Leicesters and the Sherwood Foresters, along with what remained of his battalion, to form a scratch unit. Throughout 22 March Prior's unit fought a rearguard action and Prior was badly wounded, so command of the unit passed to Captain Failes, of C Company. Finally they were relieved that night and sent into reserve for a much-needed refit.

They were back on the Ypres front on 1 April 1918. The battalion was holding the frontline at Polybecke but when a predicted attack by the Germans came to nothing the initiative was taken by the British. On 14 April the battalion was at Dranoutre and they would launch a counterattack led by Lieutenant-Colonel F R Day. But the Germans opened up a thunderous bombardment, which began at noon on 15 April. By around 1430 the battalion could see enemy infantry advancing and half an hour later they had gained a foothold in the front trench line. B Company counterattacked, but such was the weight of numbers of the Germans that they had to fall back to a line along the railway. The battalion lost fourteen killed, 156 wounded and 254 missing. By 16 April the battalion could muster just six officers and 150 men.

The situation around Ypres was touch and go for the allies, as on 28 to 29 May the French, on the right of the 6th Division, had been forced back and the battalion's D Company was needed to protect the flank. May's casualties had been heavy, with sixteen killed, 58 wounded and twenty-three gassed.

June and July were mercifully quiet by recent standards. Colonel Prior returned to the battalion on 28 July but he was barely fit, suffering from his wounds and from the ill effects of the gas. Less than a month later he had to bow to the inevitable and leave the battalion in the capable hands of Colonel Day.

By the beginning of September 1918 the final allied offensive was well under way and the 9th Battalion arrived at Corbie, to the east of Amiens, on 2 September. After a period of training they received orders on 17 September that they would be involved in an attack the following morning. They were to assemble at Holnon Wood; it was an almost impassable area, with trees down, tracks badly rutted, shell holes and the whole area wreathed in gas. By 0900 six platoons of the battalion began their advance. It took until 1500 for the rest of the battalion to assemble and get moving. Consequently, the attack was largely rescheduled to begin at 0400 on 19 September.

It had been expected that the Germans would only be offering a token resistance and would, in effect, be fighting a rearguard action. But in reality they were determined to deny every inch of ground. Consequently officer and other rank casualties in this period were particularly high.

A draft of 150 men arrived on 1 October, allowing four companies to be created again. But the 9th was expected to throw itself at the Germans once more. The German Hindenburg line had been penetrated and the 30th American Division had formed a salient towards Bohain. The plan was for the battalion to support the 118th American Infantry Regiment in their attempt to take the village of Brancourt.

The 9th set off on 8 October 1918 at 0510 and by 0923 they had reached a line to the south of Brancourt station. The Americans were on their left and the Sherwood Foresters on their right and a company of the Leicester battalion was providing a reserve for the Norfolk battalion. At around 1500 the 9th ran into heavy machinegun fire and as the casualties mounted they were forced to retire. The battalion was thrown in again at 0230 to try and take the high ground and relieve the pressure that the Americans were facing on their front. They managed to take the high ground and continued along the railway to the west of Bohain, capturing an enormous amount of German equipment.

After one day's rest the battalion found itself once again in the frontline, working their way forward at 0530 on 11 October. Once again they ran into heavy machinegun fire, but they could bring down artillery fire on the German machinegun nests. They were working in cooperation with tanks and they

Officers of the 1st Battalion, taken in 1913

managed to force the Germans out of a copse.

After receiving a draft of 260 men on 20 October 1918 the battalion once again returned to the frontline. Their target this time was a red line about 400m beyond the southwest edge of the Bois de l'Evêque. In the thick mist they pushed forward at 0120 and four hours later it was clear that a combination of machineguns, wired hedges and fences and walling had prevented the 9th from getting any more than 400m forward. Some tanks had actually managed to get to the objective, but in the absence of any infantry had had to turn back. A pair of the tanks was now detailed to break through the obstructions stopping the 9th from moving forward.

Meanwhile, the battalion had spent the day trying to work around and get towards the target from a different direction, but by the time they were ready darkness had fallen. The operation had cost them two officers killed and seven other ranks, sixty-six wounded and a further sixty missing.

This was to be the 9th's last battle and they were in Bohain on Armistice Day. This was not, however, to be the last actions of the 9th, as they would have the satisfaction of being part of the army of occupation. From 14 November they

Officers of the 3rd Battalion at Felixstowe in 1916

began their march to the Rhine. It terminated deep into Germany at Brühl, in late December 1918. This was a few miles to the south of Cologne and they had covered a distance of 246 miles. It was their first Christmas in peace since 1913.

The Other Norfolk Battalions

It is important not to forget the other Norfolk battalions that were in existence during the First World War. Admittedly most of them were tasked with the role of training and despatching drafts overseas. The 3rd (Special Reserve) Battalion was mobilized on 8 August 1914 and with a strength of 600 it marched to Felixstowe for the defence of the coastline. At times the size of this battalion reached 100 officers and 3,000 other ranks, but constantly they had to provide drafts for not only other Norfolk battalions but also other units, including the 3rd Duke of Cornwall's Light Infantry and the Essex Regiment. During the First World War 724 officers passed through the 3rd Battalion.

Perhaps the most tragic incident regarding the 3rd relates to the loss of the transport *Royal Edward*. She was torpedoed and sunk in the Aegean Sea on 14 August 1915 and onboard were 1,400 men, 300 of whom were Norfolk men. One of the commanding officers of the battalion, Colonel W Corrie Tonge, DSO, contended that this was one of the best drafts that had ever passed through Felixstowe. All but eighteen of the Norfolk men were lost.

The 1/6th and 2/6th (Territorial) Battalions were formed for home defence.

Late 19th-century Norfolk Regimental football team

Some of the men would find themselves transferred, notably to the 1st Battalion and the 8th Battalion of the Norfolk Regiment. Their patrol work was extremely important. For example a platoon of men from Thetford, under Lieutenant Fison, operated at Kessingland in Suffolk. There was also a 3/6th Battalion, which was formed at Norwich and these too performed similar duties.

The 10th (Service) Battalion was created on 21 October 1914 and in March 1915 it became a reserve battalion to find drafts for the 7th, 8th and 9th (Service) Battalions. It was renamed the 10th (Second Reserve) Battalion, Norfolk Regiment and continued on as a training battalion.

The 2/4th (Reserve) Battalion, later known as the 11th Battalion, was raised in September 1914, with the Drill Hall, Chapelfield, in Norwich as its headquarters. It too was involved in home defence work, constructing gun pits, training, providing personnel for searchlights, helping with damage suffered from zeppelin raids and a host of other responsibilities. Thousands of officers and men passed through this unit to find themselves in frontline battalions.

It is a similar story for the 2/5th Battalion. The men began forming up in October 1914 at East Dereham; initially they had no rifles or equipment and only a handful of the NCOs had uniforms. They operated in Peterborough, Cambridge, Bury St Edmunds, Thetford and Brentwood and they too provided large numbers of men for the other battalions.

The final battalion was the 3/5th, which was formed in 1915 and initially based in Dereham. It was sent to Windsor and then to Halton, near Tring, providing large numbers of men for the 1/5th. In early 1916 the 3/4th and the 3/5th were amalgamated and were based in Sussex.

During the First World War every battalion lost virtually 100 per cent of its original strength. Although estimates vary, collectively the Norfolk Regiment lost 5,576 officers and men. However when we take into account the wounded and the missing the figure is in excess of 30,000. In other words, significantly more individuals than attend a home game at Carrow Road to watch Norwich City play.

6

France 1939–1940

The interwar years, to a large extent, were a return to the normality and humdrum nature of home postings, punctuated by stints overseas. In 1919 the 1st Battalion found itself back in Ireland. It was a troublesome time for Ireland, with rebellion, riots and unrest. The battalion served in Belfast, Dublin, Drogheda and Londonderry, until in 1922 they spent a year in Colchester then in the following year left, via Southampton, for the West Indies.

The West Indies was not the dangerous posting that it had been in the past and much of the disease had been eradicated. The battalion was on the move again in 1925; first based at Moascar in Egypt and then in 1926 at Cairo. By 1928 they were in Shanghai. It became a sign of manhood to cover their bodies in tattoos. For some of the old hands the tattoos separated the men from the boys.

The 1st Battalion would then spend eight years in India, from 1929. They would see service at Sialkot and on the border between British India and Kashmir. The year 1935 was a key one for the regiment. Not

J P Mostyn, the commanding officer of the 1st Battalion of the Norfolk Regiment 1928

The barracks of the 1st Battalion of the Norfolk Regiment in Egypt in 1928

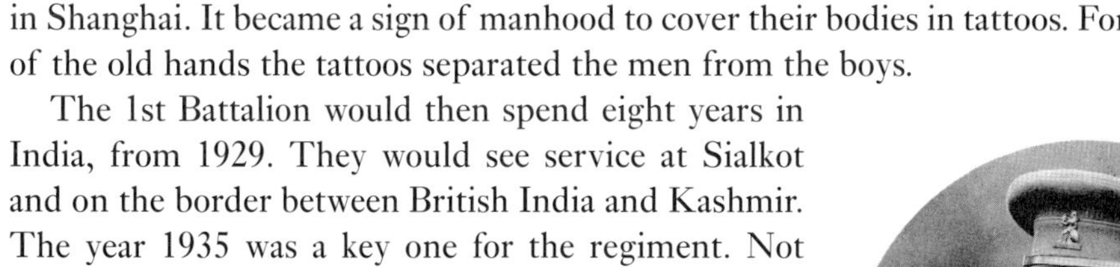

The drums and colours of the 1st Battalion of the Norfolk Regiment in Egypt in 1928

only was it the Silver Jubilee of King George V, but it was also the 250th anniversary of the raising of Cornwall's Regiment of Foot. In celebration of the events army orders in June stated:

> On the occasion of His Majesty's birthday, and in commemoration of the twenty fifth year of His Majesty's reign, the King has been graciously pleased to approve that the following regiment shall in future enjoy the distinction of 'Royal' – the Norfolk Regiment, which will henceforth be designed The Royal Norfolk Regiment.

Officers of the 1st Battalion of the Norfolk Regiment in Egypt in 1928

Officers of the 1st Battalion. This was taken on the northwest frontier in 1936. It is part of an album that was compiled by an officer of the battalion.

Men of the Norfolk Regiment taking part in a military tattoo at Olympia, London, in 1936

The 1st Battalion of the regiment giving a physical training display at the Calcutta Tattoo in 1934

In early May 1937 the 1st Royal Norfolks marched up into Waziristan for frontier duties. It was a dangerous war zone and the battalion would spend four months there, losing four men killed and three wounded in the process. The men that served for this short period of time on the northwest frontier of India would be entitled to wear a medal; a distinction for just a handful of British regiments in the past 100 years.

Portrait of the 2nd Battalion's colour party at Aldershot in 1935

Officers of the 2nd Battalion in Iraq in 1922

The 2nd Battalion had already served on the northwest frontier between 1920 and 1921. In 1922 they had spent an agonizing period hunting for the remains of Norfolk men who had fallen during the First World War fighting the Turks. In 1923 they had rushed to Baghdad, believing that the country was under threat from the Turks. In 1924 the 2nd Battalion returned to England and for thirteen years they would be stationed at Aldershot, Colchester and Devonport. From March 1937 to January 1939 they served at Gibraltar.

Group portrait of officers of the 2nd Battalion at Aldershot in 1935

Members of the anti-tank section of the 2nd Battalion at Aldershot in 1935

A view of HMS Norfolk in the waters off Devonport in 1931

The band of the 2nd Battalion posing on the deck of HMS Norfolk in 1930

Officers of the 1st Battalion in India in 1940

When the Second World War broke out on 3 September 1939 the 1st Battalion was in India and the 2nd Battalion was at Aldershot. Very quickly the Territorial Battalions, the 4th, 5th, 6th and 7th, were mobilized. In fact there were so many potential recruits that new battalions were also created: the 8/30th, the 9th and the 70th (Young Soldiers) Battalion. The number of men that would serve in the Royal Norfolks in one way, shape or form was even greater than that of those who had served during the First World War. Even the unfit, exempt, young and elderly joined the Norfolk Home Guard. Incredibly, by the middle of 1943 that had grown to seventeen battalions.

In order to prevent total confusion around the exploits of the seven active service battalions during the Second World War, it will be valuable in this chapter simply to focus on the 2nd and the 7th Battalions. Each saw service with the British Expeditionary Force in France until the fall of France and evacuation in June 1940.

Sergeant of the 1st Battalion in India in 1940

Men of B Company, of the 1st Battalion, firing field guns at the Delhi fort in India, probably late 1930s

Officers of the 1st Battalion, Christmas 1943

The 2nd Battalion in France

The story that dominates the experience of the 2nd Battalion in France from 1939 to 1940 is a tragic and unforgiveable war crime. It took place at Le Paradis, in the Pas de Calais, on 27 May 1940.

The 2nd Battalion was the first British Expeditionary Force to clamber ashore at Cherbourg on 21 September 1939. The battalion was commanded by Lieutenant-Colonel E C Hayes and it was part of the 4th Infantry Brigade Group, which at that time was concentrating around Arras. Early in October the brigade moved towards the Franco-Belgian border and the battalion set up their headquarters in the village of Rumigies. There was much work to be done to construct decent defences, dig anti-tank ditches and ready themselves for battle.

On 24 December 1939 the battalion moved up to relieve the 3rd Infantry Brigade, on the Saar front. This was a sector on the extreme left of the Maginot Line, the famed French defensive positions. The Maginot Line had been constructed by the French and ran all the way to the Swiss border. Allegedly it was impenetrable, but as the Allies were soon to become aware, it had one fatal flaw; if the enemy were to push through Belgium they could enter France around the flank of the defensive line.

It was something of an unreal period. There appeared to be some kind of agreement between the British and the Germans that they would not shell villages. Patrolling by both sides was frequent and on the night of 4 January 1940 a patrol from A Company, commanded by Captain F P Barclay, went out to have a look at the enemy positions around the railway station at Waldwisse, about 1,000m across no-man's land. It was a bright, moonlit night and the snow was thick. Barclay, along with Lance-Corporal M H Davis, took a look at a bridge coming up against barbed wire. They were spotted and there was a firefight. Barclay was awarded the Military Cross and Davis the Military Medal. These were the first awards in the BEF for gallantry.

The 2nd Battalion lost Lieutenant Everitt on 5 January; he was mortally wounded and captured, dying two days later in a German hospital. He was the first officer to be lost in the BEF.

The battalion continued in a similar vein through February to early May 1940 but by the end of April there were rumours that the Germans were about to launch a major offensive. The battalion had already been informed that they would advance to a defence line along the River Dyle if the Germans invaded Belgium. This was known as Plan D, as Lieutenant-Colonel C R Murray Brown DSO explained: 'Our role was to form part of the advance guard to the 2nd Div., and the area to be occupied was the wooded slopes behind the river near Wavre, a town some 25km se of Brussels. It was of course impossible to make any reconnaissance beforehand.'

The Germans began bypassing the Maginot Line with their lightning strike into neutral Luxembourg and Belgium on 10 May 1940. Murray Brown was on a course in Britain and Captains Elwes and Gibbons were on leave. Nonetheless the battalion began assembling to move forward. At 1730 the order was given to cross the Belgian border. It was crossed at 0130 on 11 May. Daylight saw the skies thick with enemy aircraft, but most of these were driven off by anti-aircraft guns. When the battalion reached Tombeek they tumbled out of their transport and began occupying positions before settling down to dig in. After being relieved by the 1st Royal Berkshires the 2nd Battalion moved into reserve at the Bois de Beaumont and dug in for the night.

By 13 May it was apparent that the situation in Belgium was deteriorating rapidly. Huge numbers of Belgian troops were seen to be pulling back. As a precautionary measure sappers arrived to prepare the bridges for demolition. It had already been rumoured that the Germans had crossed the Albert Canal and were making for the River Dyle. The following day the bridges were blown and German Stukas were active. There was also the bad news that the Belgian army had virtually disintegrated.

The Germans did indeed make an appearance on 15 May and C Company shot down a Stuka with their Bren guns. Although some French troops had broken on the right flank of the brigade, the British positions were still solid and intact and it came as a great surprise to the men that they were to withdraw. Orders came at 1800 on 16 May for a further withdrawal, this time to Ribstraat, near Grammont on the River Dendre.

By first light on 17 May 1940 the battalion was barely halfway there. The roads were clogged with transport vehicles and fleeing soldiers and civilians. The Germans were not far behind and the battalion arrived at Ribstraat at 1600 hours. At noon on 18 May the bridges were blown over the river and after dark it was clear that the Germans had crossed the river and that a further withdrawal would be necessary. The transports moved off at 0400 on 19 May, heading for Froidment to the west of the River Escaut. Once again thousands of refugees, broken down vehicles and other obstacles blocked the route. Many men had been lost, not as casualties, but they had been split up from the unit.

By the afternoon of 20 May the Germans were in strength at Tournai. All throughout 21 May the Germans attacked the battalion's positions. Counterattacks were mounted when possible. There was continuous pressure all along the front. The action was broken off during the night and the battalion pulled back to the wooded area of Bois de Wannenhain. The plan was for the battalion to move into reserve at La Bassée and that the French would replace them.

The 2nd Battalion moved into their new positions at 2030 on 24 May 1940. With the Germans so close behind them the battalion had to take up defensive positions. At 0330 on 26 May the Germans attacked B Company and then C Company. There was fighting in the streets of the village and already company strengths were down, but additional casualties were also inflicted during the night. By that afternoon what remained of the battalion was being desperately reorganized by the acting commanding officer, Major Ryder.

At dawn, at 0330, on 27 May a massive bombardment pounded the battalion's positions. Inevitably the Germans were about to launch a major attack. The battalion was literally overrun.

Le Paradis

One group of the 2nd Battalion, along with men from other units, had been captured at Druries Farm by No. 3 Company of the 1st Battalion, 2nd SS Totenkopf Regiment. One of the prisoners was Albert Pooley, a signaller in A Company:

> There were a hundred of us prisoners marching in column of threes. We turned off the dusty French road through a gateway and into a meadow beside the buildings of a farm. I saw, with one of the nastiest feelings I've ever had in my life, two heavy machineguns inside the meadow. They were manned and pointing at the head of our column. I felt as though an icy hand gripped my stomach. The guns began to spit fire and even as the front men began to fall I said fiercely, 'this can't be. They can't do this to us!' For a few seconds the cries and shrieks of our stricken men drowned the cracking of the guns. Men fell like grass before a scythe. The invisible blade came nearer and nearer and then swept through me. I felt a terrific searing pain in my left leg and wrist and pitched forward in a red world of tearing agony. My scream of pain mingled with the cries of my mates but even as I fell forward into a heap of dying men the thought stabbed my brain 'if I ever get out of here the swine who did this will pay for it'.

The incident had taken place on a farm belonging to Louis Creton; on the left of the pasture was the farmhouse and a long, red-brick barn. Henceforth it would be known as the Le Paradis massacre.

Pooley and just one other man, William O'Callaghan, survived the massacre. The man who was ultimately held responsible was the commander of the company, Fritz Knoechlein. He was tried for murder in October 1948 and hanged in Hamburg on 28 January 1949. Pooley could not walk and O'Callaghan dragged him out of the pasture in the pouring rain. They hid in a nearby farm and eventually they were to give themselves up, but not to the SS.

The Germans were already aware of the massacre and they launched their own investigation. The SS claimed that the massacre had been prompted by the heavy losses that they had suffered and that the British troops had been involved in unlawful fighting methods, including the use of dumdum bullets. The Germans took no further action.

Pooley was repatriated in October 1943 and O'Callaghan was released as a prisoner of war in 1945. Both of them had filed complaints and a report of what had occurred. The wheels of justice slowly turned until Knoechlein was found guilty in No. 5 Court in 1948.

Following the disastrous engagement and the subsequent massacre there was virtually nothing left of the 2nd Battalion. A handful of the men managed to make it back as far as Dunkirk. When the 2nd Battalion assembled back in England on 7 June 1940 there were just five officers and 134 other ranks. The short campaign had nearly annihilated the battalion. According to Captain Long in his report written while he was a prisoner of war: 'Total prisoners according to careful calculations made in Germany amounted to approx 150 officers and ORs. This included all captured, wounded, stragglers and survivors from 10th May–28th 1940.'

We will pick up the story of the further exploits of the 2nd Battalion in Chapter 7, when they found themselves in Burma. For a comprehensive investigation into the incident and the events that led up to Le Paradis, the authors recommend the late Richard Lane's *Last Stand at Le Paradis* (Pen & Sword, 2009).

7th Battalion in France

In the spring of 1939 the 5th Battalion of the Royal Norfolks had recruited up to double strength. Consequently, on 1 September the 7th Battalion came into existence with a battalion strength of twenty-three officers and 621 other ranks. It was commanded by Lieutenant-Colonel C A Debenham. Although the battalion's experiences on mainland Europe would be terrifying, the men taken out of the 5th Battalion to form this new battalion were in many respects the fortunate ones. Their colleagues in the 5th were to spend the bulk of the war as prisoners of the Japanese, as we will see in Chapter 7.

On 30 December 1939 an advanced party of the 7th Battalion left for Southampton, to be followed by two groups on 7 and 13 January 1940. It was a cold but uneventful journey across the English Channel to Cherbourg. On 19 January they entrained for Boisleux, some five miles to the south of Arras. The motor transport drove all the way in appalling weather, following the men. Initially they were employed in guarding an ammunition railhead and dump and generally improving the defence works. It was hard work, as the ground was virtually frozen solid.

On 1 April 1940 the whole battalion headed for Metz and were billeted in the Quartier de Vallieres barracks. The battalion was attached to 144th Infantry Brigade, 48th Division, and their first task was to set up a forward defence line and also to wire and dig a line on which German troops would be held if they managed to break through the Maginot forts. There were a number of abandoned villages near the forward defence line. C Company, under Captain Colley, made for Bizing on 2 April and D Company, under Major Wilson, towards Halstroff on 4 April.

Already the Germans were active in the area, shelling outposts and mounting patrols. A Company, under Second-Lieutenant Gill, moved up to Metzeresche and began work sorting out the village and organizing its defence. B Company, under Captain Hawkins, along with headquarters, remained in Metz.

For the remainder of the month the 7th Battalion's activities remained the same; after all it was the period that was popularly known as the Phoney War. Training was undertaken and wherever possible defence lines were improved.

By the beginning of May 1940 the Germans were even more active than before, patrolling and counter-patrolling. On 13 May they opened up on an outpost manned by D Company, killing four and wounding four others. Contact with the enemy became more frequent and from time to time there were small arms exchanges with German patrols.

Since the beginning of May the 7th Battalion had been operating with the 51st Division, primarily because one of the 51st Division's battalions was insufficiently trained. On the evening of 20 May British troops that were forward of the Maginot Line were withdrawn and the battalion moved west of the River Moselle to Jouaville. Two days later the battalion marched towards Avillers.

During the night of 24 May the bulk of the battalion marched fifteen miles to Mars La Tour; it took them four hours. They entrained for Varennes and after fifty hours of travelling the train reached Rouen. Here they made contact with the five other battalions of the 51st Division and were told to use French buses, which would collect them at 0900 on 29 May, to take them to Clais. By this stage the 51st Division was the last British division left in France. They were holding the line of the Somme, around Abbeville, with French troops on their right. The whole area was very poorly defended and they had practically no air cover or tanks.

Everything was quiet until the morning of 4 June 1940. The 51st Division, supported by the French, attacked Abbeville to deny the enemy a bridgehead that they had established there. The attack was a complete failure. In the days that would follow the fortunes of each of the companies were very different.

Battalion headquarters and the headquarters company were at Guervill on 6 June, Canehan the following day and St Germaine on 8 June. Two days later, while breakfast was being served, they were told to retreat towards St Denis as quickly as possible, as German tanks had broken through on their right.

A Company, under Captain Allen, minus 8 Platoon, was attached to the 154th Brigade at Hoquelus on 30 May. The following day part of 8 Platoon was at St Blimont and by 5 June the Germans were probing their positions. The remainder of 8 Platoon was attached to D Company, who had fallen back to the east. At around 1400 8 Platoon and D Company began to fall back through an orchard under constant attack by the Germans. On the morning of 6 June they took up a position in the grounds of a château at Belloy but were soon cut off and forced to surrender at 1800 hours on 7 June 1940. Corporal Grimes's section of 8 Platoon had managed to extricate themselves and rejoin company headquarters.

In the early hours of the morning on 5 June 9 Platoon, along with A Company, had also managed to fall back and took up positions in an orchard at Franleu. By the following day they had run out of ammunition, food and water and also had to surrender that evening.

A Company's headquarters and 7 Platoon had slipped into woodland to the south of Dargnies on 5 June. What was left of them managed to fall back through Millebosc to help defend brigade headquarters.

On the night of 9 to 10 June, still attached to the 154th Brigade, A Company was ordered to cover the line from Frecamp to Bolbec to cover the embarkation of the division at Le Havre. A Company was inexplicably missed off the operational orders for embarkation, so they headed back to link up with battalion headquarters at St Denis.

Meanwhile, B Company under Captain Hawkins was largely intact by 6 June 1940. One of the platoons was helping out with the defence of the bridgehead at Beauchamp. On 10 June, minus one platoon that was at Totes, the bulk of the company was at Ouvillers helping to guard divisional headquarters.

Captain Colley's C Company was attached to the 152nd Brigade at St Maxent until 4 June 1940. 10 and 11 Platoons had suffered heavy casualties in the attack on Abbeville on 4 June. The company began falling back, covering their withdrawal and by 9 June they too were at St Denis.

Major Wilson's D Company, attached to the 153rd Brigade, began falling back on 31 May. On 5 June they took part in repulsing a German attack on the village of Toeffles and by 9 June they were at Tourville.

By 10 June A and C Company were back under battalion command at St Denis. The bulk of B Company was in the next village and D Company was still attached to the 153rd Brigade. At about 1800 hours on 10 June the men were told to destroy everything that was not essential for fighting. They threw stores and spare parts into a stream and began falling back towards St Riquier. They reached here at 0300 but could find no trace of divisional headquarters. During the retreat a large number of demoralized and unarmed French troops had attached themselves to the battalion. By dawn on 11 June it was clear that the Germans were very close. The battalion now found out that the divisional headquarters were actually at Cailleville and they began heading there, picking up the stray B Company platoon from Totes and most of D Company.

Having regained contact with divisional headquarters the battalion was now told that they would be covering part of the so-called Corunna Line, about two miles outside of St Valery, to cover the embarkation of allied troops. By now the Germans had already started shelling the area and the prospects of embarkation looked extremely bleak. The situation was chaotic and as the battalion moved up to take their allotted places they found themselves under fire, not only from Germans but also from French. During the night of 12 June most of the division and thousands of French troops had assembled at St Valery for embarkation. The Norfolks were supposed to embark at 2345.

D Company was operating with elements of the 1st Gordon Highlanders, about two miles to the west of Cany. They had come under attack from twenty or more German tanks that literally bulldozed their way through the British positions; in effect Wilson's men were entirely cut off.

Back on the beaches near St Valery, by 0230 on 12 June, it was almost every man for himself. There was virtually no ammunition, food, vehicles or guns. Captain Colley broke up his C Company into parties of eighteen and sent them off to try and find any way to get home. Captain Colley and Second-Lieutenant Walker, with a small group of men, managed to find two boats, getting into them by sliding down the masts. There were no oars so they used spades to propel the vessels. Colley's boat had too tall a mast and it could not get underneath the bridge so he was forced to return to the beach and was killed trying to help other parties escape at Val-les-Roses.

Walker, meanwhile, having come under German machinegun fire in his boat, was finally picked up by HMS *Harvester*. He was landed at Southampton on 13 June 1940 and by then eleven more men of C Company had also been dropped off there.

D Company, meanwhile, tried to hold off determined German attacks, but it was simply a matter of time and the company was overwhelmed by German tanks and infantry. D Company was captured.

Of the entire 7th Battalion of the Royal Norfolks only thirty escaped and made it back to England. But this was not the end of the 7th; they would reform and return to exact their revenge. When the 7th Battalion was reformed in Nottingham in July 1940 the only surviving original officer was Lieutenant H J Walker. The remnants of the battalion started receiving replacements on 17 July and then received additional intakes at fortnightly intervals. Until October 1940 the battalion had virtually no equipment, but it was then moved to Grimsby to become part of the 205th Infantry Brigade of the Lincolnshire Division. It remained in Lincolnshire for the rest of the year, constructing defences and later taking part in large-scale exercises.

By 1942 the battalion had moved to Norfolk, with headquarters variously at North Walsham, Stalham, Happisburg and Sheringham. The commander, Lieutenant-Colonel F W Clowes, was replaced in July 1942 by Lieutenant-Colonel H Long, MC, and the battalion joined 176th Brigade of the 59th Infantry Division in Northern Ireland. This was to be the unit in which they would fight once again in France.

In March 1943 Long was posted to the Middle East and Lieutenant-Colonel

D M Fitzgerald took over until July, when he was replaced by Lieutenant-Colonel T G L Charles. By now the battalion was in Kent, preparing for the liberation of Europe. Training continued all the way through until six weeks before D-Day in June 1944, by which time the new battalion commander was Lieutenant-Colonel I H Freeland. The 7th Battalion, as part of the 59th Division, was scheduled to land in Normandy sixteen days after the initial landings.

7

Far East 1939–1945

Some 15,000 men from East Anglia were mobilized to find themselves in the 18th Infantry Division. Our focus is on the fate of the three Royal Norfolk Regiment Territorial Battalions: the 4th, 5th and 6th. The 18th Infantry Division, of which these battalions were a part, has often been referred to as the Lost Division.

At first the men busied themselves with anti-invasion duties, but by September 1941, after they had been issued with tropical kit, the rumour was that they were heading for the Middle East. These ill-fated battalions were actually bound for Singapore, 20,000 miles away. They sailed from Liverpool to Halifax in Canada and then on to Cape Town and then Bombay, arriving there on 27 December 1941.

As the three battalions embarked at Bombay bound for their final destination of Singapore the last British troops were pulling out of Malaya. The Causeway across the Johor Straits was blown up behind the remnants of the 2nd Argyll and Sutherland Highlanders. The 18th Division, having been trained for desert warfare, and at sea for three months, was thrown into a hopeless situation. After seventeen days of fighting, what remained of the 4th, 5th and 6th Battalions of the Royal Norfolk Regiment marched into the uncertainty of captivity.

We look at the exploits of these three battalions separately before returning to see how the 2nd Battalion distinguished itself in a wholly new theatre of war – Burma.

The 4th Battalion

The 4th Battalion's headquarters was initially based at Chapelfield Drill Hall in Norwich. A and D Companies were in Great Yarmouth, B Company was at Thetford, Attleborough, Wymondham and Watton and C Company at Diss, Harleston, and Long Stratton. The commanding officer was Lieutenant-Colonel J H Jewson. At the end of September 1939 battalion headquarters and the HQ Company moved to Great Yarmouth. The officers' mess was set up at the Central Hotel in York Road. The rest of the battalion was concentrated around Great Yarmouth and Gorleston; a number of them were billeted at the Gorleston Holiday Camp. The battalion also requisitioned Great Yarmouth Race Course.

Training was well under way and men began arriving as enlisted soldiers in July 1940. Their initial training lasted for three weeks. Soon after Dunkirk there was

Group portrait of men of No. 1 Platoon, A Company, of the 4th Battalion the Norfolk Regiment posing formally outdoors with a tent in the background, dated 1921

much to be done to protect the east coast of England from invasion. The battalion was responsible for the coastline from Caister down to Hopton. They built emplacements, dug tank ditches and laid minefields. They were assisted by the Great Yarmouth detachment of the 8th Battalion of the Royal Norfolks, as well as the Home Guard and naval personnel. It was around this time that the battalion suffered its first fatalities; two men were killed from A Company while laying mines in front of the race course.

The feverish activity to protect their stretch of coastline was not achieved without some problems with local groups. When they dug a tank ditch across Great Yarmouth golf course and when the road blocks slowed down buses there was a need for a good deal of public relations work. A huge crowd gathered to watch the battalion blow a gap in Britannia Pier at Great Yarmouth, but again it was a public relations disaster because many of the houses on Marine Parade lost their windows. One of the locals, who happened to be a major shareholder in the pier, was told: 'Well, Tom, that's the first time you've seen so much of your money go up in smoke.'

The battalion was also responsible for dealing with unexploded bombs, led by Lieutenant Pringle of the 260th Field Company of the Royal Engineers. The battalion continued to man the defences until September 1940 when it was relieved by the 4th Suffolk Regiment.

By November 1940 the battalion was in Cambridge undergoing training but in January 1941 the men were warned that they were to head for Hawick in Scotland. They were housed in an old prisoner of war camp called Stobbs Camp, about five miles from Hawick. It was also around this time that, despite deep snow, the battalion was issued with tropical kit and granted embarkation leave.

In April 1941 the battalion moved to Blackburn and after yet more training they moved to Ross-on-Wye in the July. By now the battalion was very well trained and highly motivated. There were fresh rumours by the autumn about overseas postings and in October 1941 Jewson was promoted and succeeded by the second in command, Lieutenant-Colonel A E Knights, MC MM.

The battalion entrained for Liverpool on 28 October and in the morning of the following day embarked on HMT *Andes*. There was still no clue as to their final destination. They eventually saw the southern tip of Iceland and, according to Knights himself:

> The voyage was uneventful until one morning in November, at daybreak, aircraft bearing the markings of the United States of America came swooping over the convoy. A dropped message contained a welcome from the US Navy. Then over the horizon, steaming towards the convoy appeared what seemed to be a veritable armada. This new escort consisted of one battleship, one aircraft carrier, two cruisers and several destroyers.

At this point the Royal Navy turned around to head for home.

Under US protection the 4th sailed into Halifax on 8 November. The battalion was accommodated on USS *Wakefield* and there was no shore leave. Soon afterwards they sailed south towards the West Indies, stopping off at Trinidad for refuelling. The convoy then passed around Cape St Roque, the most easterly point of South America, and then made for Cape Town. It was on 8 December, a day out from Cape Town that word was received that the Japanese had attacked Pearl Harbor and that Britain and the United States were now at war with the Japanese.

The convoy left Cape Town on 13 December 1941, heading into the Indian Ocean and then making towards Mombasa. The battalion spent Christmas Day in the Indian Ocean and on 27 December they entered the harbour of Bombay.

The battalion entrained to Ahmednagar on 28 December, but by 14 January 1942 they were back, heading for Bombay once more. Once again they clambered aboard USS *Wakefield*. Their first sight of the enemy occurred on 28 January when a solitary Japanese aircraft flew over the convoy.

The following day they were in Keppel Harbour in Singapore, amidst an air raid. The mainland of Malaya had been abandoned on the night of 30 January and the battalion was allocated a tented camp, known as Hill 85. At first the battalion, part of 54th Brigade, was put into reserve and this gave them a chance to acquaint themselves with the countryside. Part of the brigade's responsibility was the island of Pulau Ubin, between the mainland and the island of Singapore.

A platoon from the battalion was sent to guard the island, under Lieutenant J B Hayne. All the platoon could do was to fight a delaying action, as around 1,000 Japanese invaded the island on the night of 7 to 8 February 1942.

A patrol commanded by Lieutenant P C Barr went out to the island on the night of 8 to 9 February; he had two missions. First he was to take a Japanese prisoner and secondly he had to try and find four men who had gone missing the previous night. They found that the island had been abandoned by the Japanese, or perhaps just a small section remained and hid from Barr and his men.

On the same night the Japanese had landed on the western side of Singapore Island and at 1000 hours on 10 February the battalion became part of Tom Force, under the command of Lieutenant-Colonel Thomas, DSO, of the Royal Northumberland Fusiliers. They were to proceed to an area southeast of the Singapore race course. As soon as they got there the battalion sent a patrol up the road as far as Bukit Pajang village. The road was clear of the enemy, but during the night of 10 to 11 February the Japanese took the village and at 0500 on 11 February the battalion was ordered to advance up the road and clear the Japanese from the village. The area was thickly wooded and the advance was difficult.

The first objective was to secure the high ground a mile north of the northern end of the race course. The battalion soon came under attack from low-flying enemy aircraft; they dropped bombs and smoke signals to indicate the Norfolks' position. The Japanese infantry opened up with machinegun and mortar fire, causing a number of casualties in B and C Companies. B Company, however, continued to advance on the village, but it was now clear that the Japanese were advancing in force on the right flank of the battalion, heading towards McRitchie Reservoir. It was decided that the battalion should withdraw back to its start positions near the race course.

No sooner had they done this than the Japanese began to surround the area. At dawn on 12 February 1942 Captain Gripper, at the head of a carrier patrol, set off to find the positions of the enemy. His section was overwhelmed and they were captured.

The Japanese then launched a major attack on A Company's position, led by tanks. A Company conducted a fighting withdrawal and the bulk of the battalion fell back to a new defence line to the north of Adam Road. This would be the last stand before Singapore.

By the morning of 13 February the battalion positions were under heavy fire and enemy shelling continued throughout the day and into the night. Some plans were afoot regarding evacuation from Singapore to India, but they led to nothing. Patrols were sent out at dawn on 14 February and at around 0800 hours once again the battalion positions came under heavy fire. A major Japanese attack developed at 2000; Japanese tanks and infantry broke through about a mile to the battalion's right.

At 0100 on 15 February, after another Japanese attack, it was clear that a counterattack had to be mounted to gain the ground that had been lost. What remained of B and C Companies stormed the high ground around Adam Road, taking the objectives by 1100. Two cars appeared at around 1200; one of them was flying a white flag over the Union Jack. Brigade headquarters was called and they confirmed that no firing would take place after 1600, but this was later pushed back to 2000. Having lost seventy-five officers and men killed, seventeen more having died of their wounds, sixty-five missing and 124 wounded, the battalion became prisoners of war.

The 5th Battalion

The 5th Battalion of the Royal Norfolk Regiment initially had its headquarters at King's Lynn, with men based at Dereham, Aylsham, North Walsham and Holt. But by November 1939 the battalion was concentrated around Holt. Shortly afterwards the battalion was moved to Weybourne's anti-aircraft practice camp. Following Dunkirk the battalion was responsible for defence work and in September 1940 went into reserve at Holt. The bulk of the battalion was based at Gresham School, by November they were in King's Lynn and billeted in warehouses on the docks. Finally, in January 1941 they were on the move to Scotland, via Doncaster, Catterick and Carlisle, then in March 1941 the battalion was sent to Cheshire; most of the battalion was accommodated at Marbury Hall, Northwich. In the September orders were received to prepare to go overseas.

The battalion embarked from the Clyde on 28 October 1941, on board SS *Duchess of Atholl*. They experienced a very similar journey to that of the 4th Battalion and they disembarked at Singapore on Friday 13 January 1942. The commander of the battalion, Lieutenant-Colonel E C Prattley, readied the men for imminent combat. The battalion took up defensive positions in the village of Yongpeng on 16 January; they were to move up to their primary position at Jemaluang on the east coast of Johor the following morning.

By 21 January the battalion patrols had made contact with the Japanese. Initially they were responsible for holding open the road to Batu Pahat, on the west coast. The story is taken up by Major H T Crane, who was adjutant of the battalion from 1936 to 1939. He went overseas with the battalion and was taken prisoner at Singapore:

> During the evening [21 January] the road to Batu–Pahat on the west coast was reported blocked. At dawn on the 22nd, patrols made contact with the troops from Batu Pahat at the 73rd milestone and reported the road open. The battalion was ordered to keep the road open throughout the day. At about 1600 hours, D Company made contact with the enemy near the 73rd milestone. One platoon was ambushed and Captain Boardman was killed. Orders for the battalion to move into Batu Pahat were received about 17.30 hours. In the meantime, it was reported that the road was again blocked.

The battalion was then ordered to concentrate for the night near the 72nd milestone and move on to Batu Pahat next morning. On the morning of the 23rd, at dawn the advance guard encountered a strongly defended road block. B Company attacked the block but was unsuccessful, suffering several casualties including Lieutenant McKean killed and Lieutenant G H Pallister seriously wounded (later died of wounds). C Company attacked round the south flank and got two platoons round the block but had not again reached the road, when at 11.30 the Div. Commander ordered the battalion to withdraw back to Ayer Hitam.

At around 1300 hours the battalion was told to move to Batu Pahat and then head towards Skudai. They arrived there only to be told, on 24 January, to move back towards Batu Pahat. Most of the town had been abandoned and now the battalion was ordered to retake the positions. They succeeded, with the exception of some high ground to the east of the main road. At 0400 on 25 January 1942 C Company and the remnants of a company from the 2nd Cambridgeshire Regiment tried to storm the high ground. Owing to heavy enemy fire they again failed, but by 1300 new orders told the battalion to hold its present position and cover the withdrawal of the 2nd Cambridgeshire Regiment before pulling back themselves. By 2100 they had abandoned the position and were concentrating round the nearby airfield.

Alarming news was received by the battalion the following morning, 26 January; the road to their rear had been blocked by the Japanese. There were around 250 vehicles trying to get through, but the blocks had not been cleared. At 1745 the brigade commander ordered all the transport to be destroyed and for the men to work their way south through the jungle. A bridge across the river was blown at 1830 and by 27 January, under the command of Major Wood and ably assisted by Captain F Wallace (one of the interpreters), about 500 members of the battalion had reached Bennut. Another party from the battalion, under Captain Schulman (of A Company), had made it to the coast and were taken off by the Royal Navy.

By 28 January 1942 the bulk of the 5th Battalion was in Singapore, at the Serangoon Road camp. For the next couple of days they were reorganized, but on 3 February they headed towards the north of the island to help protect the naval base. On 4 February the battalion worked feverishly to improve the defence works. The Japanese, however, had started to shell the area and this continued through to 7 February. The shelling wounded Major C P Wood, of C Company, and Major Crane left to take command of the 6th Battalion of the Royal Norfolks.

On 12 February 1942 the battalion was ordered to withdraw and take up their position in the defensive perimeter around Singapore City. The Japanese had landed on the west coast of the island and the retreat was a perilous one, as the Japanese had complete air superiority. On 13 February the battalion had taken up its positions in the Braddell Road area. The Japanese attacked the forward platoon of A Company that night.

Early on 14 February the Japanese launched a major attack on the 2nd Cambridgeshire Regiment, forcing them out of position and leaving the 4th Battalion's left flank exposed. A counterattack by the 2nd Cambridgeshires readjusted the line. During the night Japanese troops infiltrated the left of the battalion, around the positions held by C Company.

The Japanese threw themselves at the 5th Battalion's frontline from dawn until 1600 hours on 15 February. Shortly afterwards the order to cease fire was received; the British troops would surrender with immediate effect. At this stage the battalion had thirty officers and 660 other ranks, although more would turn up later in captivity.

The 6th Battalion

When war broke out in 1939 the 6th Battalion was known as the City of Norwich Battalion. It was mobilized at the Aylsham Road Drill Hall in Norwich, under the command of Lieutenant-Colonel D G Buxton. To begin with it was a very weak battalion and there were insufficient men to form a D Company. As soon as the 6th was mobilized A and B Companies were despatched to Hemsby and billeted at the holiday camp. C Company assumed guard duties at Watton airfield and the remainder of the men stayed in billets in Norwich. Around the middle of November 1939 the 6th was ordered to Aylsham and training took place in Blickling Park. After a fortnight the battalion moved to Sheringham and were quartered in hotels and private houses in the town. Christmas dinner was enjoyed in the basement of the Grand Hotel. On the evening of Christmas Day, when around a quarter of the unit was on leave, a stand to was ordered and they had to man positions along the coast for several hours.

Most of the transport being used by the battalion was in fact civilian vehicles. They trained throughout the early months of 1940, preparing themselves for war. By the end of May 1940 Buxton was replaced by Lieutenant-Colonel F L Cubitt. The battalion had already made its first contribution to the war effort; a Lewis gun post at East Runton had shot down a German aircraft and it had come down to the east of Cromer. 140 new reinforcements arrived in June 1940 from the Northamptonshire and the Essex Regiment. The 6th was now close to full strength.

Towards the end of August 1940 the 6th was relieved by the 2nd Battalion of the Cambridgeshire Regiment and moved to Holt, where it was quartered in the buildings and grounds of Gresham School. In the October, the 6th Battalion moved to Weybourne, taking over coastal defences from the 5th Battalion of the Royal Norfolk Regiment. The battalion was back in reserve and stationed at Swaffham in November and this is where they spent their second Christmas.

On 5 January 1941 the battalion moved up to Scotland. They arrived in Dumfries and were quartered in a large mill on the outskirts of the town. Training continued and the battalion took part in exercises as far away as Berwick and Edinburgh. They had been issued with tropical kit, but they were not to go abroad straight away; instead they were transferred to Western Command and stationed in the Northwich district and carried out exercises around Shrewsbury and Birmingham. By this stage Buxton had been replaced by Lieutenant-Colonel J F Ross and he in turn had been replaced in May by Lieutenant-Colonel I C G Lywood.

More exercises followed throughout the summer of 1941 but finally the battalion moved to entrain, bound for Gourock, near Inverclyde in Scotland on the Firth of Clyde, on 27 October. Here they boarded the *Duchess of Atholl*, along with the 5th Battalion. They disembarked on Singapore Island on 13 January 1942, having travelled to Canada, Trinidad, Cape Town, India and the Maldives.

To begin with the battalion thought that they were going to be moving on to the mainland of Malaya for training in jungle warfare. They also needed additional training, as they had spent three months at sea. However this was not to be the case; they were immediately given a defensive position astride the Muar to Yong Peng road. They were based on a ridge ten miles to the south of Muar. It was an important position because it covered the lines of communication for the 45th Infantry Brigade who were based at Muar and under heavy attack from the Japanese.

18 January saw the battalion's baptism of fire when Japanese aircraft dive-bombed C and D Company, as well as the battalion headquarters. On the same day forward patrols from the battalion ran into Japanese probes to the west. There was worrying news from retreating Australian troops that Japanese infantry had cut off the 43rd Infantry Brigade and attacked the rear units of the Australian troops only six miles to the north.

The following day Japanese troops attacked C Company on the left or west flank of the battalion. They overran C Company and seized the road at the top of the ridge behind D Company. They were counterattacked by Indian troops and B Company, but to no avail. Punjabi troops moved up for another counterattack that night and threw in an attack at dawn on 20 January but they were beaten back with heavy casualties. Lywood was evacuated and Major A B Cubitt took over command. Effectively he just had A and B Companies and the remnants of C Company.

The whole brigade began falling back at around midday on 23 January. The 6th Battalion operated as the rearguard. The Japanese were at their throats the whole time and the battalion fended off enemy attacks until 1930, when they were able to withdraw to Yong Peng.

Lieutenant-Colonel (then Major) H S Ling, MC, takes up the story:

On the night of 24/25 January, the battalion moved to Sanggarang with battalion HQ and B Company, leaving A Company at Rengit, nine miles south of Sanggarang. The battalion was to hold the river crossings at both places in support of the 15th Infantry Brigade at Batu Pahat, nine miles to the north on the west coast of Malaya. The 15th Infantry Brigade was composed of 5th Royal Norfolk, 2nd Cambridgeshire, and the British Battalion (composed of the amalgamated Leicestershire and East Surrey regular battalions), and this was the first occasion during the battle when other units of the 53rd Brigade were near at hand. Information was received that there were no enemy south of Batu Pahat, but soon after dawn on arrival at Sanggarang, the enemy attacked from the south, and established road blocks between Sanggarang and Rengit. A force composed of 6th Battalion reinforcements from Singapore, armoured cars, a section of 4.5 Howitzers, endeavoured unsuccessfully to clear the road blocks from Rengit and suffered very severe casualties. Rengit was attacked soon afterwards, and A Company having held off all the attacks, was ordered by Brigade HQ to withdraw to Benut by the jungle, which they accomplished very successfully.

The 6th Battalion struggled their way through nearly impossible terrain and managed to get themselves to the west coast. To their horror they discovered that Benut was already in Japanese hands and they were evacuated by gunboats to Singapore.

By the time the battalion was reorganized and re-equipped it was 3 February 1942. Effectively the battalion had just three companies; A, B and C. The remnants of D Company, who had managed to get back to the battalion, had been allocated to the other three companies. For the next nine days they worked hard to protect their part of the defensive line on the north coast of Singapore Island, close to the River Seletar. Despite the setbacks morale was high and the men were confident that they could hold off the Japanese.

Regrettably the attack did not come from this direction; instead the Japanese attacked to the west of the causeway, which meant that the brigade had to withdraw as soon as possible, otherwise they would be cut off. The 6th covered the brigade's withdrawal over the River Seletar and they took up a position at the 7th milestone on the road from the naval base to Singapore City. They stood alongside the 2nd Cambridgeshire Regiment and the 2/19 Australian Battalion.

On 13 February 1942 the Japanese attacked in force and managed to infiltrate their way through the defensive positions in the jungle. By dawn on 14 February the battalion was forced to withdraw towards the Braddell Road. It was here that they received the shocking news that there was to be an end of hostilities at 1600 on 15 February. Two days later the battalion marched to Changi Barracks, on the east coast of Singapore Island, to begin three and a half years as prisoners of war.

Prisoners of War

The 6th Battalion's experiences as prisoners of war are typical of those suffered by the other two battalions. At first the barracks at Changi were adequate; there was not enough room or sufficient food and very quickly vegetable gardens were started. In April 1942 the Japanese started to demand that work parties go out to salvage, reconstruct and to load ships. As many as 1,000 men at a time were sent out on these duties.

Once again Ling takes up the story:

> In August [1942] all officers of the rank of full colonel and above left for Japan. The remaining officers were not segregated from the troops until the last eight months of captivity, and were thus able to carry out the necessary administration and welfare of the troops as far as was practicable. In June a party under Captain Goddard proceeded to Thailand (Siam) to build a railway. We had then no idea it was the commencement of the famous Thailand-Burma railway that so many of us were to take part in. Troops started to be paid for work by the Japanese. October saw the beginning of the exodus to Thailand both from Singapore and Changi. Those few left behind at Changi all felt rather desolate and depressed. Little was known then of the destination of the large numbers who had left the island for the mainland, nor of the work on which they were to be employed, but it was thought that any change must be for the better, and that the ration position could not be worse than Changi.

As so many of us now already know, conditions on the Thailand to Burma railway, the aptly named Railway of Hell, relied on forced labour. The brutal conditions under which the troops lived, with inadequate rations, non-existent medical care, appalling cross-country treks and countless examples of mindless violence, were to become the realities for the men, as Ling explained:

> We were housed in bamboo huts with attap [palm leaf] roofs, and allowed one metre per man sleeping accommodation. The railway track followed the river, or close to it, so that water and bathing facilities were at hand. The main food was rice, with vegetables and occasionally meat. Two great boons were the big Siamese duck farms which allowed us to purchase eggs, and tobacco for cigarettes which we rolled ourselves. At the end of the year 1942, officers were forced to work. As the railway progressed so working parties went further up country into the jungle and hills. Here supplies were not so good and food consisted mostly of rice and dried vegetables. Troops lived in tents in many cases, quite unrainproof and were thus never dry in the monsoon. The one redeeming feature was the warm climate so that the lack of clothing and bedding was a little offset. Most of the men

had possibly one pair of shorts, some old boots or wooden sandals. The Japs issued practically no clothing during the whole time. The first casualties commenced with the spiked bamboos which had to be cleared. These invariably produced ulcers, and as the Japs refused to let the men rest, they became appalling, many men having to have their legs amputated. As we moved up country, malaria started and remained with us for all the time. Shortage of quinine did not assist. Then came cholera, diphtheria, beri-beri, amoebic dysentery and chronic diarrhoea.

The railway, which was completed in October 1943, had cost the lives of at least 13,000 prisoners.

As soon as the railway was finished the camps were broken up and many of the men had a short period of time in which to try to recuperate. But by June 1944 an entirely new horror faced the captives. Many were to be sent to Japan or to Formosa, Taiwan. One of the ships was sunk by allied naval forces and Lieutenant Cox and sixteen other ranks of the 6th Battalion were lost.

For the remnants of the 6th their first sight of allied forces came with a daytime bombing attack on the bridge near Tamakan Camp. It put the men in great heart and three raids later the bridge was smashed to pieces, as was the railway line and several railway engines. Ling described the last months of captivity:

In Nov. 1944, officers were segregated from the troops, which was a very definite sign that all was far from well with the enemy. What a change from their bombastic attitude at the beginning. All officers went to Cajanburie Camp and the Warrant Officers were left in charge of the Other Ranks Camp with RSM Middeton at Petburie and CSM Rudling at Saigon in Indochina, where a party had gone from Singapore. All during this time we had wireless sets made and maintained in many ingenious ways. It was tricky to disseminate news in the large camps, with the fear that someone might be overheard discussing current news. The 6th of June 1944 was a great days news, after we had been feverishly awaiting for the hoped landing. Only one wireless set was found by the Japs after many searches by the Kempi (Jap Gestapo) and it was known that two or three officers were beaten to death during the searches. So it went on till 15th of August, 1945 when rumours flew around and finally it was known that the war was over. At once an HQ was set up at Bangkok and officers posted to all OR Camps to take over from the Jap guards and organise the evacuation. Officers and supplies from Burma were parachuted by Dakotas on camps. On return to England the battalion held a reunion party at the Sampson and Hercules in Norwich on the 21st January 1946. It was organised by Lieutenant-Colonel D G Buxton, the first CO of the battalion. The other CO present being the last, Lieutenant-Colonel A B Cubitt. Relations and friends were asked and some 700 were present.

The casualties for the battalion during the Malayan campaign and during their period as prisoners of war were fourteen officers killed or died and 310 other ranks.

The 2nd Battalion in Britain

We left what remained of the 2nd Battalion back in England on 7 June 1940. The battalion was by no means done and it was quickly replenished with a draft of 350 men sent from Blandford Camp in Dorset. The battalion was concentrated on the outskirts of Bradford in Yorkshire and many of the new men were from Essex or from Berkshire. They also received a draft of NCOs from the 1st Battalion of the Royal Norfolk Regiment. As the battalion trained and reorganized it was stationed at Hessle, near the Humber, where it could see the terrifying German air raids on Hull.

The battalion was responsible for coastal defence duties and in January 1941 they moved to Scotland to try out new landing craft. They also took part in manœuvres and exercises on Ilkley Moors. By December 1941 they were moved down to Fairford in Gloucestershire and had been issued with tropical kit; the strong rumour was that they were headed for India as part of the British 2nd Infantry Division.

The 2nd Battalion in the Far East

The battalion sailed onboard the former tramp steamer, SS *Orbita*, from Glasgow on 15 April 1942. It was one of the largest convoys that had ever left Britain and the men were in cramped conditions, sleeping in hammocks. The convoy sailed along the west coast of Africa and on to Cape Town, leaving South Africa on 19 May 1942. The battalion eventually arrived at Bombay and were entrained for Chinchwad Camp.

In early July 1942 they moved to Kharkvasla for a variety of exercises. They were then to move to their home base of Ahmednagar. The battalion was involved in internal security operations in August 1942 and continued training through to the beginning of January 1943. By this time the battalion had been fully rebuilt and was a mixture of conscripts, territorial and regulars.

The situation in the Far East was very dangerous; in stages the Japanese had systematically overrun Burma and by the spring of 1944 they had even penetrated the border region of India. It would be at Kohima where the battalion would show its mettle and go some way in erasing the debacle that had led to the evacuation at Dunkirk.

The British and Commonwealth forces based in India are often referred to as the Forgotten Army. The allies had adopted a Germany-first policy; in other words, the majority of manpower and resources would be thrown at knocking the Germans out of the war before any serious attempt to roll back the Japanese was to be made. Consequently it was a period of frustration for the allies in the Far East. There was an inadequate number of men, they were last in line for equipment and even relatively modest offensive plans ended up being shelved due to lack of resources.

The Japanese had tried to invade India in February 1944, but now, in the March, they threw three divisions across the River Chindwin; their objectives were to capture the base of the British IV Corps at Imphal and to seize Dimapur, in order to cut communications into the Assam Valley. Effectively this would have cut off allied forces in north Burma and, at the same time, stopped the allies from flying in supplies from the airfields in Assam to China. The Japanese 15th and 33rd Divisions were tasked with the capture of Imphal, the 31st Division would cut the road from Imphal to Kohima, then move on Kohima and take Dimapur. By 5 April 1944 the road to Kohima had been cut and the Japanese were close to Kohima. The allied 2nd Division was rushed north, 875 miles by rail and then another 600 miles by aircraft, to Dimapur. They would now have to make their way to Kohima, still 45 miles distant. The roads were not only dreadful, but incredibly steep.

As part of the 6th Brigade the battalion began digging in at Nichuguard, some seven miles from Dimapur, in order to defend the base. Based on notes written by Lieutenant-Colonel C R Murray Brown, DSO:

> By 10th April the battalion was organised and B Company was ordered forward to Ghorpani, a village 13 miles up the road. Japanese had been reported there and in fact a small patrol was later learned to have penetrated as far as the railway. B Company reported Japanese round their wire during the night of 10/11 April but no action took place. A Company was pushed up to Priphema, milestone 28, to relieve troops of 5 Brigade and on 11th April the battalion less B Company was installed there. The battalion transport had not yet arrived, and the journey in ramshackle motor transport with Indian drivers was something of an experience.

For some members of the battalion a chance to get to grips with the enemy would not be far off. It was to come on 15 April 1944, as Murray Brown recounted:

> There was at that time so little information and so much of an exercise atmosphere, and a very badly umpired exercise at that, that news of a successful attack by 1 Camerons of 5 Brigade on 14 April provided an excellent tonic; although the constant arduous patrolling on which the battalion was engaged from Priphema though providing excellent toughening training, was not relieved by any contact with the enemy. On the night of 15th April, however, No. 18 Platoon of D Company commanded by Sergeant Hazell, which had been sent up the road as an escort to a troop of tanks, was heavily attacked in harbour by a platoon plus of Japanese. Sergeant Hazell held his fire until the last moment, with excellent results and his platoon got quite a good bag at the cost of Private Woodward, died of wounds, and one other casualty.

In fact Hazell's men had been set upon by 100 Japanese and they had managed to kill around thirty of them. Hazell himself recalled the incident:

> After the first few shots they dived into the trees and returned the fire. The whole exchange of fire must have lasted about an hour and then it petered out. I had three of the lads hit. We had no idea of how many we'd killed. Someone from the 5th Brigade was aware of what was going on and had sent for the ambulances. The three wounded were taken away. One of them had been wounded in France, during the retreat to Dunkirk he got shot in the backside. As he passed me on his stretcher he sort of sat up, beamed at me and said, 'I've been shot in the arse again!' I wondered if it was his custom to stick his arse in the air to get it shot at.

The battalion continued to make aggressive patrols, hunting for Japanese infiltrators.

Kohima

On 21 April 1944 troops of the 6th Brigade entered Kohima and took over from the defenders. The defenders around Kohima had been subjected to constant fire and had suffered heavy casualties. All of the time, the Japanese had squeezed the box into which the defenders were trapped, but gallantly they had held on. It was still a highly confused and dangerous situation.

Japanese attacks along the Kohima ridge still continued and it culminated in a major Japanese assault on 23 April. By then the defenders were almost at breaking point, but the enemy were thrown back with tremendous losses. From that point onward the Japanese had to content themselves with trying to hold onto what ground they had gained and launch counterattacks whenever they could. The men that the Japanese had lost around Kohima meant fewer men for their assault on Imphal.

The commander of the 2nd Division, Major-General John Grover, now ordered Operation Strident. This would aim to cut the Japanese off by holding the road between Kohima and Imphal. Many members of the battalion referred to the operation as 'the trek'. They were to march into almost impenetrable jungle in order to cut the road behind the Japanese main lines. Murray Brown takes up the story:

> Each officer and man carried 100 rounds or its equivalent, two days light scale rations, half a blanket, gas cape, water sterilising tablets, a dah [a knife of Burmese origin] and his personal weapon and two grenades, with in addition a pick and shovel to every three men. The battalion moved off with 24 officers and 549 ORs strong. Surprise being the essence of the operation, brigade ordered the start at last light and the first stage of some

3 miles to Khonoma from the Iron Bridge on the Dimapur-Kohima road at milestone 40 which was under Japanese observation from across the valley, was begun at 1930. The going was slow and tedious, and Khonoma has many and steep entrances. In the pitch dark guides could not be found, and time and tempers were lost on all sides. Dawn had broken before the last of B Company arrived and it was some time before the battalion and much later before the column had been sorted out. The column had had little or no rest; the men were very heavily laden and the march had been carried out over strange country in pitch darkness and although the start of the next stage was delayed until after noon it was a tired column which moved off.

The battalion continued to make its way on 26 April 1944, cutting their way through virgin jungle and traversing steep hills. By now the column was behind Japanese lines. All of the movement could now be by day and the men soon learned to shave bamboo very finely in order to make smokeless fires to cook. After two days on half rations food began to run out and they now ate tinned fruit and milk and used Indian pattern rations.

By 1 May the battalion emerged on the second highest feature overlooking Kohima; they were to attack and capture the so-called GPT ridge, so named as it had been the location of the General Purposes Transport Company, one of the first positions the Japanese had captured when they attacked Kohima. From the battalion's new position they could call in artillery fire onto previously unobserved Japanese positions. The men were at around 7,000ft and the air was cold and clear and mercifully it was not raining. They could see the whole of the Kohima battlefield laid out below them. They spent 1 May reorganizing and sorting loads.

On 2 May 1944 they made for Oaks Hill, which would be the jumping off point for the assault. By now the Japanese were perfectly well aware of their presence, but by the afternoon of 2 May the battalion was installed on Oaks Hill. From here they could see virtually nothing. Allied patrols worked their way forward to discover the position of the Japanese.

With A Company in the lead the battalion moved down Oaks Hill on the morning of 4 May. Soon the battalion ran into fire and casualties began to mount. The men were told to conserve their ammunition until they could see a decent target. But every time a Japanese fired at them they received a burst of fire in return. The men began covering their advance by throwing grenades and cheering broke out when any Japanese were confronted. Murray Brown explained what happened next:

D Company were magnificent; running into a clear patch in the middle of which was a large Jap bunker, they never wavered but overran the position and mowed down those Japs who tried to escape. The speed of D Company had become so rapid that the rest of the column was somewhat strung out and in consequence the CO ordered a temporary halt to reorganise.

At around 1500 under the cover of a creeping barrage the men began to move forward again. Any Japanese foolish enough to have remained were bayoneted. The men surged forward, led by the commanding officer, brandishing a Japanese sword. They charged towards their objective using Bren guns, rifles and bayonets and an enormous number of Japanese were killed.

On the left parts of A and B Company ran into heavy machinegun fire from a bunker about 40 yards to their front. This was to become known as Norfolk Bunker. It had to be overrun to clear the line of communication down to the main road. Murray Brown explained its significance:

> Firstly there was the obvious fact that the longer it was left the stronger it would become. Secondly, it was unsound to evacuate temporarily the position captured in order to permit gunner support for an attack on Norfolk Bunker; the battalion was almost in a direct line with the bunker and the gun lines.

What the Norfolks did not know was that the bunker that had caused so much trouble was only the first of a series of them. After dark the carrier platoon made the assault, crossing a narrow ridge and knocking out the bunker. It then came under heavy machinegun fire and was forced to withdraw. The men were exhausted and had suffered fairly heavy casualties and to add to their misery there was now torrential rain, which filled their trenches with water.

Despite this everyone was determined to capture Norfolk Bunker and a strong attempt was made on 5 May, but the Japanese positions were far too strong and the storming party suffered 50 per cent casualties. The Ghurkhas tried on 7 May but they also failed. At this point the battalion was to go into reserve for rest before launching an attack on another hill, but Lieutenant-Colonel Scott, the commanding officer, was determined that the Norfolks should stay and try again to take the Norfolk Bunker.

A gun pit was dug on the night of 9 May and the gun brought up and camouflaged. An hour before dark the gun crew of the 100th Anti-tank Regiment crept into the gun pit. A second gun was brought up to just below the crest, to the north of the Norfolk Bunker. They began to open fire. As it grew dark C Company infiltrated a platoon over the crest but the Japanese counterattacked and thus another attempt to take the bunker had failed. The following day, on 11 May, the British launched an attack on Jail Hill, with the Norfolks giving supporting fire.

Still the Japanese stubbornly resisted, holding on to their defensive positions. This war of attrition had cost the battalion dearly and by 24 May they were down to fourteen officers and 366 men. A major assault was ordered at 0430 on 28 May.

C Company came under fire at around 0730 from the bunker positions. A Company was also pinned down. B Company moved forward and A and C companies dropped back to reserve. The Japanese positions were plastered by every available weapon, but they still came under withering fire as they forced their way forward. Scott led from the front, throwing grenades at the Japanese positions until he was severely wounded. By now the battalion had reached the reverse slope of the Japanese positions. Murray Brown took over temporary command of the battalion and, finally, on 30 May, the battalion moved back to Dimapur for a rest period. This ended their fighting at Kohima, but it had been at a heavy cost; seven officers and seventy-nine other ranks had been killed and thirteen officers and 150 other ranks wounded.

Within a week the 2nd Battalion was fighting on another ridge and this was just the beginning of what would be several months of fighting in Burma. On 10 April 1945 the battalion had moved to Myingyan with a view to being airlifted to Chittagong. By 15 April they were close to Calcutta and planning was well under way for an amphibious invasion to capture Rangoon in Burma. Preparations were well in hand when it was discovered that the Japanese had abandoned the city and that XV Indian Corps had occupied it without firing a shot. By this stage the battalion was no longer required for these operations, so they settled down near to Calcutta.

Large detachments of the battalion went off to assist XXXIV Indian Corps in the preparations for the liberation of Malaya; they were near Calcutta when the Japanese formally surrendered on 2 September 1945.

A small remnant of the battalion was left behind when the bulk of the men headed for Kalyan, near modern-day Mumbai, on the first stage of their journey home on 18 October 1945. In the period April 1944 to April 1945 the battalion had won a Victoria Cross, two Distinguished Service Orders, four Military Crosses, three Distinguished Conduct Medals, eight Military Medals and twenty-eight men had been mentioned in dispatches, including Sergeant Hazell, and two men had been given a Gallantry Certificate.

Chapter 8

Normandy to the Rhineland 1944–1945

The 1st Battalion had been training for their part in the invasion of Europe. They had spent a month at Inveraray in May 1943, followed by three weeks' training in the western Highlands then another fortnight at Tigabruich. They then moved into winter quarters in Nissen huts near Lockerbie. It was here that they shared the camp with the 2nd Battalion of the Royal Warwickshire Regiment. This battalion was to accompany them in almost every battle they would fight in the future. Their commander, Lieutenant-Colonel R H Bellamy also joined the 1st Battalion at around this time. They had a three-day break at Christmas 1943 and in January 1944 they moved to the east coast of Scotland for further training. The coastline around Burghead Bay, near Forres, bore a striking resemblance to a stretch of the Normandy coast that would be their objective.

They continued to carry out brigade and divisional level exercises and by the spring it was clear that the invasion was not only on, but it was also imminent. In mid-April they moved down to southern England to Hayward's Heath and it was here that the battalion received its final issues of equipment and reinforcement to bring them up to full strength. They carried out secret exercises and practised embarkation; these were the last dress rehearsals. The battalion band even came down from Norwich for a parade.

On 26 May the battalion camp was sealed and no one was allowed in or out. There was no mail and no access to a telephone. The men likened their existence at this time to being prisoners of war. Briefings began and all of the objectives and place names were given code names. The battalion's role was to push inland from the beach head gained by the assault brigade, link up with glider-borne British troops and push towards Caen.

The 1st Battalion and D-Day

On 1 June the battalion headed for their embarkation ports. The rifle companies A, B and C embarked on their landing craft and D Company and the tactical battalion headquarters were split so that if one of the craft should fail the battalion would still have command units. On Monday 4 June there was a twenty-four-hour cancellation due to poor weather, but the battalion set sail on

Royal Norfolks at Lion Sur Mer on D-Day, 6 June 1944

the morning of 5 June 1944.

As D-Day dawned the battalion was still well out from the Normandy coast. Overhead were supporting aircraft and troop carriers taking in the parachute brigades of the 6th Airborne Division. As they approached the coast they could hear naval shells smacking into the German defensive positions and see columns of smoke rising into the air. The men could spot some of the landmarks: a water tower and a strangely shaped white house. They approached the shore with German machinegun bullets hitting the water around the landing craft. One of the craft was hit just as the last man left it. From the battalion history the story is taken up:

> The beach – not the inferno all had imagined, was still not a healthy place. Many wounded were lying around, and mortar bombs still dropping regularly. A shred of white tape marked a safe lane through the coastal minefield then the first glimpse of enemy dead, killed in the preliminary bombardment and by the assault brigade, a quick close up of the water tower, and the battalion striking inland to its first assembly area. After a quick reorganisation, the unit was off again in the preordained march, passing the first column of enemy prisoners being escorted back to the beach – always an encouraging sight. And so into the first village, Hermanville. Here shelling was fairly intense, and several men were hit round an unpleasant crossroads.

The battalion continued to drive inland, but the progress was slower. The Germans were still in strong positions and the battalion dug itself in for its first night on enemy-held territory. The first night passed fairly quietly and they patiently waited for orders to move on. They finally advanced at around midday, through the village of Benouville, which was still infested with German snipers.

Orders were received that the Warwickshires were in difficulties in a wooded area called Lebisey. The Norfolk battalion moved toward the enemy-held ridge in the face of machinegun fire. C Company got into the wood but it was immediately apparent that without artillery support the Germans could not be forced out of their positions. The battalion withdrew at last light, having assisted the Warwickshires also to pull back.

By this stage it was apparent that the primary target of Caen would not be reached, but the allies had secured a major bridgehead and the troops were massing. The 1st Battalion had been blooded.

Caen

The battalion now found itself holding a 2,000m front. Three platoons covered the front line with a carrier platoon in support. This was an excellent position for patrols and the position became known as Duffers Drift. The Germans clearly did not know about the battalion's position and over the course of a week a large number of German troops, oblivious to the danger, motored down the road and were captured by the battalion.

D Company was sent out on a raid on 12 June 1944 and a week later a second was launched. Patrolling would be the main task for the time being, as they built up intelligence about the German positions in the area.

Preparing maps and air photographs for attack on Caen

Brigade HQ Command Post, July 1944

On the night of 7 to 8 July, under a full moon, the battalion moved up to an assembly area in order to launch a surprise attack on Lebisey. At 0400 the barrage began. The previous night the area had been softened up by the Royal Air Force. The men moved forward, making for their objectives at 0600 and four hours later Lebisey wood contained just dead Germans and there was no sign of an impending counterattack. The men dug in under heavy mortar and shell fire.

After four days rest the battalion marched across the Orne River and the Caen Canal and set up their HQ at Ranville. A detachment was placed at Escoville, which was mortared on a regular basis. A determined effort was being made to shatter the German defensive lines around Caen and, as the battalion history described, it was an unforgettable experience:

At dawn on 18th July the bombers started to come. It was an amazing sight to see about a thousand bombers unloading their bombs, and through field glasses the actual bombs could be seen falling. Behind this bombing came the armour: three divisions, 7th, 11th and Guards were all to have a hand. It was the big breakout from the bridgehead, the

*South of Escoville, 8 Brigade
attacks towards Troarn*

*Standing on a knocked out
German Mark IV tank*

Battery Command in Mandeville Wood

Questioning a deserter outside Troarn

country being chosen to suit the armour, with the hope of bringing the enemy army to battle on ground of our own choosing; 3 Div. was to follow the armour, and for once the battalion was reserve in the brigade.

The battalion got under way at 1400 and three and a half hours later they were ordered to assault a wood, again in support of the Warwickshires. They took their objectives and dug in for the night, expecting a dawn attack. But the Germans had withdrawn and the battalion advanced into Mandeville wood. The signs of the heavy bombing were plain to see; an upturned Tiger tank, dead and wounded horses and the surrounding countryside pockmarked like the moon.

After withstanding sporadic German artillery fire for several days the battalion was finally relieved by the Durham Light Infantry. They could have four days of real rest, and the battalion left I Corps to become part of Army Reserve.

Plans were now well advanced for the breakout and the drive through France and the 1st Battalion would play a major role in this operation. The breakout to the south of Caumont had been going on for three days when the battalion joined on the extreme right of VIII Corps. At first light on the morning of 3 August 1944 the battalion pushed reconnaissance parties out to link up with US forces. By nightfall they were at Le Reculay; effectively under the command of the 11th Armoured Division and closing with the new German forward defensive line.

On 4 August the battalion launched an assault on La Bistiere. The enemy was well prepared and held the battalion off, but at dawn the following day, under an artillery barrage, the village was stormed.

By now the 11th Division had driven a deep salient into the German lines. The 1st Battalion was relieved by the Royal Ulster Rifles and they moved up to relieve the 3rd Monmouthshires of the 159th Infantry Brigade. By the morning of 6 August 1944 the battalion was some four miles from Sourdevalle. The battalion was to advance on the village, but they would have to overcome a hill known to be held by the enemy near a village called Burcy. The battalion history explained the situation:

> Just after the leading company got into Burcy the fog lifted, to reveal the bulk of the battalion moving down this long forward slope. Although well dispersed, and with vehicles moving at a crawl to avoid dust, we must have been a sitting target for the enemy, and he took advantage of it. A Company got lost altogether trying to avoid the death trap of Burcy, and lost two officers and fifteen other ranks in doing so, not arriving at Sourdevalle till after the counterattack. C Company also got badly hit coming up, losing some key personnel.

Despite the setbacks, by 1700 the battalion was still surging forward. They watched as allied artillery pummelled the German positions. There were blazing vehicles and dead everywhere. In the chaos and confusion Thunderbolt aircraft

Mine prodders in Belgium, February 1945

shot up the battalion's positions. The Germans were pushing forward with their own counterattack and despite the bombardment they tried to close with the battalion. It was touch and go until 1930, when twenty or more Shermans of the Fife and Forfar Yeomanry arrived. This was the tipping point and by 2130, leaving behind enormous numbers of dead and wounded, the Germans had fled.

The men spent the night bathed in the light thrown out by the fires of burning vehicles. The engagement had cost them 160 killed and wounded and the battalion was down to 390 men. The battalion held the same position for five more days, under constant mortar and shell fire. They were eventually relieved on the night of 11 to 12 August and they had won their first major battle.

A reconnaissance party tackle a problem in map reading at Assen, Holland

Element of the 11th Armoured Division pass through Assen

Valkenswaard, Holland, the first Dutch village to be liberated by advanced units of the 2nd Army

Awaiting orders at Helmond, in southern Holland. The 1st Battalion was to take over positions from the Suffolks in September 1944.

Digging in, in Holland, 17 November 1944

At 0500 on 12 August 1944 the men were still sound asleep in an orchard near Le Reculay when orders were received that the Germans were in retreat and that all available units should begin the pursuit immediately. By 13 August the battalion was well on their way towards Tinchebray, settling in at the small village of La Masierie at 2000 hours.

Exactly twenty-four hours later the Royal Warwicks put in an attack against the German positions. They came under tremendous mortar fire and the attack broke up. Consequently the 1st Battalion was thrown in to relieve them. As night fell 1st Battalion patrols could find nothing of the enemy; again they had slipped away. The battalion was on the move again on 17 August and this time they moved into Tinchebray.

A patrol leaving Wijnhoverhof in Holland in January 1945

Belgium and Holland

Reinforcements had arrived in the August and by the end of the month the battalion was moving up again, in the wake of British and Commonwealth units surging across the Belgian frontier, liberating Brussels and forcing their way to the Dutch frontier. The battalion had been left out of this chase, but by 3 September 1944 they were at Viller en Vexin, around twenty miles to the north of Rouen. They received orders to move on the night of 17 to 18 September. Advance parties would move towards Brussels.

The battalion was engaged in operations to round up isolated German units in Holland. On 23 September they made their way to Asten in southern Holland. The Germans had not been cleared out of the area and the town was still under mortar and artillery fire. B Company received a shell straight through its HQ, but no one was hurt. After three days they were ordered to occupy the town of Helmond. Allied armour had moved through the outskirts but no one had been into the town itself. With a reconnaissance unit in the lead the battalion passed through a thick belt of woodland on the way to the town. By midday on 25 September they had reached the outskirts of the town and were met by a despatch rider. The orders were to advance on foot. The battalion expected the worst and advanced with caution, weapons ready. Instead of meeting a grimly determined German garrison the battalion was overwhelmed by jubilant Dutch civilians.

Crossing a Dutch river in 1944

D Company, supported by tanks and armoured fighting vehicles, ready to launch an attack near Lingen in Lower Saxony, Germany, in 1945

Officers of the 1st Battalion planning the final assault on Bremen

A 1st Battalion patrol in the shattered streets of Bremen in April 1945

Germany

Three days later the battalion was once again on the move, setting up camp about two miles to the northeast. They were close now to the German frontier and the battalion headed over the Grave Bridge on 3 October 1944 and into another wooded area. They were now no further than 3,000m from Germany itself. The battalion took over from US airborne troops that had been here since Operation Market Garden. The battalion was given a sector to overlook the massive Reichwald Forest, strongly held by German troops. Their orders were to dominate no-man's land. By 9 October the battalion was back heading towards Grave and then they headed south, across the River Maas.

Very few members of the battalion and for that matter not many readers will have heard of the tiny German village of Pfalzdorf, but it was in this village on 25 February 1945 that the 1st Battalion set foot on German soil. The whole village was jammed with allied men, vehicles and equipment. The battalion's objective was across flat and open ground, swept by German machineguns and mortars and the target was the town of Kerveheim.

The commander of the battalion, Lieutenant-Colonel Peter Barclay, DSO MC, led his men across the open ground, through outlying farm buildings and into the streets, forcing out or killing every German soldier that they found. A Company was decimated in the attack but the other three companies had a firm

Officers and men of S Company at Lubbecke, near Minden in Germany in 1945

D Company at Espelkamp, near Minden, after the German surrender in May 1945

hold and held it against all German counterattacks. It was only when two companies from the 2nd Lincolnshire Regiment arrived to lend a hand, on 2 March, that Barclay was finally able to confirm that the town was in allied hands.

The battalion then pushed on, taking Haus Winkel, then Emmerich and finally Dornich. It was then across the Rhine to Lingen. Soon after they were eight miles south of Bremen, at Barrien and in mid-April 1945 they were at a small village called Leeste. The fighting was still fierce.

One of the men, Johnnie Cowan, had been in the Royal Warwickshire Regiment, but had transferred to the 1st Battalion and joined B Company as a Bren gunner in time for the Normandy invasions in 1944. Cowan was blinded in both eyes by machinegun fire and two of his colleagues, Jack Pratt and Horace Reid, under the cover of smoke grenades, retrieved his body.

German resistance at times was still fanatical but the 1st Battalion pressed on to nearby Brinkum and then into Bremen itself. On the morning of 5 May 1945 the men were in what remained of the town of Delmenhorst when they received the following signal from brigade headquarters: 'To 1 Norfolk from 185 Brigade. Restricted. Cancel ALL offensive ops forthwith and CEASE FIRE 0800 hours 5 May 1945. Further details later.'

The men received the news with a sense of relief; since landing on the Normandy beaches fifteen officers and 235 men had been killed, forty-seven officers and 785 other ranks had been wounded, forty-six of them were missing and two officers and 148 men had been worn down to utter exhaustion.

The 7th Battalion and Normandy

We left the 7th Battalion in Kent, in the early summer of 1944, under the command of Lieutenant-Colonel I H Freeland. As part of the 176th Brigade of the 59th Division they were due to land in Normandy sixteen days after the initial invasion. They continued training right up until the last minute. The battalion was split into four parties for their move to Normandy; elements of the battalion would leave from Newhaven, Tilbury and Margate. The battalion would establish itself at Le Manoir, beginning on 28 June and this was seven miles to the northeast of Bayeux.

The 7th Battalion would be involved in the planned assault on Caen, which was due to be launched at 0420 on 8 July 1944. The attack was due to be in three phases, with the final phase being the capture of Caen itself. The primary objective allotted to the 7th was the village of Epron, in phase two of the operation. The village was two miles to the north of Caen. The battalion would be entirely reliant on other units having reached their objectives first. They knew that they would be advancing across open cornfields.

The battalion assembled north of Anguerny on 2 July and they launched reconnaissance patrols on 4 and 5 July and on the 6th practised moving through crops. Lieutenant-Colonel Freeland summarized the plan:

> The battalion would march to the forming up place early in the night 7/8 July and would dig itself in by first light on a slight reverse slope in the cornfields clear of the woods, which were registered enemy defensive fire targets. The high corn would hide the battalion from enemy observation at Lebisey. The forming up place and start line, a hedge, were well back from the present forward defended localities as it was essential to get the battalion well deployed and going strong before coming out into the open in front of 1 Suffolk.

All of the men were well prepared for their first taste of battle. At 0620 on 8 July they received orders that they were to get under way at 0730. It was assumed that phase one of the operation had been successful. No sooner had the leading companies got into the open than they came under heavy machinegun fire. The Bren gunners tried to fire back but the Germans had them virtually pinned down. The attack was a total and bloody failure, yet success could be achieved if the village of La Bijude could be captured.

Fifty men of the battalion were collected together to form a composite company. At around 1400 D Company, supported by tanks, began advancing on the village. One of the lead tanks was almost immediately hit by a German anti-tank weapon and the infantry began running into heavy fire. After around an hour D Company had established itself on the southern outskirts of the village and anti-tank guns were brought up. By now D Company was down to two officers and sixty-five other ranks; they were far too weak to try to take Epron.

There was still confusion; brigade thought Epron had been taken and new orders demanded that the battalion press on, clear La Bijude and then press onto Epron. What remained of the battalion started off again at 2030, closely supported by tanks. Freeland described the action:

> D Company quickly reached Auberge and reorganised, but A Company having more houses to clear, took longer [Auberge was a village to the south of Epron]. By 2200 hours the village was clear except for the odd sniper. Opposition had been slight apart from consistent shelling. By last light the battalion was firmly reorganised, with anti-tank guns and medium machineguns in position, and was ready for the expected counterattack. However, reconnaissance patrols during darkness brought back only negative information and so it appeared that the enemy had withdrawn out of contact after taking a terrific hammering. The dead left behind proved that beyond doubt.

On 9 July, with no counterattack having developed, A Company advanced into the abandoned village of Couvre-Chef. There was momentary confusion in Auberge when a squadron of British tanks supporting the 3rd Division attacked the 7th Battalion believing that the town was still in German hands. Luckily no casualties were sustained. The battalion remained for another day and a half at Epron, clearing up the battlefield and performing a memorial service for their casualties. Ten officers had been killed, were missing or had been wounded along with 142 other ranks. On 11 July the whole division moved back to Ryes, close to Arromanches, for rest, re-equipping and recuperation. The battalion spent three days there, receiving new officers and several men were promoted to replace lost men.

On 14 July 1944 the 59th Division came under the command of XXX Corps. The plan was to make thrusts towards the south, aiming for Thury Harcourt. It was intended that this would pin the bulk of the German forces in the area and allow a breakout. The 59th Division itself began concentrating north of Fontenay-le-Pesnil with orders to capture Noyers. This was on the main road from Caen to Villers Bocage. The area around Noyers was held by the British 49th Division and for two weeks they had been engaged in a struggle to capture Fontenay-le-Pesnil and Rauray.

The 7th, as part of the 176th Brigade, readied itself in reserve at Au Drieu, some three miles to the northeast of Tilly on 14 July. After waiting for thirty-six hours they moved forward and dug into cornfields, whilst the other two brigades attacked Noyers. The first attack had only limited success and on 17 July the order to attack was halted and the 59th Division was told to take up a defensive position, with all three brigades in line. The 176th Brigade moved up, without incident, and found themselves in bocage country; a patchwork of tiny fields, with high hedges and deep lanes. The battalion had to be constantly alert for enemy patrols and infiltration. The battalion deployed across a crossroads and the hamlet of Tessel Bretteville, with D and C Companies in the frontline and A Company and the carriers in reserve. For the next seven days they carried out aggressive patrolling against the German 986th Grenadier Regiment.

A typical incident involved a reconnaissance patrol of C Company, under the command of Lance-Sergeant Clarke:

> Coming upon enemy positions suddenly in the thick country this patrol killed three Germans without loss to themselves and gained much accurate information. The mortar platoon and Vickers guns carried out many harassing shoots, the former gaining much useful experience.

On 25 July the battalion was relieved and moved back into divisional reserve. The battalion would now have a new role, as Freeland explained:

> The battalion was given five counterattack tasks for which it was to be supported by 9R Tanks who were next to the battalion. When the

necessary reconnaissances had been carried out and the plans formulated both units got down to infantry and tank cooperation training. As a result an excellent liaison was formed and both units were confident in each other, especially as they had been told to expect to fight the next battle together when the attack on Villiers Bocage took place. While the battalion was in reserve, plans for the breakout were being made. On 2nd August the battalion moved to an assembly area west of Vendes in readiness for the attack of Villiers Bocage.

Villiers Bocage

The main weight of the German army in Normandy was around Caen and Villiers Bocage. The allies knew that in order to destroy the German 5th Panzer Army and the German 7th Army they would have to come to grips with them and pin them while the Americans broke south from the Cherbourg peninsula and then headed east. If the Americans could achieve this while the British held the Germans' attention then the enemy's line of retreat to the River Seine would be cut. The British and Commonwealth troops were under no illusions that this was going to be a very tough fight and that the Germans would resist every attempt to dislodge them. The 59th Division, now attached to XII Corps, was tasked with destroying the Germans covering Villiers Bocage and then to drive for the River Orne, around Thury Harcourt and hopefully get across the river. The 59th Division was flanked by the 50th on the right and the 53rd on the left. As soon as XII Corps got under way the 1st Canadian Army would attack Falaise from the north.

For the capture of Villiers Bocage the 176th Brigade, of which the 7th Battalion was a part, would initially be in reserve. It would be their role to pass through the other two brigades, capture Villiers Bocage itself and then drive to the River Orne. First the 197th Brigade would need to capture the high ground to the north of Villiers Bocage, while the 177th Brigade would hold the line to the north of Noyers.

The 197th's attack went well and on 3 August 1944, riding on top of Churchill tanks of the 9th Royal Tank Regiment, the battalion led the brigade to the northern outskirts of Villiers Bocage. By nightfall the brigade was five miles to the southeast of the town. During the night the 9th Royal Tank Regiment was replaced by CVII Royal Armoured Corps, which delayed the advance the following morning. Nonetheless, with B Company in the lead on Churchills, accompanied by two troops of Flails tanks (designed to set off mines) belonging to the Westminster Dragoons, and a troop of Royal Engineers, the advance began on 4 August.

As they approached the river they came under machinegun and mortar fire. Two of the Churchills were knocked out by a German 88mm anti-tank gun hidden on the far bank. B Company deployed to clear the Germans from their side of the bank and the battalion seized Ouffieres. The Germans had turned a group of houses close to the bank into a strongpoint. The riverbank was steep and wooded and difficult to get across. The Royal Engineers' tanks were brought up and assisted B Company in overwhelming the German strongpoint. By the end of the day the Germans had been completely cleared from the British side of the river. C Company was brought up on the left, with B and D Companies in reserve and A Company guarding the right.

River Orne

Plans now had to be made to cross the river. Reconnaissance was to be launched on the night of 5 to 6 August and tentatively the crossing would take place on the night of 6 to 7 August. The men, however, were absolutely exhausted and had not slept for forty-eight hours. Freeland described how the battalion carried out the reconnaissance:

> The Orne was known to be fordable in places, but difficult to bridge on account of its steep banks. The immediate requirements were therefore to find a place or places to wade across and a site to build a Class 40 bridge [a Bailey bridge capable of taking the weight of 40 tons]. Two patrols were sent out during the night 5/6 August. A fighting patrol from A Company under Lieutenant Paul covered a reconnaissance by an RE officer of the most likely crossing place, where the banks were not so steep as elsewhere. Further upstream C Company provided a covering patrol for a reconnaissance by an RE sergeant. This patrol was commanded by Major Walker the company commander. The RE sergeant was unsuccessful in his reconnaissance so Major Walker and Captain Jamieson tested the height of the bank in a very unorthodox manner. Captain Jamieson, who is 6ft 5inches tall, hung over the bank while Major Walker held his ankles. Being unable to reach the water Captain Jamieson proved that the banks were too steep for an assault crossing or a bridge building at that point.

Major Adderson of A Company also took out a patrol in the early morning, using mist as cover. Anderson took one man with him and they waded across the river, which was only 3ft deep at that point. They went 150m inland and discovered useful intelligence about the Germans defending this stretch of the river.

The decision was made for the whole of the 176th Brigade to wade the river. The 7th Norfolks would be last across, behind the 7th South Staffords and the 6th North Staffords. They would form a bridgehead just west of the Grimbosq Forest. A bridge would then be built at Le Bas. The initial crossing achieved total surprise and the two Stafford battalions achieved their objectives. By 0100 on 7 August the whole of the 7th Battalion was also across the river, with no casualties. The companies advanced towards their objectives. The Germans had been taken completely by surprise. Before the night was out, however, there was heavy fighting as the Germans began to respond.

Major Adderson, of the 7th, described what happened to his company that night:

> A Company advanced from the start line without incident, but on getting within 50 yards of their suspected objective very heavy fire was opened by the enemy. At 0340 hours the enemy counterattacked from the orchards to the left, but the attack was smashed by well controlled fire and the Germans withdrew in disorder. Sergeant Raynor was badly wounded in this attack, but gallantly remained in command of his platoon. A patrol was sent out to try to contact D Company on the left, but it ran into strong enemy positions and had to return after suffering casualties. For the rest of the night the company position was under continuous heavy close-range fire and it was impossible to dig in. At 0445 hours the enemy tried to work around to the right of 8 Platoon but were forced to withdrawn by accurate 2inch mortar and Bren fire. As soon as dawn broke, the enemy made a determined counterattack from the front. This was driven off with heavy loss. The enemy now proceeded to subject the position to intense mortar and Spandau fire and at 0815 hours, while the early morning mist was still about, the end came with an overwhelming attack from the right and rear. The last remaining Bren of 9 Platoon was kept in action until the end through the devotion to duty of Corporal Vasey, who, although three times wounded, kept the gun supplied with ammunition and inflicted heavy casualties upon the enemy. The remnants of the company were soon overrun and taken prisoner, their ammunition being exhausted.

A Company had fought to the bitter end; sixteen of them had been killed and three-quarters of all of the others had been wounded. Major Adderson, however, was only to be a prisoner of war for a short time, as he was liberated by American troops in Paris on 23 August 1944. C Company had tried their hardest to link up with A Company. By 0900 A Company's radio was no longer functioning. The battalion tried to find them throughout the day, but to no avail.

Meanwhile a bridge had been built across the river and tanks and anti-tank guns were beginning to arrive. They immediately came under fire from the Germans and suffered heavy casualties. The anti-tank guns were quickly deployed and a troop of Shermans arrived with D Company, with the remainder of the squadron in reserve behind battalion headquarters, which had dug in, in an orchard to the east of the road. The regimental aid post was set up in a nearby farmhouse. D Company was sent forward to clear houses to the south of Grimbosq, supported by a troop of Royal Engineer tanks. They came back with twelve prisoners from the German 271st Infantry Division. Lieutenant Buckerfield and the carrier platoon were stationed between C and D Companies. By midday the whole battalion was dug in, but now down to three companies they were in a precarious situation.

Spirits were raised at 1600 hours when hot food arrived; this was to be the last meal the men would have until the battle ended on 8 August 1944. Towards the end of the day Sergeant Smith took a patrol out from C Company with a troop of tanks to try and find A Company. They ran into Germans massing for a counterattack. Smith's men and the tanks managed to kill around twenty Germans before withdrawing, not having found any sign of A Company.

The Germans launched their major counterattack under the cover of darkness, primarily aimed at D Company. This action went on until around 2200 hours. A small German party broke through between D Company and the carrier sections, but they were counterattacked by a handful of men from battalion headquarters. Further to the right the Germans managed to get close to the bridge and German tanks started shelling the 7th Battalion's headquarters area. A sizeable number of Churchill tanks were knocked out and by now there were at least fifty wounded in the regimental aid post.

During the night the battalion launched patrols to warn of another possible attack. The men could hear German tanks moving around in the forest. As dawn broke on 8 August there was heavy mist and the Germans postponed their next attack until 0800 hours. This was preceded by heavy artillery and mortar fire. They focused on the anti-tank guns and on the Churchill tanks. The bulk of the German attack fell on D Company, as Freeland recalled:

> The Bosche infantry worked round through Grimbosq village and attacked D Company from two sides. The forward platoon was soon overrun and Lieutenant Bushell killed, whilst Sergeant Courtman, firing his last remaining gun alone under intense fire of all kinds, was killed by a tank shell. So died one of the bravest men of all times, who by his magnificent example had inspired the men of the D Company around him to superhuman efforts. A very confused situation now arose and Captain Jamieson, the only officer left in D Company, quickly reorganised the remnants of his two forward platoons round company headquarters, his reserve platoon and the remaining Churchill. A fierce fight now ensued at close range and it was while climbing up on the outside of the Churchill to attract the tank commander's attention towards an important target that Captain Jamieson was wounded near the right eye and in the left forearm.

Colour Sergeant-Major Jones took over command and Jamieson, after he had had his wounds dressed, and despite being in enormous pain, rushed back to rejoin the company. Together they held the Germans back, inflicting huge casualties. The Germans tried several more times that morning to overwhelm D Company. Jamieson stayed with his men and refused to be evacuated until his company was safe.

C Company, meanwhile, had been pummelled with shells and mortars and had suffered around seventy-five casualties. It was impossible for any of the wounded to be evacuated, as the Germans dominated the road towards the bridge. By the afternoon the ferocity of the German attacks abated, however there was still shelling and small arms fire and German tanks could still be heard.

At 1700 hours two companies of the 7th South Staffordshires, under Major A J C Prickett, of the Royal Norfolk Regiment, came under the command of the 7th Norfolks. One of the companies relieved D Company and the other cleared Grimbosq and another squadron of Churchills also arrived. The battalion had faced the 12th SS Hitler Jugend Panzer Division and the Germans had been badly mauled by the battalion; they were in retreat towards Falaise.

The main German attacks had been made the previous evening by the 26th Panzer Grenadier Regiment. The attacks during the morning of 8 August had been by the 25th Panzer Grenadier Regiment. One of the German prisoners captured admitted that of the 400 men of the 25th Panzer Grenadiers only

The regiment's 2nd Battalion band playing in a town square in Italy in 1945

thirty were left.

Jamieson was later awarded the Victoria Cross and collectively the battalion was praised for its courage and dogged determination. The whole forest area was strewn with German bodies. The 12th SS had dashed themselves to death trying to dislodge the 7th.

The whole operation against the Germans in this sector had sapped the strength of the British and Commonwealth units. Reinforcements were at a premium and, consequently, a great deal of reorganization had to be done. The battalion now became part of 177th Brigade when 176th Brigade was disbanded. To replace A Company the whole of A Company of the 7th South Staffordshires was transferred to the 7th Norfolks.

Falaise

The battalion joined 177th Brigade on 13 August 1944 and by then the destruction of the German 7th Army in the Falaise pocket had commenced. 197th Brigade was in the lead and had reached the high ground at Ouilly on the main road running west from Falaise. 177th Brigade would now pass through

Officers of the 30th Battalion in Italy in 1946, at the time of the battalion's disbandment

them and advance parallel to the River Orne, but on the east side. The battalion moved up by motor transport some ten miles northwest of Falaise and reached Ouilly at around 0300 on 17 August. The battalion would now operate as the advance guard.

Under Major Walker C Company marched on foot ahead of the column, starting off at 1000 hours on 18 August 1944. Freeland described the situation:

> The country was beautiful and there appeared to be no enemy about for the whole battalion moved down along open road, across a bridge over a tributary of the Orne at the bottom of the valley and up the open road on the far side without any opposition. However, the enemy was being very cunning for as soon as the vanguard reached the high ground west of Les Isles Bardel considerable Spandau fire was encountered and mortars and a battery of enemy guns shelled the road. C Company fought their way slowly to a sunken road with some casualties, but were unable to get any further. The enemy was on very dominating ground which completely overlooked all the approaches. It was also very difficult to pinpoint enemy positions and to select objectives, while the launching of a battalion attack from such disadvantageous ground would be a difficult undertaking. However, a complete battalion attack was obviously necessary to dislodge the enemy rearguard from such a strong position. Prisoners and civilians gave conflicting estimates of the enemy strength.

A squadron of Churchill tanks was called up and all the battalion could do was to wait. The Churchills would support an attack on the right made by A Company, with D Company following them up. C Company would give covering fire and B Company and the carriers would be held in reserve. British artillery would drop smoke onto enemy positions.

The attack went in without a hitch. A Company overwhelmed the German positions, suffering six casualties; D Company came up against no enemy opposition and A Company pushed on another 1,000m.

The following morning, 19 August, the battalion was ordered to clear a large wood 1,500m in front of the 5th South Staffordshires. This too was accomplished without incident. It allowed the South Staffordshires to advance another two miles before they ran into enemy positions. The 7th moved up that day to support the Staffordshires in case the Germans launched a counterattack, but on 20 August, as the South Staffordshires advanced slowly, the battalion worked around the left to take the high ground to the west of Bazoches. This position overlooked the main road from Falaise to Putanges. The battalion advanced around six miles and it was apparent that the Germans were withdrawing in disorder. There were broken-down vehicles and abandoned equipment and ammunition everywhere. A patrol from C Company also

Officers of the 1st Battalion, June 1945

managed to capture the intelligence officer of the German 374th Infantry Division. He had fallen asleep when his division had withdrawn and he confirmed the disastrous state that the German army was in.

On 21 August the battalion would carry out its final operation. It was to mop up an area and capture a German field dressing station, along with staff and a large number of wounded British prisoners. At the end of the day the 59th Division would be broken up and the infantry battalions would be dispersed to provide reinforcements for other units.

The battalion mustered for the last time at the scene of its greatest triumph, around the banks of the Orne. D Company would go to the 1st Battalion of the Royal Norfolks, B Company to the 1st Battalion of the Suffolks, C Company to the 1st Oxfordshire and Buckinghamshire and A Company to the 2nd Monmouthshires. The bulk of the headquarters company would go to either the 1st Battalion of the Norfolks or the 1st Battalion of the Suffolks. In effect the 7th Battalion ceased to exist on 26 August 1944. Freeland summarized their short but illustrious contribution:

During its short active service career for the second time in the war the 7th Battalion had made a name for itself which was in keeping with the highest traditions of the regiment. At the time of its dispersal, in spite of severe casualties, its morale and fighting record was of such a high order that it was singled out for special praise by not only the Divisional Commander, but by the Commander-in-Chief himself. In the two months fighting the battalion had been awarded one VC, two DSOs, one MC, ten MMs and five Mentions-in-Dispatches. In spite of the dispersal of its members the spirit of the battalion lived on and the success of all ranks in their new units can be determined by the following illustrations. On VE Day, three out of six CSMs in the 1st Battalion were ex 7th Battalion. The most notable decorations to be awarded to ex-members of the battalion were the DSO to Major H I Walker who finished as second in command 1 Oxfords and Bucks, the MC to Captain G Duxbury, 2 Gordons, and the DCM to C S M Langford of 1st Battalion. The 7th Battalion owes much to those members of the regiment, and other regiments, who helped to train it in England since 1940, but who were deprived of the privilege of fighting with it and sharing in its glory. The breaking up of a good battalion at the height of its success was a very bitter blow to all ranks. In spite of this all members felt that they had done their duty and had contributed a little towards the superb war record of the Royal Norfolk Regiment.

Chapter 9

Becoming the 1st East Anglian Regiment 1946–1964

The 1st Battalion in Germany

The 1st Battalion was in Bremen in May 1945 and shortly after it moved to Soligen to become part of the Allied Army of Occupation. In March the following year a battalion memorial was unveiled at Kervenheim and at the end of the month the battalion moved to Volksdorf, near Hamburg, where it joined the 7th Armoured Division.

Many of the men were due to be demobilized; some of them had skills that were needed back in civilian life, so these were the ones that were demobbed first. As for the rest, it was a question of first-in, first-out. This made it very difficult for the battalion, as National Service men were coming to replace them, all of whom would need considerable training.

The battalion settled down to its occupational duties and found new challenges in divisional sports. The tug of war team, for example, managed to win the Rhine Army Championship. After four months the battalion moved to Neuhaus, near Paderborn in Westphalia, into a former German cavalry barracks. Here it would remain until June 1947 and its duties included providing the demonstration company for the school of infantry of the British Army of the Rhine Training Centre.

New colours were presented to the battalion on 7 November 1946 and King George VI became the colonel-in-chief of the regiment on 31 January 1947. His father, George V, had been the colonel-in-chief for twenty-seven years, between 1910 and 1937.

Lieutenant-Colonel F P Barclay left the battalion in January 1947 to be taken over, until the September, by Lieutenant-Colonel A B Cubitt. He in turn was replaced by Lieutenant-Colonel G R Turner-Cain, DSO. By November 1947 the battalion had been posted to Berlin, where it was responsible for the city districts of the Tiergarten and Wilmersdorf. Relations with the Russians were strained at this time and particularly during the Berlin air lift period. During this time Lieutenant-Colonel R P Freeman-Taylor took over as commander of the battalion.

The battalion marching with fixed bayonets, with the band in the background, taken in Berlin in 1948

The battalion headquarters guard section being inspected by Field Marshal Montgomery in Berlin, Germany between 1947 and 1948

The 1st Battalion on parade at Sennelager, in the city of Paderborn in Germany in 1949

In the spring of 1949 the 1st Battalion was flown out from Gatow to Lubeck and then they took the train to Dusseldorf and spent the summer training there. The battalion's service in Germany came to an end in early 1951. Initially it was believed that they were bound for Malaya and other rumours suggested Hong Kong.

The battalion arrived at Dover in February 1951 and after a period of reinforcement and training they were mobilized for service in Korea. They sailed from Southampton on 30 August 1951, by which time the new commanding officer was Lieutenant-Colonel J H R Orlebar, who had taken over on 12 May.

A line of soldiers with fixed bayonets being inspected by Manny Shinwell then the Secretary of State for War, a position he held until 1950. This photograph was taken in Berlin between 1947 and 1948.

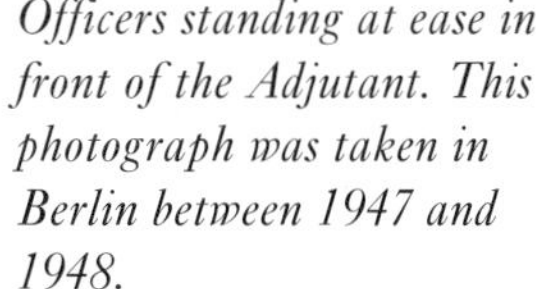

Officers standing at ease in front of the Adjutant. This photograph was taken in Berlin between 1947 and 1948.

The regimental colour marched off by Sergeant Fowler, Second Lieutenant Berney and Sergeant Jeery at Hubbelrath, near Dusseldorf in 1950

The saluting base with four officers. Lieutenant-Colonel Butler is on horseback and a sergeant holds a small flag. This photograph was taken at Dusseldorf in 1950.

The 2nd Battalion in India

Meanwhile, the 2nd Battalion, having been withdrawn from Burma in April 1945 for a possible amphibious landing at Japan, found itself in Kamaredi by October. From here around 70 per cent of the whole of the battalion was demobilized. By January 1946, after some changes in commander and the receiving of reinforcements, they were at Ramgarh, in Bihar Province, in a former Italian prisoner of war camp. The battalion was deployed in August 1946 to deal with civil disorder in Calcutta. The battalion was fully employed throughout the first half of 1947, dealing with civil disorder arising out of the creation of newly independent India and Pakistan. The decision had been taken to withdraw all troops from India and consequently on 3 August the lead elements of the battalion were onboard trains heading for Bombay. They would embark on HMT *Georgic* on 16 August. The battalion paraded on the quay on 17 August and was addressed by Lord Mountbatten, the Viceroy and Governor General. The ship docked at Liverpool on 3 September 1947.

In the post-war period it had been decided that all of the regiments would be reduced to one battalion and, as a consequence, the 2nd was due to be disbanded. The final disbandment took place in March 1948. The 2nd Battalion colours were laid up at Sandringham Church on 13 June 1948. This was the third time that the 2nd had been disbanded (1802 and 1815). This time they had served for ninety-one years.

Officers of the 2nd Battalion at Sialkot in the northeast of the Punjab (now Pakistan) in 1946

Saying farewell to General Strickland in 1946. Strickland had been commissioned in the Norfolk Regiment in 1888 and he saw service in Burma, Sudan, India, Nigeria, the western front in the First World War, Ireland and then again in Egypt. His full title was Sir Peter Strickland, KCB, KBE, CMG, DSO.

An inspection of the 1st Battalion by King George VI at Sandringham in 1947

The 4th Battalion in Greece

The 4th Battalion came back into existence in November 1945. Lieutenant-Colonel R P Freeman-Taylor became the commanding officer and the battalion was reformed at Morley Hall Camp in Wymondham. They received orders in January 1946 to prepare for overseas duties. There was confusion as to where the battalion would be deployed, but in the end they left Liverpool in May 1946 and arrived in Athens on 16 May. There was considerable civil disorder in Greece. The 4th was sent to Patras on the northwest coast of the Peloponnese as part of 179th Infantry Brigade.

After three months the battalion was broken up, with many of the men dispersed to other units. But early in 1947 it was decided to reform the battalion, as part of the new Territorial Army. In effect it would become the Territorial Infantry Battalion for Norfolk. Recruitment began on 1 May 1947. A former prisoner of the Japanese and member of the 4th Battalion, Lieutenant-Colonel R F Humphrey, became the new commanding officer, based at Norwich. The battalion had detachments at Great Yarmouth, Loddon, Harleston, Diss, Attleborough and Wymondham. Recruitment was slow and even by early 1950 there were still just twenty-two officers and ninety-one other ranks. National Service had proved to be a considerable obstacle in obtaining sufficient recruits.

Reorganization

During 1950 the battalion headquarters was moved to the Britannia Barracks in Norwich, which had been the regiment's home since 1887. Lieutenant-Colonel J F Wilkins took over command and the strength of the battalion had grown by July 1951 to twenty-five officers and 264 other ranks (135 National Service men).

Before looking at the further postings and exploits of the battalions, it is valuable to look at a strange organization that existed for just five years, between 1946 and 1951. Its existence causes some confusion. In October 1946 the British regiments were reorganized. Under this system regiments were grouped on a territorial or a traditional basis. The Royal Norfolk Regiment joined what became known as the East Anglian Brigade Group. In effect they joined the Suffolk, Essex, Bedfordshire and Hertfordshire and Northamptonshire Regiments. The idea was that new recruits would be centrally trained and the men would be put through a six-week course before joining the regiment. In June 1951 this system was abolished; although none of the regiments at the time would know it, a prototype template of merged regiments had been tested and would point towards the future for the regiment.

The 1st Battalion in Korea

The 1st Battalion arrived at Pusan in Korea on board the *Empire Orwell* on 30 September 1951 and joined the 29th Infantry Brigade, to relieve the 1st Battalion of the Royal Ulster Rifles. The situation in Korea had been born out of the Second World War. Almost arbitrarily the Russians had occupied the north and the Americans the south, splitting the country along the 38th Parallel. Five years of negotiations went on to try to reunify the country. The Russians and the Americans had withdrawn in 1949, leaving behind them two bitterly opposed factions.

When the 1st Battalion arrived Operation Commando was under way. This was aiming to establish a stronger bridgehead to the west of the Imjin River. The battalion had very little time to acclimatize itself. A Company moved up to relieve a company of the 1st Battalion of the King's Own Scottish Borderers at 1200 hours on 8 October 1951. They took over a hilltop position called Kowang-San.

On the following day the rest of the battalion moved up into line, taking over from the 1st Battalion of the Royal Northumberland Fusiliers. To their left was the 25th Canadian Infantry Brigade and to their right the 28th Commonwealth Infantry Brigade. Temporarily the 1st Battalion was attached to the 28th Commonwealth Infantry Brigade. This was a period of relative calm and the battalion stayed in line from 11 October to 23 November, improving their defences and carrying out patrols.

All during the period the enemy probed the defensive lines and on 21 November the battalion received orders to take over from a French unit overlooking the Sami-Ch'On Valley. A and B Companies moved instantly and C and D Companies made their way the following day. This was to be where the battalion would spend the winter months. Peace negotiations were under way during this time, but in the meantime Chinese troops tried to gain as much territorial advantage as possible to give their negotiators a stronger hand in the talks.

The winter conditions were brutal, with biting cold, but the men quickly developed new ideas to keep themselves warm and comfortable. Each of the companies even had a bath house with hot, running water. The rations were American and much of the cold weather equipment was courtesy of the US Army. Comforts did arrive from home in the shape of woollen clothes, food and books courtesy of the Korea Comforts Fund, which was fully supported by the Eastern Daily Press and the people of Norfolk. The battalion had a short period out of line on 14 December, but they were back by the 19th and into a regular routine of more patrols and constant watch for the enemy.

The battalion suffered a death on the night of 23 December 1951 when Private T Watkins was killed while on patrol. His body had to be left until the following day when Second-Lieutenant M F Reynolds and another patrol tried to recover his body. This failed but later Major B D Chapman, A Company's commander, led another patrol that recovered Watkins's body.

By January 1952 the winter temperatures had dropped dramatically and men would return from patrol with their clothes frozen almost solid to them. Throughout January and into the February the battalion slowly haemorrhaged men, due to the constant patrolling and dreadful conditions. On one occasion, at

2030 hours on 19 February, a patrol from D Company, commanded by Second-Lieutenant T H Keen, ran into an enemy force. Keen was wounded in the head and Corporal Willmott took over, with Private R S Critcher, the Bren gunner, firing his weapon from the hip to cover the withdrawal. Critcher was hit but continued firing and was awarded the Military Medal for gallantry. Two members of the battalion, from A Company, were captured on the afternoon of 29 February. Corporal Ashlin managed to stun his guard with a stone and he and Private Pantrini both managed to escape.

There was another example of extreme bravery on 3 March, just after dark. Second-Lieutenant T J B Henson, along with twelve men from C Company, left their positions to set up an ambush point on a bridge over the Sami-Ch'On River. It was a clear night and the patrol was about 500m from the river when they detected movement. Henson decided to press on but minutes later the left-hand group came under fire. Henson rushed forward with his group to assist and found themselves amidst enemy soldiers. They fought hand to hand and eventually the enemy fled. C Company commander quickly sent a relief patrol and they clambered into jeeps, reaching the village of Taraktae, around 600m from Henson's position. Henson's casualties, three killed and six wounded, were quickly evacuated and Henson was awarded the Military Cross. Private A E Tearle, Henson's radio operator, was mentioned in dispatches.

The battalion came out of the line on 9 March 1952, returning just over a month later on 19 April. This time they replaced the 3rd Battalion of the 15th US Infantry Regiment in an area to the east of Kowang-San. The first major action on their part of the front took place on 30 April, with heavy shelling and there was more shelling on 5 and 9 May.

The 1st Battalion mounted patrols throughout May 1952 and was engaged in a major action on 29 May, which cost the battalion a number of casualties. On the night of 26 to 27 June a patrol from B Company inadvertently strayed into a minefield; five men were killed and four wounded. The company commander, Major B D Chapman, was determined to retrieve his men and led a patrol into the minefield to get them out. He was awarded the Distinguished Service Order for his courage.

The 1st launched Operation Yarmouth on 7 July, with the purpose of capturing one of the enemy. A platoon outpost was established about 500m from the main line. The position lay at the east end of a ridge nicknamed Crete, but the 1st Battalion preferred to call it Bunker Hill. The hope was that the enemy would find the position too intriguing not to send a patrol out to look at it. But there was no reaction, so another position was built 700m from the nearest Chinese outpost, on Hill 118. The new operation would be called Cromer and it got under way on 23 July 1952. Second-Lieutenant Henson, MC, moved up onto the hill to dig positions ready for Lieutenant Berney and his men. First they had to dislodge the enemy from the top of the hill; this was achieved by Lieutenant Shuttleworth and his platoon, who then took up defensive positions. Henson's men dug a new position and Berney and his platoon arrived before first light. Everything was ready by 0400 on July 24. Patrols up to 2200 hours had failed to notice any enemy activity, but at 2225 forty Chinese made for the new position. Berney's men were outnumbered two to one and they fought a fighting withdrawal, with Private G R Reed using his Bren gun to hold the enemy off. He was awarded the Military Medal. It was an even more courageous act than could possibly be expected because Reed, a National Service man, was due to go home the following week. Berney, realizing that not all of his men were with him, ran back to the top of the hill. It was the last time he was seen alive and his body was found the following day, still with his pistol in his hand. Two men were never found but were presumed killed.

So the cat and mouse games continued around Hill 118. Another group of Norfolks occupied the hill during daylight hours with ambush patrols ready to grab a prisoner at night. The waiting continued until the night of 2 to 3 August, as Second-Lieutenant Reynolds recalled:

> We had been in position approximately two to three minutes when the corporal of my north section attracted my attention. I called over and saw straight away approximately twelve Chinese moving towards us at half double. At a range of about 20 yards I gave the order to fire. A fierce fight developed with many grenades being thrown by both sides. The flashes were very blinding but it was obvious they were attempting to rush us from the north and northeast. About a minute after we opened fire the enemy put up a green veri light. By the small amount of light this gave it was possible to see a considerable number of enemy in some disorder. The fire fight continued for several minutes after which I found myself to have only one magazine and no grenades left. I also knew we had suffered considerable casualties. I gave the order collect the casualties and get back up the hill. This order was obeyed. About five men remained with me to cover the others out but at this stage I myself was wounded and was unable to get back and reorganise my patrol. My intention was to collect the unwounded men, redistribute ammunition and go back down the hill, as I was certain that those Chinese that were left were in a state of confusion. This was afterwards borne out by the fact that only a small party (about six) of Chinese searched the area for our wounded.

After they were reinforced a number of badly wounded Chinese soldiers were captured, but all of them died before they could be questioned. At first light the following day the battalion's dead and wounded were recovered. This was to be the culmination of their tour of duty in Korea. Bunker Hill was evacuated on 3 August and by 2330 on 8 August the battalion had been withdrawn to reserve positions. They headed back for Pusan. Some thirty-three men of the battalion were buried at the UN cemetery. The battalion finally left for Hong Kong on 28 September 1952.

The 1st Battalion in Hong Kong

The *Empire Orwell*, with the 1st Battalion on board, docked at Kowloon on 30 September 1952. The battalion was to go into barracks at the Norwegian Farm Camp, only 2,000m from the frontier with the Peoples' Republic of China. From the very moment the battalion arrived in Hong Kong National Service men began to be demobbed and by March 1943 the bulk of the original Royal Norfolks were in B and C Companies, with A and D Companies primarily former members of the King's (Liverpool) Regiment.

Despite the upheavals and lack of men, work still had to be done and training continued. At the end of May 1953 the commander of the battalion, Orlebar, handed over to Lieutenant-Colonel G R Turner-Cain, DSO, who had been the commanding officer in 1947 to 1948. Training and exercises continued until the battalion learned that it would be leaving for England in August 1954. Advance parties left on 22 July and the battalion finally commenced embarkation on 31 August. It took them five weeks to get home via Singapore, Colombo and Aden. HMT *Devonshire* docked in Liverpool on 5 October 1954.

Men of the regiment march past Norwich City Hall, with the Lord Lieutenant taking the salute in 1954

Colour party and guard marching through Norwich in 1954

The regimental band playing outside Norwich Cathedral. Two lines of troops are marching out of Cathedral Close. This was taken in Norwich in 1954.

Display of the 4th Battalion's colours and silver around the time of the amalgamation.

The 1st Battalion in Cyprus

The battalion now moved to Colchester to take over Roman Way Camp. It would be placed in reserve as part of the 3rd Infantry Division and it needed to prepare for potential deployment in Europe. Consequently new training was necessary. The training cycle continued through to October 1955, when the battalion was put on seventy-two hours notice to move. This was reduced to forty-eight hours shortly afterwards and the battalion was ready for any posting by 14 October. The 1st Battalion learned at 0300 on 15 October 1955 that they would be flying out to Cyprus the following Monday. They left Colchester on 16 October and the first aircraft took off from RAF Lyneham at 0800 on the following day, with the last leaving at 1730.

The situation in Cyprus was potentially explosive. The island had belonged to Turkey until 1923 and had then become a British Crown Colony. Around 20 per cent of the population was Turkish. The majority of the population wanted a closer relationship with Greece; in fact they wanted political union. On 28 July 1954 the British government announced that it was unlikely for Cyprus to become independent. This was seen as a huge provocation. The leader of the group known as Enosis, which favoured union with Greece, was the Greek Orthodox Archbishop Makarios. He had gone as far as recruiting a Greek army colonel, George Grivas, to set up a fighting wing for the movement. The relations between Britain and the Cypriots deteriorated and it was not long before the National Organization of Cypriot Fighters (EOKA), led by Grivas, became active. There were isolated riots, murders, intimidation, ambushes and attacks on isolated police stations. The 1st Battalion arrived in Nicosia on 18 October 1955, to become part of Operation Brazen, with the mission to restore peace.

It was not long before the battalion was thrown into operations. They would carry out searches, set up cordons and carry out patrols. They would have to be ever watchful of potential ambushes. They also had to provide guards for headquarters, government offices and barracks, along with airfields, the homes of the military and prisons. Curfews also had to be enforced, along with the setting up of instant roadblocks to try and catch EOKA operatives. On 9 December 1955 the battalion suffered its first casualty in Cyprus when Private Peaks was slightly injured when a bomb was thrown at an observation post on Metaxas Square in Nicosia.

By January 1956 the battalion had moved to Limassol. They occupied Thorny Camp, just outside of Limassol and came under operational command of 3 Commando Brigade, Royal Marines. Soldiers would have to be placed at local police stations and roadblocks set up to search for arms, ammunition and explosives. In one such operation in January C Company was sent into remote villages in the outlying district to collect licensed shotguns; they seized 250 weapons.

Field Marshal Sir John Harding and Second Lieutenant M E Buckley in Cyprus in 1956

A particularly successful mission was Operation Little Chicago, which took place on 6 and 7 February 1956. For some time the village of Pakna, some twenty miles to the northwest of Limassol, had had something of a bad reputation. There were some 1,600 inhabitants of the village that lay in the foothills of the Troodos Mountains. The entire battalion was deployed, along with other British units, to encircle the village. This was completed by 0450 and at 0520 three figures could be seen making their way out of the village. They approached the cordon held by B Company and, despite the EOKA men's attempt to bribe a lance-corporal, they were taken prisoner. A search found a number of weapons and ammunition. Two of the men were wanted for attempted murder. The battalion began searching the village at 0610 and found a good deal of EOKA propaganda, equipment for making ammunition and more suspects. By 1130 it was all over and the men could return to camp.

A Company of the 1st Battalion was also directly involved in a failed assassination attempt on Governor Harding. A bomb was found in the governor's bed on 21 March 1956. Second-Lieutenant M E Buckley took the bomb out of the house on a shovel and put it into a weapons' pit, where it exploded. Buckley was later awarded the MBE.

There were more operations, particularly in the Troodos Mountains, which aimed to break up EOKA cells. The 1st Battalion was due to leave Cyprus in July

1956, but the Suez crisis changed all this and Cyprus became a major staging post for British and French troops and equipment *en route* to Egypt. This delayed the 1st Battalion's move and it also meant that, as men were needed elsewhere, the battalion began to shrink, as new drafts were smaller. Nonetheless they continued with their internal security duties until they finally received orders to leave Cyprus for Germany in mid-November 1956.

The advance party began arriving at Aldershot barracks in Iserlohn in mid-December 1956. They would share a large barracks with the headquarters of the 5th Infantry Brigade. Most of the buildings were taken over by the 1st Battalion during January 1957 and after a period of leave the bulk of the battalion began to arrive to commence training in the February. Once again the battalion had to learn new techniques, as their role in Germany would be entirely different. Instead of facing EOKA terrorists in an isolated mountain village they would now have to adapt to the prospect of preparing for a major conventional war.

Amalgamation

In late July 1957 the battalion learned that there might be an amalgamation with the Suffolk Regiment. The colonel of the regiment, Lieutenant-Colonel W H Brinkley, had been told by the Chief of the Imperial General Staff. There were major changes coming for the army, most of which had been spelled out in the Defence White Paper that had been published in April 1957. Added to this, National Service would end in 1960.

By August 1958 the three undersized companies were reduced to two strong companies, A and B Company. C Company would now have the mortar platoon, the machinegun platoon, the anti-tank platoon and the signals platoon. D Company was disbanded. The Suffolk Regiment was due to join them at Iserlohn in the summer of 1959, so amalgamation appeared imminent. In December 1958 the East Anglian regimental cap badge had been brought into use. The Britannia badge, which had been worn by the regiment for generations, now disappeared. The men could see the shape of things to come, as in February 1959 the 1st Battalion of the Essex Regiment, which was also at Iserlohn, was amalgamated with the 1st Battalion of the Bedfordshire and Hertfordshire Regiment to form the 3rd East Anglian Regiment.

The 1st Battalion celebrated Almanza Day on 9 May 1959 instead of the usual 25 April. This was a particularly important celebration for the regiment, as it commemorated the exploits of the 9th Regiment of Foot at that battle in 1707. They could not celebrate on the normal day due to their training schedule. The last trooping of the colour by the 1st Battalion went ahead in the certain knowledge that amalgamation was only weeks away.

The 4th Battalion

The 4th Battalion had been one of those that had been captured at Singapore in February 1942. It came back into existence in April 1947, as the 4th (Territorial Army) Battalion. Recruitment began on 1 May 1947. The first post-war commander of the battalion was Lieutenant-Colonel R F Humphrey, who had served with the battalion and had been captured at Singapore. Battalion HQ and the support company, along with one Rifle Company, were based at the Chapelfield Road Drill Hall in Norwich. Two rifle companies, along with the anti-tank platoon, would be based at Great Yarmouth with a platoon detached at Loddon. The fourth company was split between Diss and Harleston. The battalion became part of the 161st (TA) Infantry Brigade, along with the 4th Battalion of the Essex Regiment and the 4th Battalion of the Suffolk Regiment. The battalion's colours were officially handed back on 30 June 1947.

Recruitment continued into 1948, with C Company focusing on Attleborough and Wymondham. Recruitment was quite slow and by June there were still only ten officers and fifty-eight men in the battalion. D Company was formed in October 1949 at North Walsham and by the end of the year the battalion had grown in strength to twenty-two officers and ninety-one other ranks.

In 1950 there were significant changes; National Service men would now have to serve for three years in the Territorial Army after their full-time service. Also, on 1 December 1950 Humphrey handed over command of the battalion to Lieutenant-Colonel J F Wilkins. Humphrey had had a long association with the battalion, as he had first joined it in 1926. The battalion expanded throughout 1951 and by the middle of the year there were twenty-five officers and 264 other ranks.

Group portrait of the colonels of the East Anglian Brigade dated 1952

Around half of the men were National Service men. There was another change in command in January 1953, with Lieutenant-Colonel M R Braithwaite taking over.

Training on new equipment and regular exercises continued and at the end of 1955 the battalion's strength was hit due to a change in government policy. Former National Service men would now only be required to attend a single annual camp. This meant drill nights were no longer compulsory. The government had also decided to downgrade the role of the Territorial Army; they would now be involved in civil defence and supporting the police. In early 1956 Lieutenant-Colonel N F Read became the new commanding officer of the 4th Battalion. He was a former 1st Battalion man, where he had served as second in command.

By April 1957 it was clear that the regular 1st Battalion would amalgamate with the Suffolk Regiment. However the 4th Battalion would be allowed to continue to wear the Britannia cap badge and retain the Royal Norfolk Regiment as its title. By January 1959 command of the battalion had passed to Lieutenant-Colonel W D Flower and on 11 July a ceremony took place at the Britannia Barracks in Norwich, where the depot was formally handed over to the battalion, although they did not reoccupy the barracks until 6 November of that year. By this time the 4th had been involved in the ceremony commemorating the freedom of Lowestoft for the 1st East Anglian Regiment the previous June. The 4th Battalion had risen in strength to around 340 men and was the strongest battalion in the division.

New colours were presented to the battalion at Britannia Barracks on 8 July 1962 by Princess Margaret who was then the colonel-in-chief of the 1st East Anglian

Amalgamation ceremony

Regiment. These would replace the colours that had been presented to the battalion back in 1909 by King Edward VII on Mousehold Heath. In the previous month Lieutenant-Colonel Flower had handed over command of the battalion to Lieutenant-Colonel A J Robertson. On 15 February 1962 the battalion was involved in the ceremony that saw the borough of Great Yarmouth grant freedom to the 1st East Anglian Regiment. December 1963 saw the old battalion colours, along with those of the 1st Battalion, laid up at Norwich Cathedral. They were placed in the Regimental Chapel.

The merging of the Royal Leicestershire Regiment with the 1st, 2nd and 3rd East Anglian Regiments in September 1964 had no bearing on the 4th Battalion. The new title of the merged regiments was the Royal Anglian Regiment, but the 4th continued to be the 4th Royal Norfolk Regiment.

The colours of the 1st East Anglian Regime being laid up at Norwich Cathedral

The amalgamations had been a long time coming. The 2nd battalions of all regiments had been disbanded in 1947. They had initially been created in 1881 with the idea that they would be used to garrison India. The Royal Norfolk Regiment's own 2nd Battalion disappeared in March 1948. Nonetheless, the army found itself grossly under strength during the 1950s; men were needed in Korea, Malaya, Kenya and Cyprus, as well as troops for the British Army of the Rhine. Suez had just been another major problem, but post-Suez there was a call for a reduction in both spending and in manpower. Detailed plans were announced on 24 July 1957; across the army fifteen infantry battalions would be lost.

There were to be a number of amalgamations. The Royal Norfolk and Royal Suffolk Regiments would be amalgamated, the Bedfordshire and Hertfordshire with Essex and the Royal Lincolnshire with the Northamptonshire Regiment. Effectively, the three new regiments would be part of the East Anglian Brigade.

There were arguments despite the inevitability of the decision. The Royal Norfolk Regiment would have preferred to have been called, in its new form, the Royal Norfolk and Suffolk Regiment, but instead they had to accept the 1st East Anglian Regiment as its title. The Lincolnshire and Northamptonshire Regiments did not associate themselves with East Anglia at all, but they became the 2nd East Anglian Regiment. There was even argument about the cap badge. Clearly the Royal Norfolks would have preferred to have retained Britannia, but in the end the colonels of the regiment voted for a Gibraltar castle and key on a garter star. The castle and the key were associated with three of the regiments and the garter star with the Bedfordshire and Hertfordshire and the Royal Lincolnshire.

As amalgamation day loomed the depot at Britannia Barracks was closed down and the 1st Battalion at Iserlohn prepared for the arrival and assimilation of the Suffolk Regiment. Both of the regiments had served their country for nearly 300 years; henceforth they would serve together.

Chapter 10

The Royal Anglians 1964–2010

The history of the East Anglian Regiment was to be extremely short. As early as 1962, there were rumblings of further amalgamations and streamlining. Infantry regiments would have to accept being a part of far larger regiments to avoid extinction. The three regiments that made up the East Anglian Brigade would now face another reorganization. In May 1963 the Royal Leicestershire Regiment joined the East Anglian Brigade. It maintained its own identity but adopted the brigade cap badge and other common items of dress.

It was always intended that, whatever became of the regiments, they would maintain their county connections in some way. To begin with there was considerable debate over what the new, amalgamated regiment would be called. Options ran from Queen Elizabeth's Own Royal Regiment to the Royal Regiment of Anglia. As it transpired, it would be called the Royal East Anglian Regiment. There would be four battalions; the 1st (Norfolk and Suffolk), the 2nd (Duchess of Gloucester's Own Lincolnshire and Northamptonshire), the 3rd (16th and 44th Foot) and the 4th (Leicestershire). Formation day was 1 September 1964.

Yet the Royal Anglians were not an entirely new regiment. Not only did the regiment have the tradition of the Royal Norfolk Regiment stretching back into history, but it also had the cumulative history and identity of all of the other regiments that were part of the amalgamation. There was a bewildering list of battle honours, won by the individual regiments, stretching back to 1695. Ancient emblems ranging from Britannia, the Sphinx, the French Eagle, the Royal Tiger to the Castle and Key of Gibraltar were dear to the regiments.

In order to continue our focus on the Norfolk element of this newly amalgamated regiment, we will from this point concentrate on the 1st (Norfolk and Suffolk) Battalion and the associated 4th Battalion of the Royal Norfolk Regiment, as a part of the Territorial Army. There is also the question of the title of the battalion. When it was formed in 1964 Norfolk and Suffolk were in brackets. The brackets were dropped entirely in July 1968 and at times between 1959 and 1968 it was referred to as the Royal Norfolk and Suffolk Regiment. In 1978 to 1992 the battalion often had Norfolk, Suffolk, Cambridgeshire in brackets as a part of its title. But whatever it was called between these dates, we are still referring to the 1st Battalion of the Royal Anglians.

Aden

As the 1st East Anglian Regiment the battalion had arrived in Aden for garrison duty in early 1964. They were based at Thumeir, under the command of Lieutenant-Colonel Dye. This was the Radfan region. By September 1964, now formally as the 1st (Norfolk and Suffolk) Battalion of the Royal Anglian Regiment, they were rotating companies amongst a number of detachments and outposts across Aden.

Aden was one of the many Crown colony oddities dotted around the world. It was a valuable port and had vital oil refineries. Supported by the Egyptians, many of the inhabitants of Aden wanted union with the Yemen and it was the Radfan, and particularly the Dhala region, which was volatile. The battalion spent Christmas away from the fighting, but returned towards the end of December 1964, when Private Frazer was killed by a land mine and two more of the men were wounded.

Dye, having been awarded the OBE, handed over the battalion to Lieutenant-Colonel T M Creasey on 17 February 1965. The enemy facing the battalion consisted of the National Liberation Front (NLF) and the Front for the Liberation of Occupied South Yemen (FLOSY). Both of them were backed by the Egyptians. They were well armed and not frightened to come to grips with British regulars.

Between mid-February and mid-March 1965 the battalion was responsible for internal security duties in Steamer Point, Maalla, Crater, Khormaksar and Sheikh Othman. B Company was at this point in Mukeiras but terrorist attacks became more common and B Company was returned to bolster the battalion. On 12 March a rocket was fired at the Sheikh Othman police station and it hit a room occupied by the headquarters unit of 7 Platoon of B Company. Two of the men were wounded. Private Kent saved the life of Sergeant Smith by giving him first aid and keeping him conscious until help arrived. Both of the men were awarded the BEM for their gallantry.

The Crater area was particularly difficult to police and often operations were carried out at night, with roadblocks and vehicle checks. Between February and September 1965 some 35,000 local people were searched, along with 8,000 vehicles, and a number of grenades, mines, pistols and other weapons were seized.

On 19 June 1965, at around 2230, two terrorists had thrown a grenade into the seaman's mission at Steamer Point. As luck would have it Second-Lieutenant Hawkins was being driven by Private Richardson and he saw three men get into a car and drive off. The two soldiers followed the car until it came to a stop in a cul-de-sac. Hawkins grabbed one of the men and sat on him amidst a hostile crowd, whilst Richardson went to get help. Hawkins was awarded the MBE and Richardson the Queen's Commendation for Brave Conduct.

The battalion's sixth and last tour in the Radfan took place between 28 July and 22 August 1965. They suffered two attacks during the tour, the first on 3 August, which saw a firefight that killed two terrorists and wounded a third. Another took place on 12 August with no casualties.

Germany

The battalion formally handed over duties on 21 September and left for Germany, where it would join the 7th Armoured Brigade at Celle. It was an enormous shock to the system; the climate was radically different, as were the living conditions and it also meant that the battalion would have to learn to become an armoured infantry unit. By January 1966 the battalion, equipped with eighty armoured personnel carriers, had begun its conversion and could take part in training exercises as mechanized infantry.

The men still retained their close association with marches and three officers and thirty-five soldiers of A Company took part in a 100-mile march around Nijmegen in Holland, winning three team medals and thirty-eight individual medals. The battalion took part in a major exercise in October 1967, just a month after Lieutenant-Colonel Emsden had replaced Creasey. This large exercise incorporated four battle groups, including the 1st Royal Anglian, the 11th Hussars, the 2nd Royal Tank Regiment and the 1st Black Watch.

The battalion left Celle and the 7th Armoured Brigade in February 1968, bound for Catterick and the 6th Infantry Brigade. They were now in the Alma and Bourlon Barracks and a new training cycle began. The battalion would be expected to return to Germany each September, for annual training, but after they had carried this out in 1969 they were told that not only would they have a new commanding officer, Lieutenant-Colonel Jackson, but they were due to go on an emergency tour to Northern Ireland. In the event the emergency tour was cancelled, but the likelihood was they would have a two-year tour beginning in July 1970.

It was around this time that the 1st Battalion began to adopt the nickname The Vikings. Certainly, their new social centre became known as the Viking Club, which was opened on 24 February 1971 by Anne Shelton. In fact according to the battalion journal, the name had been adopted by Lieutenant-Colonel A Campbell, the commanding officer of the 1st East Anglians, in Berlin back in 1959. It was supposed to reflect the Viking heritage of the east coast of England. The battalion's journal said:

> Some of you may be wondering now about references in the press to the Vikings. This is the nickname the 1st Battalion has acquired in Berlin. It has been the cry of our spectators on the touchline and at the ringside. It is a nickname by which we are also known to all our neighbouring units in Berlin. We are adopting a nickname which has appealed to the battalion's imagination and fired off a new enthusiasm.

Ireland

The battalion was now to be based in Londonderry and it joined nine other infantry battalions in Ulster. The general in command, Lieutenant-General Sir Ian Freeland, was an old Royal Norfolk man. Freeland finally retired in 1971 with the award of the GBE, although seven months later he would take over as honorary colonel of the regiment and continue his long association.

The 1st Battalion had to adapt once again, so the three rifle companies and the support companies became four internal security companies, each with three platoons and a company headquarters. The 1st Battalion, now under the command of Lieutenant-Colonel Jackson, moved into Ebrington Barracks on 30 July 1970. The barracks were wholly unsuitable and they moved across the River Foyle to Duncreggan Camp, which had last been used by the British army in 1935.

The battalion had its first call out just ten minutes after being put on immediate standby at 2200 hours. As the battalion's correspondent in the *Castle* described:

> With two Saracens [armoured personnel carriers] in support from the 17th/21st Lancers and 9 Platoon up, we had to crash through a blazing barricade made up of cars, vans and debris etc, with rioters throwing missiles from either side. Permission from the CO was given to use CS gas. We fired thirty five rounds, broke through the blazing inferno and drove the rioters back into the Bogside.

In August the battalion also had the dubious honour of being the first British unit to fire baton rounds, or rubber bullets.

The tension began to subside in Londonderry and in February 1971 the battalion moved little by little to Belfast. Here they faced shootings and nail bombs and they operated in conjunction with the 2nd Battalion of the Royal Anglians. But while the battalion had been away Londonderry had seen more rioting and the battalion went straight back into action, trying to bring peace back to Bogside. Stones and bottles had given way to bombs and bullets. Internment was brought in during August 1971 and in the same month, as once again the *Castle* described, training, alertness and luck often meant the difference between life and death:

> C Company had a very successful engagement with a gunman, who, armed with a pistol, tried to outshoot three SLRs [self-loading rifles]. Needless to say he lost. The Bogside and Creggan barracked themselves in for a while until they were shown how ineffective their barricades were. Since then the sniping, nail bombing and petrol bombing has continued unceasingly. There is no quicker way of making a soldier out of a recruit than shooting at him. Indeed even the newest recruit has picked up field craft quickly and all sentries have kept alert and watchful knowing that at any moment a bullet could be directed towards them. It could be a well aimed shot. It could be a ricochet.

There were two events that overshadowed the year and these were the tragic deaths of Private Wilkins and Lance-Corporal Curtis, as *Castle* recalled:

> Wilkins was on duty in an observation post in the Brandywell location on 27th September when he came under intense fire from at least three positions. Over fifty rounds were fired at the post. He died of his wounds on 11th October. He was the first soldier in the battalion to die as a result of enemy action since September 1965. The Brandywell, being on the edge of the Bogside and in low ground, has become a favourite target for attacks by the IRA. It has a single narrow, vulnerable line of communication which has to be patrolled to prevent mining. On 9th November during one of these patrols Lance Corporal Curtis was moving across a gap in a wall, covered by two other members of the patrol when a single shot struck him in the chest. Covering fire was given by one soldier as the other went to his aid. Lance Corporal Curtis died on the way to hospital. This murder occurred less than twenty four hours before the battalion was to go on leave.

The battalion knew that it was due to leave Ulster in March 1972 and once it had had its leave it would do its last tour of Londonderry. Each day, however, there was a sigh of relief when the report came through on the radio 'No CAS' (no casualties). On 21 December 1971 the battalion withdrew from the city and was responsible for policing duties around the county. It is important to bear in mind that many of the families were actually in Northern Ireland with the men and there was the constant threat that they could become victims of terrorism.

The final operation took place on 6 March 1972, on the border with the Irish Republic, at the village of Clady. A battalion roadblock came under fire and Colour Sergeant-Major Watson of B Company was hit in the leg with splinters from an armour-piercing bullet. Watson insisted on walking to the helicopter himself, claiming he had only been grazed, but the doctors in the hospital took two weeks to remove all the fragments from his leg.

Cyprus

The move out of Londonderry went smoothly. By 6 March all of the baggage had been despatched to Cyprus in containers and the battalion advance party flew there on the night of 21 to 22 March, with the main body flying out between 10 and 20 April. By 14 April the battalion was once again on operational duties in Cyprus and involved in a major training exercise around Akrotiri airfield, with a Ghurkha battalion. The battalion remained in Cyprus until May 1974, although for training exercises August to October 1973 was spent in Kenya and another group visited Sharjah, one of the emirates of the United Arab Emirates.

The 1st Battalion now found itself operating in three different roles within six months. First there was the hot climate of Cyprus then the arctic warfare training at Tidworth and finally a four-month emergency tour of Northern Ireland, operating in Portadown, Lurgan, Armagh and Dungannon. The first three months of 1975 saw the battalion involved in Exercise Hardfall, a major training exercise in Norway. Further exercises took place in Denmark, Italy and Turkey. The same hectic schedule continued in 1976, with two major exercises, one in Norway and another on Salisbury Plain, while there was also additional training on Sardinia. If anything 1977 had an even more exotic and varied collection of different locations for the battalion, with Norway, Italy, Jamaica, Guyana and Denmark all on the itinerary. The busy year ended in Norway and for the battalion Norway was once again the destination for the first part of 1978.

By May 1978 the battalion was preparing for a mechanized role in the British Army of the Rhine. The last time they had used armoured personnel carriers was back in June 1969. Soon the battalion was back in Celle in West Germany, with training continuing despite six weeks of uninterrupted rain. The battalion, however, knew that it was soon to be transferred back to Northern Ireland for another stint.

Ireland

They returned to Northern Ireland and to the city of Belfast between 12 May and 16 September 1979. Operation Banner, as the posting was named, was extremely successful despite numerous shooting and bombing incidents. The battalion suffered no casualties but confiscated a number of rifles, pistols, rounds of ammunition, bombs, bomb-making equipment and radios. One notable mistake was when the battalion arrested a High Court judge in error. The battalion enjoyed a period of leave on their return from Northern Ireland.

As 1980 dawned A Company went off to Denmark, C Company to Canada and B and D Companies went to Sennelager near Paderborn in West Germany, for field firing. Between August 1981 and January 1982 the 1st Battalion were operating once again in Northern Ireland, in Fermanagh. A Company, according to *Castle*:

> The Big Red A is now manning outposts in SE Fermanagh, which, in appearance, resemble World War One dugouts and in role are similar to the Ops of the Khyber Pass. BAOR [British Army of the Rhine] now seems an incredibly long way away and memories of tracked, mobile homes are fading fast.

B Company, meanwhile, was carrying out vehicle checks and searches at Aughnacloy, some miles to the east of the rest of the battalion. By now the battalion had learned to tread the line between firmness and diplomacy:

> Chat procedure reached a new dimension when Corporal Nigel Dowd

called at the house of a Mrs Rafferty whose husband had been lifted a few days earlier in connection with a culvert mine. After receiving a very unfriendly reception he accurately weighed up the situation: 'I suppose that ruins my chance of a cup of tea Mrs Rafferty?'

D Company meanwhile was based in northwest and southwest Fermanagh, controlling an area with 125km of border to patrol and responsibility for six outstations. They worked long hours in extremely wet weather.

The 1st Battalion brought its Fermanagh tour to a successful end in late January 1982 and returned to Celle, then onto Oakington, where it arrived in the May, with a new commanding officer, second in command and company commanders. They then went underwent intensive training for their tour to Belize. Major-General Jack Dye formally handed over the regiment to General Sir Timothy Creasey, who had formerly been the commander of the 1st Battalion, on 6 November 1982.

The year 1983 was the 75th anniversary of the founding of the Territorial Army. The Royal Anglian Regiment had one of the largest TA infantry organizations in the whole army. It had three battalions across the east of England, running from Scunthorpe to the Thames and from Hinckley to Norwich. There were thirty different Royal Anglian TA centres, all catering for the volunteers that made up the 5th, 6th and 7th Battalions. At the time the 5th and 7th were part of a reserve for the British Army of the Rhine, while the 6th was responsible for home–based security.

The 1st Battalion was to remain in Belize until April 1983, carrying out patrol programmes through difficult jungle terrain. For many years the battalion had had a formal affiliation with HMS *Norfolk*, but she had been sold to the Chilean navy. Now the battalion established a relationship with HMS *Yarmouth*. There was an exchange of an arctic warrior statuette from the battalion with a plaque from HMS *Yarmouth*.

The battalion returned to duty at Oakington Barracks on 25 April, but the following month they were called out to RAF Upper Heyford. This was at the height of the Campaign for Nuclear Disarmament protests against the deployment of cruise missiles. Thousands of CND supporters were expected and the battalion was to be deployed within the perimeter. In the event fewer CND supporters turned up and despite the poor living conditions for the battalion in one of the accommodation hangars the Americans at the base looked after the men very well.

For the first time in a number of years not only was the 1st Battalion based in the Home Counties, but so too were the other two regular battalions. This allowed the regiment as a whole to rekindle its relationship with various parts of East Anglia and events were held during 1983 at King's Lynn, Wisbech, Lowestoft, Colchester, Dunstable, Lincoln, Northampton and Watford.

From December 1984 to January 1987 the 1st was based at Ebrington Barracks in Londonderry. The battalion was in place by 4 December and although it was busy there were no serious attacks. Life in Ulster continued, but with an increase in terrorist activity by 1985, as the *Castle* recalled:

> May proved a busy period for the city company (A Company) with a number of vehicle hijackings and burnings, leading to two shooting incidents on the 24th, when a foot patrol had a single high velocity shot fired at it – the shot passing between Lieutenant Kendall and Corporal Osbourne. Later the same day approximately twelve shots were fired at a joint army/RUC [Royal Ulster Constabulary] patrol and in the follow up operation two terrorist rifles were recovered by 2nd Platoon on 25 May.

The battalion lost Cambridge-born Private Martin Patten when he was shot in the early hours of Sunday 22 September 1985. This was during a period of even more intense terrorist activity in Northern Ireland.

By 1986 the 1st Battalion was halfway through their two-year tour of Londonderry. But during the year they were joined by the other two regular battalions, the Poachers (2nd Battalion) and the Pompadours (3rd Battalion). The almost matter of fact description of some events in 1986 in the *Castle* belies the danger that the men were in during this period in Londonderry:

> The routine workload involving bomb hoaxes, real bomb clearances and support to the RUC during search operations received a smart injection of adrenalin in late February [1986] when a Viking foot patrol, after some quick thinking by the commander, shot and killed a terrorist and wounded and captured a second after they had attacked Fort George [a base]. This was the first direct terrorist death by uniformed troops for some considerable time. In early March a bomb was detonated near a Viking foot patrol as they passed a library in the city and Private Milne was lucky to receive only a slight cut to his left ear.

Later in the year a potential disaster was averted:

> In the early hours of 25 July, a civilian worker, while his family were held hostage, was forced to drive his car containing a bomb into Fort George. On arrival he passed through the gate and declared the car a proxy bomb. Prompt action by the guard commander quickly cleared the area and after two controlled explosions, the area was finally declared clear. A plastic drum containing 1000kg of home-made explosive and a number of smaller bags containing a total of 10kg of explosive were recovered from the car.

In December 1986 the 1st Battalion spent their third Christmas in Londonderry. On 23 September 1986 A Company, on their penultimate tour of the city itself, had helped to uncover a cache of bomb-making equipment. B Company came under attack from an improvised grenade launcher at 1915 on 9 October 1986 and fortunately nobody was hit. These were typical encounters for the battalion.

Gibraltar

By January 1987 the battalion was in an altogether different location, with new responsibilities and challenges. They had been posted to Gibraltar and were in situ at the Lathbury Barracks. A Company was responsible for the naval dockyard area and B Company deployed to RAF Gibraltar. Both of the companies were responsible for the defence of key points vital to the operations of the other two services. With no regular battalion available to replace them, the summer of 1988 saw the three rifle companies carry out a four-week training programme at Stanford, while the rest of the battalion covered their commitments at Gibraltar.

As 1988 turned to 1989 the battalion prepared for a move back to Colchester and to 19 Brigade. For many of the soldiers this was a return to real soldiering and commitments with NATO and in Germany. From the beginning of April the battalion began forming up at Hyderabad Barracks in Colchester and after just a week all three rifle companies went off for training: A Company to Catterick and B and C Companies to Salisbury Plain. The battalion was now preparing for another trip to Northern Ireland. Such had been the turnover of officers and men that less than half of the battalion that had served in Londonderry between 1984 and 1987 had ever served in Ireland before. There were very few of them left from the tour in Fermanagh in 1983.

Ireland

In August 1989 the battalion spent their last few days in Colchester with their families and were in South Armagh by 25 August, just in time for the first incident of the tour, as the *Castle* explained:

> Just as the last of the main body was arriving at RAF Aldergrove our first major IRA incident occurred. On a misty summer's day, at about 5pm, four Mark II mortars were fired at the Creevekeeran permanent observation post. The mortars which were fired from the back of a Hiace van travelled about 250m and missed the OP by a fairly narrow margin.

In the last few months of 1989 there were six more serious terrorist incidents. One of the last ones, on 26 October, was described by the *Castle*:

> The last incident in this period was a mortar attack on the Barouki Sangar in Crossmaglen Square. At 1215 hours on 26 October a tractor and trailer drove up and parked about 15ft from the Sangar. Three mortars were fired at point blank range into the side of the Sangar with one mortar remaining unfired. The Sangar itself was quite badly damaged but luckily the six soldiers inside were unharmed.

The remainder of the tour saw scattered incidents throughout the battalion's area of responsibility. On 19 January 1990 the battalion said farewell to their commanding officer, Lieutenant-Colonel John Sutherell, MBE, and in February they welcomed a new commanding officer, Lieutenant-Colonel David Phipps. After a well-earned period of leave the Vikings reassembled at Colchester. In fact 1990 was a year that was dominated by tours of Northern Ireland. On returning to Colchester they began almost immediate training for another six-month tour of Fermanagh, which would begin in May 1991.

It had been ten years since the battalion had been in Fermanagh. They carried out the full spectrum of rural operations: searches, patrols and monitoring. Although the majority of the time was relatively peaceful, as the *Castle* recalled it was interspersed with major incidents:

> Gunmen along the border were engaged by the battalion on a number of occasions. The first incident involved members of a patrol who engaged a number of gunmen in the vicinity of the border near Rosslea. The second incident involved two soldiers in a B Company multiple at Killybilly PVCP [Permanent Vehicle Check Point] who engaged two gunmen whilst they were moving into a position to attack them as they allowed a car through the PVCP.

The battalion endured rocket and machinegun attacks and a monstrous 8,800lb tractor bomb. There was another huge 3,500lb bomb; this was all fitted into steel drums with additional fertilizer bags. It would have caused enormous damage. The tractor bomb became stuck in a drainage ditch, which undoubtedly prevented certain fatalities. Wessex helicopters were fired at by rocket-propelled grenades and the battalion also had to contend with vehicle booby traps.

The Vikings handed over to 42 Commando and said goodbye to Permanent Vehicle Check Points, patrolling and the border and settled back to life with their families at the end of 1991. They had five weeks post-tour leave to enjoy.

Mergers

From 5 October 1992 the Royal Anglian Regiment was reduced from three to two regular battalions. The colonel of the regiment sent the following message to the colonel-in-chief, HM Queen Elizabeth the Queen Mother:

> The Colonel of the Regiment and all ranks of the Royal Anglian Regiment send their loyal greetings to our Colonel-in-Chief on the occasion of the merging of the 3rd (Bedfordshire, Hertfordshire and Essex) Battalion the Royal Anglian Regiment with the 1st (Norfolk, Suffolk and Cambridgeshire) Battalion the Royal Anglian Regiment and the 2nd (Lincolnshire, Leicestershire and Northamptonshire) Battalion the Royal

Anglian Regiment to form the new 1st and 2nd Battalions of the Regiment on 5 Oct 1992.

The Queen Mother replied:

> The Regiment is once again going through a period of change – and it is to me a source of very real sorrow that the 3rd Battalion is to lose its individual identity. The splendid record of achievements of this battalion have added lustre to the proud record of the regiment.

The 3rd Battalion's colours were laid up at Warley on 5 October. From this point the regiment would consist of two regular and three volunteer battalions. This all of course meant change for the two surviving regular battalions, both of which became overstrength literally overnight.

As the newly merged 1st Battalion began to reorganize itself it had little chance to catch breath as training and exercises were still the order of the day. In early 1993 the battalion undertook an intensive six-month training programme, learning how to become fully air mobile. They also moved from 19 Infantry Brigade to the Air Mobile Brigade in March. Air mobile exercises continued throughout the year, but after August the battalion began to prepare for another six-month tour of East Tyrone in Northern Ireland. The training was carried out from October to early December; already the battalion knew that they would be spending Christmas in East Tyrone. The Vikings took over from the 2nd Battalion the Light Infantry and they knew that, as soon as the tour ended, as members of the 24 Air Mobile Brigade, they would have an exhausting schedule of exercises to complete.

The year 1994 started with a double attack on Dungannon and Cookstown. The highlight of March was finding 481kg of home-made explosive; several arrests were made. The Vikings returned to Colchester in July 1994 and they would have to relearn old skills and have them tested on exercise. Before putting East Tyrone to the back of their minds, 160 members of the battalion received General Service Medals. When they returned from leave they went on exercises on Salisbury Plain. There was speculation that the battalion was about to be deployed overseas, but instead they continued training until they were put on seven days notice to move, on 29 May 1995, to Bosnia.

Bosnia

They deployed at the beginning of July to the port of Ploce in Croatia. The first troops reached Split on 31 July. When the bulk of the troops arrived in Ploce they found a dilapidated port with very few facilities for the 3,500 British troops. The main body of the battalion had left Ploce by 5 August and their main mission in Croatia was to act as a theatre reserve. They were able to get into Bosnia and train in an area just north of Tomislavgrad. Although this deployment only lasted until

October 1995, it was not until 21 December that the last elements of the battalion arrived back in Colchester. Prior to Christmas 1995 there was another change in command, with Lieutenant-Colonel Roger Brunt being replaced by Lieutenant-Colonel Richard Harrold. Again there was much speculation and excitement about where the battalion would move to next; it ranged from Northern Ireland to the Cayman Islands. But in reality the battalion remained at Colchester. The battalion was based at Oakington Barracks between July 1996 and May 1999, with another tour of Belfast from November 1996 to May 1997.

A number of parades were mounted in 1997 across the East Anglian region, not only to reaffirm the regiment's close affinity with the area, but also as a major recruitment drive. Consequently a series of freedom parades were carried out, the last of which took place in Chelmsford on 18 July.

Ireland

As exercises and training continued in 1998 the battalion was preparing for their forthcoming tour to Londonderry. They were expecting an unusually demanding time and that the battalion, instead of focusing on one area, would probably have to cope with operations across the whole of the country. The lead elements of the battalion had already begun to establish themselves at Ebrington Barracks as early as September 1998.

Although the political climate in Northern Ireland was changing there were still attacks in February and March 2000 in County Fermanagh and County Londonderry. There was an increased threat from dissident Republicans and in order to interdict terrorist movement into and out of Londonderry patrols were inserted by boat or helicopter.

By this time the companies making up the 1st Battalion had firmly established their identities. A Company was most closely associated with Norfolk, B Company with Suffolk, C Company with Essex and D Company with Cambridgeshire. The battalion was perfectly well aware that they would have to adapt once again to a new mechanized role in May 2001 when they would be shifted to the Elizabeth Barracks at Pirbright. The battalion was looking forward to the opportunities of combined arms work and the fact that Pirbright had excellent training and social facilities. But first they would have to see another Christmas on active operations around Londonderry. The Fort George base was also due to close and the last soldiers had left there in October 2000. The fort had had a long association with the British Army and from 1973 no fewer than sixteen battalions had used it as an operational base. The 1st Battalion of the Royal Anglians had used it on at least two separate occasions.

The battalion still had to be on its toes until the very last moment before redeployment. On 23 January 2001, at 0014, a single mortar bomb was fired onto Ebrington Barracks, hitting the corner of the officers' mess building. The *Castle* explained what happened:

> Fortunately it failed to detonate and all personnel were safely evacuated from this building and the surrounding residential area, which was under threat. The mortar was launched from a van parked in a side street some 70m from the perimeter fence. Obviously the possibility of a secondary was of concern and all soldiers involved were very alert and deployed in the Waterside to provide the necessary additional security.

Afghanistan

It was highly likely that, given the developing international situation, the battalion would be required to serve in Afghanistan in the not too distant future. Meanwhile all the battalion could do was to bring themselves up to the greatest state of readiness possible.

The commanding officer of the 1st Battalion, Lieutenant-Colonel P D Jones, MBE, explained what was in store for the battalion in the *Castle*:

> Within days of returning from leave the barracks emptied of soldiers and the pace of life picked up to full sprint. Four platoons have been sent to reinforce the King's Royal Hussars for their tour of East Tyrone but our expedition to Kabul did happen and it is worth reflecting on what it was all about. The International Security Assistance Force mandate, given to it

The mortar platoon under training in 2005

The Commanding Officer of the 1st Battalion addresses the battle group at the end of a three-week training programme on Salisbury Plain in 2004

following the Bonn Agreement of late 2001, was to provide security assistance in Kabul to the Afghan Interim Administration from December 2001 to 22 June 2002. The Vikings followed 2 Para into the largest, most violent, most unstable and most destroyed part of Kabul. The battalion's area covered five police districts, over a million people, over half the ground area of Kabul, and much of the Northern Alliance forces that had made it as far as the city. The once affluent and beautiful southern half of the city had been almost completely destroyed by the civil war of the mid-90s and all that was left were the people, the weapons, the criminals and heaps of rubble.

The three rifle companies reinforced by support platoons deployed to company patrol bases in the south of the city, known as Camp Eagle, Suffolk House and Norfolk House. The battalion's mission was to provide security and a degree of stability. The task was known as Operation Fingal. There was a tragic, accidental shooting on 9 April 2002 that cost the life of Private Darren George of the 1st Battalion. He was the first British casualty in Afghanistan for many years.

The battalion would not see overseas active service duty again until April 2005, but in the meantime there was the continual annual round of training and exercises. Private Facal of 10 Platoon of the 1st Battalion described a typical experience for the men in the *Castle*:

The first exercise that I would take part in with the battalion was going to be in Turkey. Everyone was really looking forward to it. The flight took about four hours in an RAF TriStar. When we arrived it was strange to see armed guards accompany us everywhere with loaded rifles. The exercise was strange, not like any I have been on in the UK. The Turkish army had erected tents and provided shower facilities, toilets and a bakery. The catering in the field was excellent – apparently the Turkish army don't use ration packs! The Turkish soldiers wouldn't lie down when they were shot. The observer controllers would reset people who were shot almost immediately. We won in the end but feel that the Turkish soldiers weren't really playing the game at times.

This provides a useful personal perspective of a private soldier shortly after he had joined the 1st Battalion in December 2004.

Basra

After three months of preparatory training, followed by a couple of weeks leave, the 1st Battalion headed for a six-month tour of Iraq in April 2005. They were to be deployed on Operation Telic 6 and based in Basra. The battalion was responsible for some 12,000 square kilometres: to put it into perspective, about the same size as Cambridgeshire, Norfolk and Suffolk together.

A note left at the memorial at Sandringham on the ninetieth anniversary of the Gallipoli campaign

Members of A Company manning a sangar

The year 2005 was the ninetieth anniversary of the Royal Norfolk Regiment's 2nd Battalion's involvement in the Battle of Sh'Aibah (Shaiba), which took place from 11 to 15 April 1915. Consequently, the 1st Battalion called their camp Britannia Lines. In 1915, also, the 5th (Territorial Battalion) of the Royal Norfolk Regiment had sailed from Liverpool and landed at Sulva Bay on the Gallipoli peninsular on 10 August. As you will recall, many of these men vanished and their bodies were never identified.

The posting lasted until October 2005. It was a successful tour and although there were no major overseas postings in 2006, it was nonetheless another busy year full of training exercises and there was even time for some men to help train the Estonian army for a forthcoming tour of Afghanistan. A and B Companies spent six weeks in Canada, C Company completed freedom parades in Chelmsford, Colchester and Thurrock, but the men's thoughts were dominated by the fact that they would be redeployed to Afghanistan in 2007, as they were to take over from 45 Commando in Helmand in the April.

Afghanistan

Operation Herrick ended up being one of the most demanding tours the battalion had ever had to mount. They were fortunate that they had had a year's notice before the tour had commenced, but they would be involved in over 350 engagements with the enemy and the battle group, around 1,500 strong, claimed around 1,000 Taliban killed during the operation. Lieutenant-Colonel Stuart Carver, then the commanding officer of the 1st Battalion, wrote in December 2007:

> The first major operation was Operation Silicon on 29 April which had the objective of clearing a known Taliban stronghold to the northeast of Gereshk in order to remove the indirect fire threat from the town. By the end of the first day of intensive fighting, six kilometres had been cleared and around ninety five Taliban had been killed.

This was just the first of many major operations during the tour of duty. The successes came at a cost; nine members of the battalion were killed and across the whole battle group another three were killed (two Estonians and one Dane) and fifty-seven were wounded.

Lieutenant-Colonel Carver pointed out that the average member of the battalion had been involved in at least forty significant engagements and went on to say:

> Despite the casualties, morale remained high throughout the tour and the robustness and willingness to fight, over such an extended period, was impressive. The support we have received from the wider regimental family and the people of East Anglia has been outstanding. Letters of support have poured in from regimental officers both serving and retired, the associations and mayors and councils across the region. These have been particularly well received and have provided a welcome boost to morale.

Major D S J Biddick, MBE, the commander of the Norfolk Company (A Company), added:

> Nothing worth achieving in this life comes without cost, and so it has proved with this mission. Tragically we lost Private Chris Gray on Friday 13 April: killed in action as he bravely engaged in a fire fight at close quarters in the treacherous Nowzad terrain. His courageous section commander, Corporal Billy Moore, was also shot that day, as was Private Craig Fisher; fortunately they have both now made a full recovery and Corporal Moore is back on operations in Sangin. Just seven hours into the eleven days of Operation Lastay Kulang in the Sangin Valley Corporal Daz Bonner was also killed in action when his vehicle hit an anti-tank mine.

The battalion left Afghanistan in October 2007 and after post-operational leave they were put on standby for public order duties for Northern Ireland. The battalion was also warned to provide a company for Kosovo from March 2009; at this stage they had no idea where the rest of the battalion would be deployed. A

(Norfolk) Company took part in a freedom parade through Great Yarmouth on 22 January 2008, as Second-Lieutenant Harry Willies wrote in the *Castle*:

> Having been granted the freedom to march through the town with colours flying, drums beating and bayonets fixed, we set off and were immediately greeted by thousands of people and hundreds of flying union flags. Along the route more and more people turned out and the cheers rose in the afternoon sky and our spirits with them. After the parade, we made our way to Great Yarmouth Parish Church, in which all 3,000 seats were filled. After the service there was time to mingle with the people of Great Yarmouth. This was a great opportunity for everyone to come together under one roof and talk about the company's experiences in Afghanistan.

There was a degree of frustration and uncertainty throughout the rest of 2008 and into the beginning of 2009, when it was unclear whether or not the battalion would be deployed abroad, either to Kosovo or to Afghanistan. In fact in the middle

Members of the 1st Battalion marching through Norwich in 2007, exercising their freedom of the city

of 2008 there were even rumours about going back to Iraq.

As it was A (Norfolk) Company, along with C and D Companies, returned to Helmand Province in October 2009 for a six-month tour to support the 11th Light Brigade. They were to provide nearly 400 men to assist in counter-insurgency operations. This meant that August and September 2009 were both hectic and challenging. The battalion had to receive additional training, learn new tactics and be issued with new equipment for the posting in Afghanistan. They received an in-depth package of training based at Thetford and Otterburn. The battalion's preparation included using the replica Afghan villages created at the training facility in Thetford.

Once the training was complete the men had a short leave period and were then deployed to Helmand. A Company were deployed to support the Household Cavalry battle group at Musa Qala, C Company was deployed to Nad Ali to support the Grenadier Guards battle group and D Company was attached to the Danish battle group based around Gereshk.

The 1st Battalion was officially deployed for Operation Herrick 11. At the time of completing this book the weekly situation update for the week ending Friday 20 November 2009 had just been released as an unclassified document. It clearly describes precisely what A (Norfolk) Company had to contend with on a daily basis:

> A Company conducted op Mar Brus 2, this was a company level joint Afghan National Army and ISAF [International Security Assistance Force] search operation that involved assets from across their battle group. Several compounds were searched during the day resulting in a number of finds of bomb making equipment. During the operation, 3 Platoon conducted a joint patrol with the Afghan National Army Platoon based with them to provide security for the Counter-Improvised Explosive Device (IED) Team to investigate and destroy an IED found previously. Both platoons were engaged with enemy machinegun fire from several firing points as this was undertaken. The two platoons remained in contact with the enemy for nearly five hours keeping him in place while the company used 105mm direct role artillery, 81mm mortars, and an A10 aircraft to support them. Also as 1 and 2 Platoon returned from a patrol to Roshan Tower, Patrol Base Woqab was engaged by small arms fire and rocket propelled grenades. The firing points were suppressed from the base Sangars and 81mm mortars. An Apache gunship and two Tornadoes were used to help identify and neutralise the threat to the base.

As this title was in its final stages of completion the news of the tragic death of Lance-Corporal Adam Drane from Bury St Edmunds, of the 1st Battalion of the Royal Anglian Regiment, was released. The lance-corporal was in 6 Platoon of C (Essex) Company, on his second tour of Afghanistan. This was the eleventh battalion fatality in Iraq since first deployment in 2002.

The 1st Battalion of the Royal Anglian Regiment, and in particular A (Norfolk) Company, can trace an unbroken line of military service all the way back to 1685. Despite the rationalizations, mergers and amalgamations, the traditions of the 9th Foot, the Norfolk Regiment and the Royal Norfolk Regiment continue in A Company of the 1st Battalion. From the Battle of the Boyne (1689) through the Seven Years' War, the Napoleonic Wars, innumerable colonial conflicts, both World Wars, Korea, Northern Ireland, Cyprus, Bosnia, Iraq and Afghanistan the spirit of the men that became the Holy Boys and ultimately the Vikings fights on.

Bibliography

Barthorp, Michael. *Crater to the Creggan*, Pen & Sword, 1978

Britannia Regimental Magazine

Burton, Reginald. *Railway of Hell*, Pen & Sword, 2002

Carew, Tim. *The Royal Norfolk Regiment*, Royal Norfolk Regiment Association, 1991

Castle Regimental Magazine

Godfrey, F A. *History of the Royal Norfolk Regiment 1951–1969*, vol. 4, Regimental Association of the Royal Norfolk Regiment, 1993

Hart, Peter. *At the Sharp End: From Le Paradis to Kohima*, Pen & Sword, 1998

Kemp, P K. *History of the Royal Norfolk Regiment 1919–1951, vol. 3, Regimental Association of the Royal Norfolk Regiment, 1953*

Lane, Richard. Last Stand at Le Paradis, *Pen & Sword, 2009*

Lincoln, John. Thank God and the Infantry: From D-Day to VE Day with the 1st Battalion the Royal Norfolk Regiment, *Amberley Publishing, 2009*

Loraine, Peter F. History of the Norfolk Regiment 1685–1900, *vol. 1, Jarrolds, 1919*

Loraine, Peter F. History of the Norfolk Regiment 1914–1918, *vol. 2, Jarrolds, 1919*

McCrery, N. The Vanished Battalion, *Simon & Schuster, 1992*

Regimental Museums

Original documents, photographs and artefacts related to the Royal Norfolk Regiment and its later incarnations are held in three different locations. Details below were correct at the time of going to press.

For information up to 1959: the Royal Norfolk Regimental Museum, Shirehall, Market Avenue, Norwich, NR1 3JQ. Telephone: 01603 493649. Email: regimental.museum@norfolk.gov.uk.

For information on the Royal Anglians to the present day, the museum is part of the Land Warfare Hall of the Imperial War Museum at Duxford. Email: info@royalanglianmuseum.co.uk.

The Royal Anglian Regiment Association's headquarters is at The Keep, Gibraltar Barracks, Bury St Edmunds, Suffolk, IP33 3RN. Telephone: 01284 752394. Email: chief-clerk@anglian.army.mod.uk. This is also the location of the Suffolk Regimental Museum.

Index

Portsmouth 2, 7, 10, 15, 44, 57, 68, 72
Portugal 30–1, 32–3
Pretoria 79–80

Q
Quebec 18
Quiberon Bay, battle of 14–15

R
Radfan 229–30
Rathmulton 4–5
Ribstraat 158
Rochester 89
Rolica, battle of 30–1
Romford 27
Royal Anglian Regiment 228–47
Royal Anglian Regiment 1st Battalion 228
Royal Anglian Regiment 4th Battalion 228
Royal Canadian Regiment 78
Rustenburg 80

S
Sabathu 51
Salamanca, battle of 36–7
Salvaterra, siege of 8
Sambre River 131–2
San Sebastian, siege of 39–40
Sannaiyat 99
Saratoga 19, 20, 21
Scunthorpe 234
Sebastopol 55–6
Sedgemoor, battle of 1
Shaiba 96
Sheringham 87, 163, 171
Sikh Wars 51–4
Sinai 107
Singapore 165, 167–9, 169–71, 172–3
Somme 123–5, 133–6, 137–9, 141–2, 161
Sorel 18
South Africa 58–65, 72, 75–85
South Armagh 236–7
Southampton 149
Southwold 23

Spain 28, 35–9
Spanish Succession, war of 7–11
Spithead 14, 15
St Helena 58
St Kitts 24
St Lucia 24, 25, 26, 44
St Peter's Lake 18
St Valery 162–3
St Vincent 44
Stalham 163
Stockport 10, 45
Stoke Newington 21
Stowmarket 27
Sudbury 27
Suez Canal 107, 111–12, 114
Suffolk Regiment 223–7
Swaffham 88, 171

T
Tezeen 50
Thetford 87, 147, 165, 246
Three Rivers 18
Tibet 64
Ticonderoga 18, 19
Tipperary 6
Tobago 44
Tombeek 158
Torres Vedras 35
Tower of London 1, 8, 27, 72
Trinidad 44, 167
Turkey 233, 241–2

U
Umbala 52
United Arab Emirates 232

V
Valencia de Alcantara, siege of 8
Valladolid 37
Vigo 31
Villiers Bocage 200–1
Vittoria 38–40

W
Walcheren Expedition 32
Warley 238